The Fear of the Visual?

'Perera is a master storyteller effortlessly weaving histories of personal family albums with sociology and anthropology's methodological anxieties about the power of photography to better represent the "real" in comparison to the text. Journeying through time, he recounts how the act of photographing was careful and conscious at an earlier time, in contrast to the present era of the digital, of casual and thoughtless selfie-taking, made possible by inbuilt cameras in mobile phones. *The Fear of the Visual?* is a wonderful and richly rewarding read.'

Rahnuma Ahmed, Anthropologist, Dhaka

'Sasanka Perera traces a fragmented history of seeing from his location in the global South. It is in response to his location, more specifically in Sri Lanka, that he is able to speak back. His directs his dialogue towards the past and present theorists of sociology, social anthropology and visual anthropology from the global North. In the process, he raises salient disciplinary concerns within visual anthropology and its fraught relationship with both sociology and social anthropology. What acts like a pivot around which he stages the disciplinary conversations is their anxiety over the visual. In fact, it is by addressing and foregrounding this fear of the visual that Perera constructs a compelling narrative of photography in which he skillfully weaves the personal and the political.

This book represents a much-needed move within postcolonial theory to deconstruct authoritative and Eurocentric histories of photography of the non-Western world, and instead it offers a nuanced counter-narrative. It helps us to imagine an iconography of a South Asian anthropologist whose response outgrows a merely combative reaction. Instead, it takes on board the poetics of the fragment, of overlooked histories and memories, and marks an important moment in decolonising visual anthropology.'

Parul Dave Mukherji, School of Arts and Aesthetics,
Jawaharlal Nehru University

‘The line, “the camera travelled from its topmost shelf to lower ones”, caught my interest. I am wary of academics who disgorge themselves of papers at conferences. This is an academic I could relate to. The absence of jargon helped, but it was the storytelling that excited me. The references to Berger, Sontag and Barthes did not appear forced; the ill-fitting clothes, I could relate to, but it was the reference to the Yashica FX3, which I was struck by. My photographic ecosystem was full of people who judged others on the basis of the camera they owned. FX3 owners were dismissed. Those with “proper” cameras were taken seriously. Such unapologetic mention of an FX3 was liberating. I remembered the family amongst the ruins of their home in Hikkaduwa, Sri Lanka after the tsunami. Perched amidst the rubble, they huddled around the family album they had found, slowly turning the pages. Unconcerned about the “valuables” they might have lost, or what could perhaps still be retrieved, they found life where life had perhaps been lost. Photography mattered. Posturing didn’t.

Here is a person looking at why photography was not being taken seriously without taking himself too seriously. Bravo.’

Shahidul Alam, Independent Photographer, Dhaka

The Fear of the Visual?

Photography, Anthropology, and Anxieties of Seeing

Sasanka Perera

Orient BlackSwan

THE FEAR OF THE VISUAL? PHOTOGRAPHY, ANTHROPOLOGY, AND ANXIETIES OF SEEING

ORIENT BLACKSWAN PRIVATE LIMITED

Registered Office
3-6-752 Himayatnagar, Hyderabad 500 029, Telangana, India
e-mail: centraloffice@orientblackswan.com

Other Offices
Bengaluru, Bhopal, Chennai, Guwahati,
Hyderabad, Jaipur, Kolkata, Lucknow, Mumbai,
New Delhi, Noida, Patna, Visakhapatnam

First published by Orient Blackswan Private Ltd. 2020

ISBN 978-93-5287-995-3

Typeset in
Minion Pro 10.5/12.6
by Le Studio Graphique, Gurgaon 122 007

Printed in India at
Yash Printographics, Noida

Published by
Orient Blackswan Private Limited
3-6-752, Himayatnagar, Hyderabad 500 029, Telangana, India
e-mail: info@orientblackswan.com

For my parents

Eric Perera (1932–2010)
&
Rohini Obeyesekere Perera (1932–2020)

For introducing me to the possibilities of photography early in life and for teaching me the value of humour, patience, sensible politics, dissent, and a clear intolerance of what is simply wrong.

Contents

Tables and Images

Tables

Images

Preface and Acknowledgements

It is self-evident that this book is as personal as it is academic. When it comes to photography, given its association with my personal biography from a very early age, and the research interest it has held for me in more recent times, an axiomatic and clinical separation between the personal and the academic is not possible. I also do not consider it necessary in the specificity of my own circumstances. In my life, the personal actually and sensibly informs the way I use the camera and deal with images in research. That is, experiences in the personal domain have taught me as much as my formal readings on photography have. In the same way, research and formal learning on visuality, photography, and ways of seeing also impact my thinking when I use the camera in times of leisure. This is because what I read on photography and the resultant reflections must necessarily impact in some way the manner in which I frame images. I cannot see how these two domains can be kept separate or why it should be done at all, if this lack of separation is maintained within conscious limits and can also be intellectually profitable. It is in this context of the inseparability of the two that I have opted to enter most chapters with one or more personal recollections, as a means to approach the academic discussion that each chapter is supposed to present.

The immediate trigger for this book in its present form was the course 'Photography and Method in Sociology and Social Anthropology', which I designed and taught my Ph.D. students for about three years from 2013 onwards. Although initially focussed on methodological concerns in a conventional sense, it rapidly became a more eclectic seminar that touched on issues of history and politics, involving photography as well as sociology and social anthropology on the one hand, and theoretical issues involving systems of knowledge within which photography, sociology and social anthropology are ultimately located, on the other. These transformations were the result of the rapid changes in my thinking as I read more and more on the subject, as well as the conversations I had with students and colleagues in and beyond the class. Much of the initial reading material was provided to me by enthusiastic students in my classes, who had more patience and the technical know-how to prowl the internet and find extremely useful texts. They were keen to share these with me, some of which were introduced to the class as well. Without this dynamic interaction, this book would not have emerged in its present form. At times, the book was also discussed in class as a possible collaborative effort. But this did not transpire in any tangible manner given the pressures of graduate school that students had to endure, and my own thankless schedule.

A limited number of forums from 2013 onwards allowed for my initial ideas to be presented and discussed as matters of discourse open to fine-tuning. One of the first such forums was the conference organised by my friend N. Jayaram on the theme, *Knowing the Social World: Challenges and Responses*, at the Indian Institute of Advanced Study, Shimla, 13–15 March 2013. In my paper for the conference, 'To Click or Not to Click: Preliminary Thoughts on Photography's Methodological Absence in Social Anthropology in South Asia', my attempt was to work out some of the key issues in the initial format of my Ph.D. course as well as to excavate the histories of photography and social anthropology to ask the question: Why was photography not considered a serious enough method of research within mainstream social anthropology? A more extensive and focussed forum to discuss some of these issues was provided at the conference, *Re-imagining Visuality: Exploring Possibilities in Photography, Theory and Practice*, organised on 28 February 2015 at my own department at South Asian University, New Delhi. This was coordinated by Kumud Bhansali, one of the Ph.D. candidates from the 2013 batch from my 'Photography and Method in Sociology and Social Anthropology' class. In a sense, the paper I presented at that conference, 'Fear of the Visual? The Presence and Absence of Photography in Social Anthropology', provided the basic initial structure for this book.

As far as I am concerned, what I have discussed in this book is not necessarily what is important to mainstream sociologists or photographers, or even to colleagues squarely located in the midst of the formal domains of visual sociology and visual anthropology. Instead, these are issues that intrigued, interested, or baffled me as a sociologist with a pronounced interest in photography, who continues to be located in a mainstream Department of Sociology, but with enough avenues to facilitate ruptures from normative academic practices. I also consider what I have written a trajectory of my own education, which may be of interest to others who might be keen to engage in academic work off the beaten track.

This book has immensely benefitted from material that have been diligently sourced and sent to me by students and colleagues. Abdullah al-Modabber at the South Asian University Library ordered many books that I was interested in, found others via inter-library loan, and also offered his help to find material online whenever I had difficulties. Ratan Kumar Roy from the Ph.D. programme in Sociology provided a lot of published material, which he had secured for his own reading. Suren Raghavan in Colombo also provided many important texts that he had secured in London. In addition, many others chipped into help by locating texts from numerous sources, which made this book possible over the years. These include Dev Nath Pathak at South Asian University, Ifthikar Dadi at Cornell University, Shukla Savant and Siddharth Mallavarapuat Jawaharlal Nehru University, Kumud Bhansali, Krishna Pandey, Mumitha Madu, Pooja Kalita, Kaushlya Kumarsinghe, and Diksha Gupta in the M.Phil and Ph.D. programmes in Sociology at South Asian University, and Rashi Bhargava at Maitreyi College, University of Delhi.

I am also thankful to Titus Marasinghe, Karnika Jayatilaka, Thanuja Perera-Childs and Kevin Childs, Lakruwan and Nadee Kariyawasam, Raihana Sayeeda Kamal, Chintan Girish Modi, Jinali Chandrika Hettiararchi, and Anula Ratnayake, who have freely shared family and personal photos from their individual collections. I am grateful to Chandra Lekamaarachi at the University of the Visual and Performing Arts in Colombo for archiving some of my own field photos in her collection, which has become immensely helpful after nearly a decade. My thanks are also due to Phillips Images in Mumbai and Plâté Limited in Colombo for giving me selected images from their collections and the necessary permission to reproduce them in this book. I appreciate the generosity of Asif Bin Ali in Dhaka and Arshad Sardar in Mumbai for their help in securing specific photographs from different places.

I am grateful to Sujata Chandra, Chani Imbulgoda, Susan Visvanathan, Sandhya A. S., P. K. Balachandran, Unnathi Samaraweera, and Sanjee Goonatilake for sharing their thoughts on selfies, which helped me in writing Chapter 4.

I am thankful to Nilanjana Majumdar and her colleagues at Orient BlackSwan for their interest in this book and for pursing it over time as I missed many deadlines, and to the anonymous reviewers for their suggestions. I greatly appreciate the courteous and professional help from Proteeti Banerjee at Orient BlackSwan and for her excellent work in editing this text, and making it more reader-friendly. Mishta Roy in Bangalore deserves special credit for doing an excellent cover design, understanding quite well my intentions in the book. My thanks are also due to the friends and colleagues from South Asia with an interest in photography and its politics for writing the endorsements for this book.

Finally, my thanks are also due to my wife Anoli for keeping constant tabs on my writing and for providing necessary, and sometimes incessant, reminders as well as offering many ideas. Some of the chapters in the book found their genesis in my many conversations with her.

January 2020

Sasanka Perera
Department of Sociology
Faculty of Social Sciences
South Asian University, New Delhi

one

Introduction

From Recollections of Biography to Initial Thoughts on Photography[1]

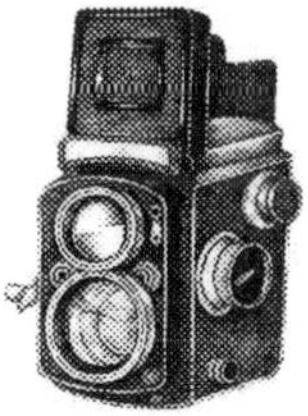

Photography is a way of feeling, of touching, of loving.
What you have caught on film is captured forever ...
it remembers little things, long after you have forgotten everything.
Aaron Siskind (1903–91)[2]

Personal Recollections of a Distant Childhood

What I have written in this book is both personal and academic at the same time. It is personal because photography has been an integral part of my life for a very long time, and that involvement began long before my academic interest in the subject. It is academic because what I discuss goes much beyond the personal and the private to deal with issues of representation, politics, power, ethics, and the aesthetics of photography, as I understand these from the perspective of my training as an anthropologist and on the basis of what I have read on the subject. Given these two ends in my life within which my interest in and practice of photography are located, I think it makes little sense to clinically remove the personal from the academic in the name of objectivity, an issue that I discuss again later in this Introduction. Without my personal involvement in photography as a matter of leisure, and being mindful of its power in the vast public and private domains in which I had seen the camera at work, I doubt if I would have approached my academic interest in photography as I have in this book. In that sense, the personal has moulded the academic to a significant extent.

I begin this Introduction with three personal childhood recollections involving photography. Overall, these are my entry points into the discussions that will follow in later chapters. In one sense, these help to create more legible signs of what I have referred to as my personal involvement with photography. But they are also openings into the not so spectacular and mundane worlds of photography in general, which are by and large not privy to the academic gaze, as opposed to what is spectacular, national, historical, and so on. Subsequent to presenting these three personal vignettes and the conceptual and theoretical frameworks within which they may be located, I proceed to discuss a number of ideas that other scholars have presented, which might help to locate photography as an important practice with its own forms of politics, rather than a mere technical act. In other words, in this brief discussion, I have tried to lay the groundwork for considering photography a serious approach to anthropological research.

The main interest that motivated me to write this book revolves around a simple question: Why is photography not taken seriously enough in contemporary mainstream social anthropology and sociology in South Asia—and to a great extent, in the rest of the world—as a possible way of conducting research or as a substantial object of research? In other words, I was curious to know why photography had not become a more conscious way of seeing the world in these disciplines, which had at the core of their intellectual engagement human actions and people's social and cultural worlds. By looking at the past and present practices of photography and its narrative possibilities with regard to social and cultural histories as well as the possibilities of theorising the visual, my hope is that I might be able to answer this question at least for myself, and if not convincingly, then at least partially. At the very least, it might open interesting questions for others to pose, repose, and explore in more detail. Naturally, my immediate context of thinking and seeing is South Asia, where I am located by choice, in whose anthropological practice such questions have not been of critical or self-reflective importance.

In the most basic sense, photography is a matter of producing images of specific objects on chemically treated surfaces through the control of light. In the digital realm, such images are initially produced upon an electronic field, which will be transferred to chemically treated surfaces only if they are to be printed. In other words, irrespective of whether we are talking of analog or digital photography, it is essentially a technical process.

For me, however (and for many others too, I suppose), photography is not merely something technical which one engages in by manipulating an impersonal apparatus. Historically, at least, it has not always been a thoughtlessly flippant activity, compared to the sensibility that many people who engage in photography today express, as a result of the democratisation of access to photography. Its use and relative familiarity to me is personal, and is woven into my personal and family histories. My sense is that this state of affairs is often shared by people of my generation and background who were born and brought up at a time when taking a photograph and developing it was still a conscious effort, which needed the investment of time, patience, and ultimately, money as well. As a result of these circumstances, there was a better opportunity for some of those moments to be more clearly etched in one's memory. By 'moments', in this context, I do not only refer to incidents that were captured within the frames of photographs, but also to moments and processes that led to the photograph in the first place. Numerous moments linked to the use of the camera from my distant childhood are still well within recallable memory. Elizabeth Thomas, in a recent recollection of her own family photographs, makes similar observations when she notes that 'opening the old family albums invokes many senses .... Just one word cannot fully describe it. Nostalgia, joy, heartache, amazement, questioning are some of the sentiments that flood through my senses' (Thomas n.d.).

In my case, I assume that such recalling is possible because photography and its results, which ended up in our family albums, must have made an impact on my consciousness without my active knowledge taking much note of the embedded nature of this experience at the time. In fact, my recollection of these memories is not unlike flipping through the pages of an old photo album. Some images are very clear, while others are somewhat faded, but not altogether lost. I remember them in much the same way a photograph would narrate its story, sometimes fully and at other times partially, needing others' intervention as well as access to numerous sources of information to complete the narrative. Since these memories make contextual sense with regard to some of the issues I would like to address as this book unfolds, some of these memories, it seems to me, are as good a place as any to begin this journey. I will begin with three recollections.

Recollection 1

Long before I started going to school, I remember a black and grey cube of an apparatus with a few knobs and lenses embedded in it safely deposited on a steel rack far above the reach of my sister and I. It was encased in a cotton cover, which my father had stitched himself. Obviously, it was a somewhat valued object in my home. Hence the protective distance given to it by my parents and the homemade cover for added safety. Later, as I started schooling, I was told that it was a 'Kodak box camera', which my parents had inherited as a wedding present in the mid-1950s. That was part of family lore, in much the same way that every other valuable item in the house had its own story. The cane couch and the chairs were bought by my parents with their first salary, and were made out of cane imported from Malaysia by local craftsmen attempting to put together something that reminded me much later of Bauhaus sensibilities. I doubt that these local carpenters knew about that European stylistic rage which influenced architecture, the interiors of built spaces, and furniture design, among others. Perhaps it was more likely the accidental but enduring impact of a wayward catalogue.

The large darkened clay jar that stood in one corner was from my grandfather's collection of medicine jars, in which he had supposedly stored his *ayurvedic* concoctions in the first half of the twentieth century. He had learnt his craft in Calcutta, and I recall the stories about his tough life in the city where he had converted an abandoned toilet to serve as his abode in the 1920s. Before its reincarnation as a receptacle for medicines, the jar had come from the Maldives, along with many other such jars, in sailboats via the southern Sri Lankan port of Galle in the late nineteenth and early twentieth century, filled with *rihaakuru*, a dark sticky delicacy made out of fish blood and eaten locally with rice. The Sinhalas called *rihaakuru* '*diyahakuru*', or liquid juggary. It is no longer a part of Sri Lankan cuisine or culinary memory, along with *bondihaluwa*, a rice-based sweet also introduced from the Maldives at the same time. Despite the loss of this culinary practice and its memory, these jars can be seen in antique stores and in some people's homes as items of curiosity along with antique value, almost completely devoid of their historical context.

The red Pyrex dessert dishes were a gift from one batch of my father's students, given on the day of their graduation from the Survey Academy in Diyathalawa, and we are no longer in touch with any of them; I have no recollection of their names or faces, except the vague memory of the genesis of the glassware in our home, as narrated by my father in the 1960s. The six tall, slender lemonade glasses with a bamboo design were a personal gift from one of those students, Uma Maheshwaran, who went on to become a well-known militant leader in the Tamil insurgency twenty-five years later. Like Maheshwaran's demise in the midst of extreme political violence, almost all the glasses are now gone as the result of much less violent domestic mishaps, except one which now has a crack that seems to accompany its original bamboo design. But its story is something only I remember now; it was never a part of my sister's memory and my mother has lost any reference to it, along with references to many other, far more important things, as she progresses well into the eightieth decade of her life.

Like all these objects with their individual stories and the incomplete recollections etched in my memory, the camera was yet another object which came into our home as one among the many wedding presents my parents received on the day of their wedding in the mid-1950s. This one came from my mother's maternal uncle, who had both the means and the sense of style and taste to offer such a gift at that time. It was only much later that I realised it was a Kodak Box

Brownie camera, which Roberts says was 'designed to produce bad pictures' because it had to be held at waist level when operating, with the photographer peering down into the viewfinder.[3] In this process, one had to be very steady to be able to take a decent photo, and had to be mindful enough to manually rewind the film roll once the camera had been clicked. If not, another image would be captured on the same negative, making the resultant print look somewhat surreal. We only had a very few of these accidental images, partly due to my father's in-built propensity to be conscious of what he was doing as well as his life-long antipathy towards wasting material, often reiterated in the hymn-like repetition of the adage, 'waste not want not'. Besides, even if double exposures occurred, studio owners in those days did not carelessly print everything. They knew which ones were errors, and thereby deliberately denied us possession of what might have been veritable artworks, albeit by mistake. The well-known Sri Lankan photographer, Lionel Wendt, had already perfected a form of art by the 1930s out of careful multiple exposures, again something I learnt much later.

Nevertheless, my father had become a master of this camera whenever he decided we could afford the black-and-white Kodak 35 mm film rolls and their processing costs. Holding it at waist level, peering into it for seemingly long moments and shouting orders to us not to move, or to move from one place to another in order to frame what he wanted, was part of growing up. Many of the prints still languishing in the solitary family album that remains in my possession have been produced from this camera. As Berger has observed, 'photographs bear witness to a human choice being exercised in given situation' (Berger 2013: 18). That is, a photograph results from the 'photographer's decision that it is worth recording that this particular event or this particular object has been seen' (ibid.). This does not necessarily mean that what is photographed is always an object or an event that has come about as the result of the natural progression of time, or that it reflects reality as it generally unfolds in a particular situation. Often, when a photographer decides that something is worth recording because it was seen by him, it is likely to be an event or an object that had been specifically prepared to be photographed.

These choices can be better understood within a discourse of selective performance. Until the arrival of digital photography, enabling everything and anything to be photographed, and thereby making photography ordinary as well as more democratic, the act of photography was a conscious decision to preserve for the future a specific moment from the past. The moment an image is frozen in time through the act of photography, it moves immediately from the present to the past, and can only continue to exist in the future as a trigger to memory and recollection. This is what Orhan Pamuk describes when he notes, 'we were having our photographs taken in anticipation of our own gaze back. When we faced the camera, we were "posing" for the future' (Pamuk 2017). But 'in posing for the future', 'we were also enhancing the present' (ibid.).

In the case of my own family, these were choices made by my father—what, where, and when to photograph. The rest of us were elements embedded within the structure of the choices he initiated. But in retrospect, given what these stories narrate about moments in my own past, specific times and circumstances, which allows for very specific narrative possibilities that otherwise would not have been possible, I am thankful for the choices he made. And I am no longer sure that the rest of us were as seemingly lacking in agency in these circumstances as it might appear. It seems more likely that we were very willing partners in these choices, and therefore perhaps willing characters in these pictorial but mute narratives, in which voices might now be found. Today, looking at these photos, I think of ourselves as actors on a stage who were self-consciously performing a family drama in which my father—and less often, my mother—was the director. As a result of my father's decision—in the Bergerian sense—that the events and objects he photographed were 'worth recording' (Berger 2013: 18), we have an incomplete, but narratable and reasonably coherent collection of photographs that document in a cartographic sense the places we had visited and seen throughout the 1960s and 1970s, and less often after the 1980s. But I stress the word *incomplete*. Not only were the events, objects, and places for the photographs carefully selected, but what went into the family albums and what kind of brief written notes might accompany some of them were also carefully thought out. If the act of photography was mostly my father's prerogative, the act of long-term preservation of family albums was mostly my mother's. As Pamuk says, 'My mother's album was like a diplomatic whitewash of our lives. In the photographs she chose, there were no traces of my fights with my brother, of our parents' arguments, of any inner turmoil, weariness, regret, debt, financial worry, or anger' (Pamuk 2017). What Pamuk describes for his own family is the kind of reality all of us have to deal with when we look at our families' photographic archives, and attempt to make sense of them so long after some of them had been recorded. They are by definition incomplete.

I have a vague recollection of seeing cameras similar to the one we had in other middle-class households at the time. Its popularity might have stemmed from its simplicity of operation. Also, despite its enhanced value in our household, it was nevertheless a relatively affordable object at the time for many middle-class people with a reasonably steady income—if they had the interest to acquire one. It was an early example of the possibilities of democratising the practice of photography up to a point, which only realised its full potential much later with the advent of digital photography and the inclusion of cameras in mobile telephones. The Kodak Brownie became a documenter of middle-class family events. Karlekar notes that in the Indian context, the Kodak Brownie played a crucial role in popularising domestic photography, in the context of which 'picnics, family holidays, birthday parties, marriages, and even deaths were recorded throughout the country' (Karlekar 2013: xvii). The situation in Sri Lanka was much the same. And like in India, domestic photography in Sri Lanka at the time was a 'middle class preoccupation', and quite often, the subjects as well as the practitioners of photography were from the same class background (ibid.).

As we grew up and became perceivably more responsible, the camera travelled from its topmost shelf to lower ones and towards our reach, opening up possibilities of experimentation—but without film. Also, by that time other, newly acquired objects in the household had come to occupy more coveted places in terms of their social as well as monetary value in the imagination of my parents. As a result, the aura of the old box camera diminished over time. This was certainly the case by the time a new Yashica FX-3 Super 2000 camera arrived in our home as a result of my father's travels in the Middle East for employment since the late 1970s.

Recollection 2

One of my mother's relatives, who had migrated from her village in Meegama in southern Sri Lanka to Colombo in the early 1960s to work as a domestic aide in her paternal uncle's house, had over time setup a small photography studio in Colombo. He became a well-known and an award-winning photographer much later. This meant that whenever my family made its regular visits to the city from places like Kandy and Diyathalawa in the mountainous regions where we used to live throughout the 1960s up to the early 1970s, a photographic record of many mundane family events and gatherings away from 'home' was maintained as a kind of a black-and-white nondescript pictorial narrative, with no plots and no master script. For Susan Sontag, such photographs would make the world look like 'a series of unrelated, free standing particles', offering a 'view of the world which denies interconnectedness, continuity, but which confers on each moment the character of a mystery' (Sontag 1977: 23). Sontag would be correct if we assume that this 'interconnectedness' and 'continuity' had to be somehow integrally generated by individual photographs, thereby not making them 'unrelated, free standing particles'. But why should this be the case? These concerns—albeit with many lapses and with no knowledge of Sontag's theoretical anxieties—were addressed by my family via their own intervention in ordering the photographs within the family albums, initially by my parents and later by me, and now, by none. The flow of a formal and pictorial recording of family history has effectively stopped. I doubt if digital photography, with its built-in capacity for saving carelessly clicked images within nondescript crevices of mass-produced hard disks or the internet, would be able to replace the more carefully crafted family albums. At least in my family circle, this is not the case. But while it lasted, the photos in our albums were not unrelated, free-standing particles, but frozen moments or appearances in a journey which made reasonable sense because they were thematically and temporally ordered, edited by careful omission, and therefore embedded with a specific storyline and a kind of continuity over time. That ordering, which was exterior to the photographs, was nevertheless undertaken in times that were approximately contemporaneous to the photographs themselves. But today, this sense of continuity has stopped because the maintenance of family albums itself has stopped. As a result, the 'character of a mystery' that Sontag says is conferred upon such photographs seems to have become a tangible reality. They become mysterious because they are beyond time, frozen at moments which are so distant from today, and as a result, they might look 'strange' or 'unbelievable'. But their ability to narrate micro-histories of my own family remains intact as long as they can be deciphered by those who survive.

Nevertheless, these photographs are by and large what Berger would have called 'banal snapshots', as opposed to 'memorable photographs' (Berger 2013: 19). They were simply not memorable from a national or global point of view, or in terms of historical and news value. On the other hand, their personal and familial memorability also tends to escape family members, including myself, as the events and people recorded in these photos become further distanced from our recallable memory as time passes by. But as a narrative, each of these photos flowed from one frame to the next, and from event to event; while some moments lingered on pictorially over a number of frames, others were very brief. Yet many others are nonexistent in our pictorial record, but perhaps languish in some form in our failing memories. These would be moments when the camera was simply not around, unhappy moments, and family scandals that no one would have dared capture for posterity. If my father's photos referred to in the first recollection narrated the incomplete story of my family's irregular travels across the country as well as the built spaces in which we lived and the people we met and saw, these latter images placed in context a similarly incomplete record of our limited encounters in Colombo.

The existence of these pictures in our family collection became possible mostly because our relative charged us nothing, or very little, for his efforts in photography as well as for developing the negatives. Some of the images were clearly posed, while others were not. Naturally, they were better exposed and framed than many of my father's photos. Once printed, we received them in our home by post. They found their due place in the family albums, with some brief notes on the backs of a selected few. As I visit via these photos the places, events, and people they refer to, I cannot but help feeling the gray areas of history we might not have privy to, simply because we have not opted to take seriously seemingly banal photographs of ordinary people's regular lives in our reconstructions of the past.

Recollection 3

The final recollection, which is clearly etched in my mind from the same time, has to do with a very different relationship with the camera. My uncle, Gananath Obeyesekere, who is an anthropologist by training, had left for the United States in the late 1960s, and my family was given the responsibility to move into his furnished house and look after the place. My parents had to 'hold the fort' until his return. One of the rooms in the house, on the first floor at the end of a corridor, was always closed and locked. I never knew where the key was hidden. But sometimes, when my father went into the room to dust its surfaces and sweep the room, I also followed and was always told not to touch anything. It was my uncle's library, with tall bookcases containing numerous volumes covering most walls. On a table in the middle of the room, inside a tightly sealed transparent plastic container, were a camera and some other equipment. I cannot recall what the other objects were. But they were free of dust. My father had told me that these were my uncle's equipment, which he would use in his work. I did not know what this meant. The equipment were taken out, cleaned thoroughly (although there was nothing to clean), and placed in the container once again and sealed. The container was then covered with a piece of thick white cotton cloth. After the entire room had been cleaned, we would leave and my father would lock the door, and the key disappeared into its secret hiding place. This ritual continued until we moved out of the place to our own house after my uncle returned.

This was not merely a locked room for me. Instead, it was a sanctified shrine with its own defied objects of seeming veneration and its own set of rituals which were routinely repeated, not too differently from the actions we sometimes performed at Buddhist temples nearby. At that time, it felt like a sacred space to which our entry was restricted, partly because I was too young to enter its hallowed womb and partly because the central object within its sanctum sanctorum was too valuable to be handled and perhaps be destroyed by children. As such, while I knew the main item that was protected here was a camera, I cannot remember what it looked like and I never felt it in my hands. It was a distant and strange reference. But it initiated a thought in my mind that cameras were valuable things and some, unlike our Kodak Box Brownie, were more valuable than others. A long time later, when I read George Orwell's *Animal Farm* and realised that 'some animals were more equal than others', as proclaimed by the pigs who had access to power, the hierarchy of cameras that was residually injected into my conscience made much more sense.

As a result of these three long-term encounters with the camera and the act of photography in my personal life, a certain familiarity with the apparatus and a detectable awe at what it can do became a natural element of my habitus. At times, the encounter waned while at other times it became entrenched, depending on circumstances, which ranged from the availability of a camera at a specific time and place, ability to afford the expenditure of developing and printing negatives, and the nature of the gaze that was possible in specific situations. More importantly, as a result of the first two encounters, an incomplete and grainy black-and-white family archive had emerged which, after the 1980s, began to include colour images, while black-and-white analog photography slowly began to fade into oblivion. Collectively, these images have recorded moments of my family history as well as some stories beyond the family's purview, which had somehow come into the intersection where my family happened to be present while the camera was at work. These stories, often captured informally and sometimes in a more structured manner in print, which ended up in family albums, included snippets of its personal networks, references to time-bound fashions and hairstyles, indications of places we had visited and their spatial politics, things about architecture we had accidentally captured, and so on. Thomas, in similar recollections, notes,

> [A]s I look at the lovely old objects in the photographs—the old painting or clock that was the family heirloom proudly displayed, mom and her friend gracefully draped in saris .... In another photo I see mom's eyes, her printed blouse and plain sari with the brooch that held the *pallu*[4] in place. (Thomas n.d.)

Beyond Recollections

While looking at what is left of my family albums, I realised long before my academic interest in photography began that each image contained a story or a snippet of a story, and these images sometimes worked as triggers for time-suppressed memories, much like the Kodak Brownie camera itself and the other household objects I had briefly described earlier had done. It is in such a situation that a photograph depicting her grandmother 'bent over the wood fire in her kitchen', 'blowing at the embers trying to get the fire to burn brighter', reminded Thomas many years later of 'the warm smells of her kitchen' as her grandmother would narrate stories (Thomas n.d.).

But what does a photograph taken in such circumstances actually mean? Berger notes that a 'photograph celebrates neither the event itself nor the faculty of sight in itself' (Berger 2013: 19). For him, 'a photograph is already a message of the event it records' (ibid.). More importantly, 'the urgency of this message is not entirely dependent on the urgency of the event', while it also cannot be completely independent of it (ibid.). What this means is that a photograph often becomes a fragmented reference to the event or object it represents, and therefore its narrative is incomplete. Nevertheless, a photograph also means that 'something' has been recorded, and therefore it means something—the message. More clearly, each story or each fragmented narrative that is inscribed in photographs might often have nothing much to do with what the objects in the images themselves represented. These objects—be they houses, cars, streets, persons, or whatever—only made sense in a specific context, if that context could be unravelled by someone who had access to the moment that was captured. But now, in the context of my family photographs, I am one of the very few who could decode and unlock those stories with an adequate degree of familial accuracy, with reference to actual incidents, moments or people. Likewise, many such pictures in other collections would also lose their personal interpreters over time with the diminishing of personal memories and the natural advent of death in family circles. In my case, too, I no longer recall some of the people in our family photographs; they have become distanced from my recollection, and therefore literally 'unknown'.

Even so, anyone who can deploy creative analytical skills—within the limits of reasonability—could still elicit much out of these kinds of mundane family images that might help to construct micro-social and cultural histories without the aid of personal interpreters. For instance, if someone pores over the images in my family album, they would notice that my sister was wearing some of the same clothes that I had been wearing when I was her age in earlier images; they might learn that we were careful with our material objects and were not ashamed to reuse clothes, as was quite common at the time. That might also suggest something about my family's income. Our Ford Anglia car, with its number plate EL 7332, is featured in many of these images, and that too might say something about my family's social status when situated in the wider social and economic milieu of the time (see Image 1.1).

The 1970s was a time when the import market was severely restricted as the result of the protectionist and closed-door economic policies of Prime Minister Sirimavo Bandaranaike's government of the time. Yet, these images show me wearing American 'cowboy' jeans of the wrong size, ending six inches above the shoes and with the socks showing, along with a striped shirt and armed with plastic revolvers and a gun belt (Image 1.2). Where would such ill-fitting but obviously cherished clothes and cultural paraphernalia come from when the market was so tightly closed to such things? One might

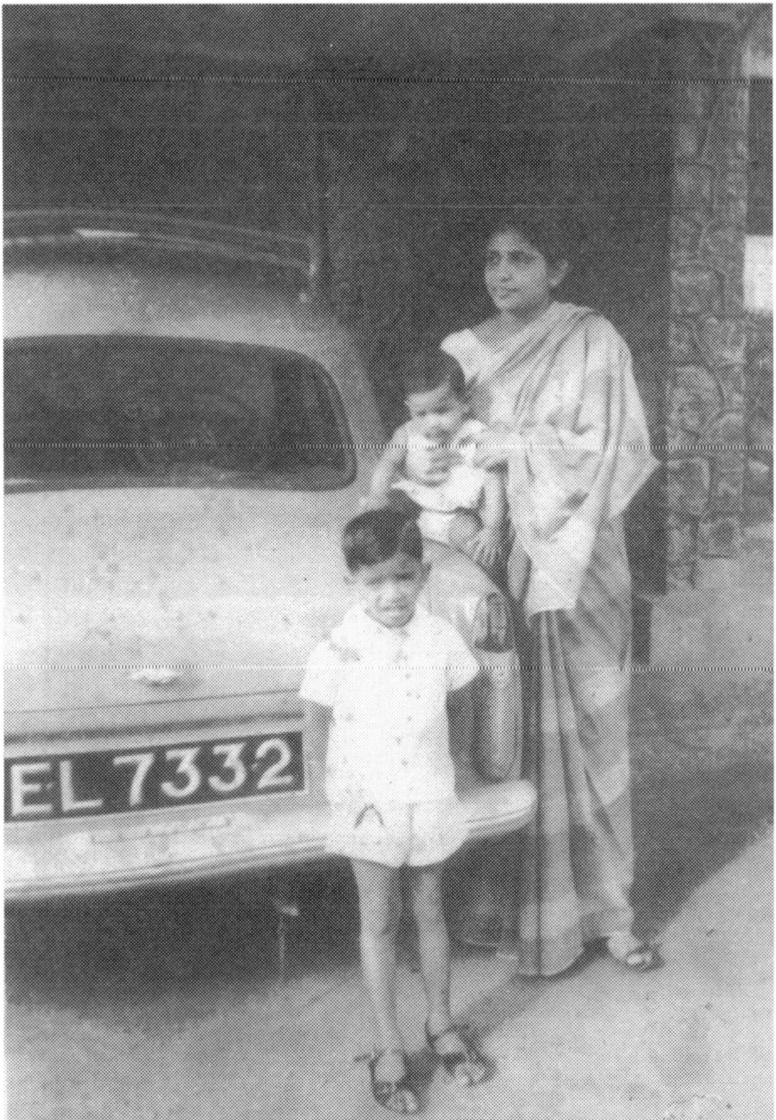

IMAGE 1.1 Author's family with their Ford Anglia car, early 1960s.
Photograph courtesy of: Author's family collection.

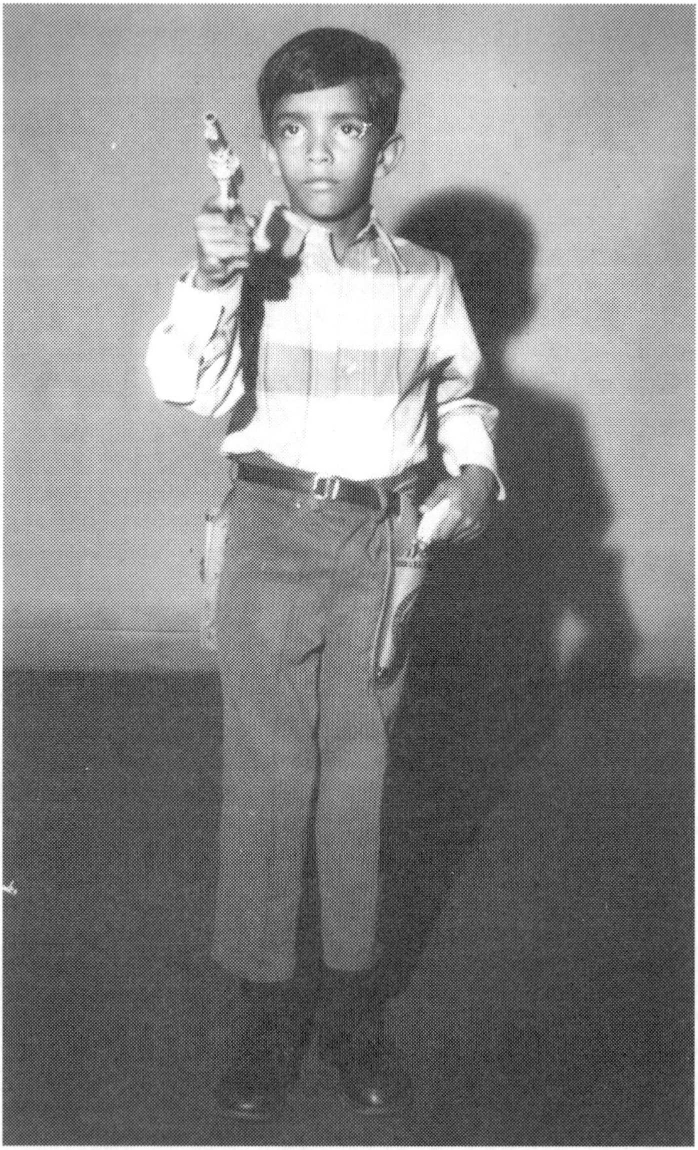

IMAGE 1.2 Author wearing American 'cowboy' jeans, mid-1960s.
Photograph courtesy of: Author's family collection.

wonder if the family had friends and relatives overseas. Although the images themselves might not be able to prove that assumption, it would remain a reasonable interpretation when situated in the realm of wider realities of the time. So the possibilities of narrating stories through photographs are considerable as long as they are carefully located in the multiple contexts and sites to which they belong, and could be interpreted by a close reading of the images themselves or by someone who had access to that world, either through systematised personal recollections or through more sustained and broader historical research.

What Thomas notes about her family photographs makes general sense in such a situation. As she notes,

> [T]hrough these old photos I see our changed lives, how some of the old values we were brought up with have modified somewhat, but what I'm most pleased and thankful for is that someone had photographed those moments .... Those moments of history are part of who you are now. (Thomas n.d.)

In the end, while accepting that objects like family photos are highly subjective and are not captured with a formal research agenda in mind, they certainly have considerably rich narrative potential, should anthropologists care to decipher and unlock their social lives and stories. It is in this potential that my interest and story begins.

As the personal stories above would indicate, long before its methodological and interpretive implications in anthropology began to interest me, photography was a minor family legacy, which later became a passion and continues to be so. As my long-term relationship with the camera evolved, and more specifically over the past fifteen or twenty years, I have often thought about its potential in research and the politics of image-making and capturing moments of the present for reference in the future. Over time, this interest pushed me to think more carefully and systematically of the photograph's possible potential in research in two specific ways—first, as a source of socio-cultural and political information, and second, as an object of research and interpretation. It is from this basic perspective that I have approached the chapters in this book.

Outline of Basic Issues: Towards Making Sense of Photographs

My relatively unstructured thoughts on the situations outlined above constitute the point of departure for my present journey as this book takes its cartographic course through personal memory, conditions in the present, moments in history, and the practice of anthropology in our region and elsewhere. Let me now outline very briefly some of the issues that have captured my attention over the past five years as I read, thought and taught on the ability of visuals to speak and narrate histories. In these conversations and monologues, my focus was both on visual culture in general and photography in particular.

Imagery, from the earliest cave paintings to more contemporary photographs and digital images, has been an integral textual category of expression in human society. It constitutes structures of narrative, not only about the fantasies of individuals, but also records anxieties, personal accounts, local events, mundane moments, important collective historical junctures, preoccupations with the self, and so on. But first, one needs to be sure of what is expected of photographs with regard to research in anthropology and what the potential of photographs are, both as objects and in terms of theoretical possibilities. As I said at the very beginning, photography is not merely a matter of controlling light in order to technically capture an image. Its potential in research, which goes beyond aesthetics, has much to do with the visual construction of the object that would be photographed, the manner in which the object was transformed into a photographic image, and the internal consistency it comes to acquire through this process. As pointed out by Pinney, the notion of 'iconicity' as outlined by Charles Sanders Peirce in the early twentieth century can explain some of the reasons for photography's popularity as a medium (Pinney 2011: 66). This is also the basis for photography's often quoted, and equally as often misunderstood, claim of authenticity in representation. For Peirce, photographs are significant because in some ways they are 'exactly like the objects they represent', and 'this resemblance is due to the photographs having been produced under such circumstances that they were physically forced to correspond point by point to nature' (ibid.). Here, 'nature' is not simply a reference to the natural environment as such, but to the original or natural state of the object that was photographed—prior to being photographed. In the sense suggested by Peirce, an icon constitutes resemblance that is independent of any physical causation (ibid.). To put it simply, resemblance and iconicity give life to photographs, based on the simple logic that they look like their referents (ibid.).

Barthes' view is not too different from this understanding of a photograph's integral ability to represent the object of its attention. For him, a photograph 'is never distinguished from its referent (from what it represents), or at least is not immediately or *generally* distinguished from its referent' (Barthes 2000: 5). This is what Sontag refers to as a 'trace, something directly stenciled off the real, like a footprint or a death mask' (Sontag 1977: 154). Nevertheless, for Barthes, 'it is not possible to perceive the photographic signifier' independently, which needs 'secondary action of knowledge or of reflection' (Barthes 2000: 5). Barthes' argument is that the 'photograph always carries its referent with itself, both affected by the same amorous or funeral immobility at the very heart of the moving world' (ibid.: 5–6). But for him, the seeming 'funeral immobility' of the photograph is a matter of concern, because in it time is frozen, while actual time moved on. For me, that immobility is also photography's strength rather than its weakness as it freezes time and space at a given moment, allowing us the ability to interpret what that frozen moment or object might mean in a world that has moved on. Without that freezing of time, the photograph would lose both its value and meaning.

Berger, on the other hand, sees photography as an activity enmeshed between two paradoxes. For him, 'a photograph is an automatic record through the mediation of light of a given event: yet it uses the *given* event to *explain* its recording', in the context of which photography becomes an act of making 'observation self-conscious' (Berger 2013: 19). But precisely because photography in most cases involves a certain element of self-conscious action, it would hardly be an 'automatic record'. Instead, a photograph is always the result of a series of conscious choices and actions. However, in more recent times—as I will discuss when I deal with the phenomenon of selfies and casual or fleeting photography later in this book—self-conscious action with regard to photography has taken a certain toll as its practice vis-à-vis some genres has become almost 'innate' and unthinking, given its easier access. In these circumstances, photography of specific genres—like selfies—might well have moved closer to what Berger has termed an 'automatic record' (ibid.).

Despite its seemingly close solidarity with the idea of representation, a photograph is not always a purveyor of 'truth', or a simple matter of representing a referent in the world beyond the photograph that defies interpretation and the more complex politics of representation. In this situation, Marion and Crowder's simple observation, 'because images always represent a particular view, images cannot accurately be seen representing reality of truth' makes more sense (Marion and Crowder 2013: 3). Although they were talking of visuals in general, this observation can be read with reference to photographs as well. That is, when reading photographs, one has to take into account the multiple subjectivities that have come into the photographs on the basis of the subjectivity of time and place, of the photographer, and of the people in the photograph. Thus, in any given context, there can be more than one reality or one truth in any photograph.

The ideas of Peirce, Barthes, and Berger that I have so far considered were presented at different times in the twin lives of the camera and the photograph. But in each of these times, it was difficult to delink the immobility of an object in a photograph from its referent. This was a world prior to the easy doctoring of images, when there was at least an anticipation that a referent to an object presented in a photograph existed somewhere in the 'real' world beyond the image. The life of a photograph is much more complicated today, with numerous possibilities of metamorphosis from the very act of its genesis onwards, which may occur with no reference to reality. After all, what would the representational sense of a photograph be in terms of 'truth' validity when the objects photographed might be stage-managed, arranged, choreographed, specifically posed, or quite simply digitally constructed or rearranged? Moreover, in the context of today's digital photography and related technologies, a photograph's claims to be authentic with regard to the objects it is supposed to represent and its claims to the truth in these references take a further toll, given the increased possibilities of creating a purely technically doctored presence through photography without any tangible reference to these photographs beyond the images themselves. Referents to such images cannot be found in the real world, but only in the mediated worlds of ideas tempered with politics. That is, in today's circumstances, we can have a photograph whose internal stories might allude to a set of seeming realities, events or objects that do not exist beyond the frame of that picture. In these circumstances, photographs become works of fiction rather than a reference to evidence or facts. Today's 'fake news' has as much to do with doctored events and accompanying stories as with its dependence on constructed (not captured in the conventional sense) photographs, which are effectively works of fiction deeply rooted in the political imaginings of people with specific vested interests. This brings to mind the question: 'Why waste time discovering the truth when you can so easily create it?'[5] These are important considerations that one must visit when looking at photography's methodological credentials, an issue that I will visit in more detail as this journey progresses.

Berger argues that the 'formal arrangement of a photograph explains nothing' and the events depicted in a photograph 'are in themselves mysterious', while 'the true content of a photograph is invisible' (Berger 2013: 19). But are photographs this mute and this difficult to decipher? Berger believes that a photograph cannot speak for itself, a concern shared by Sontag, as we have already seen (Sontag 1977). But the question is: Why should any text be so autonomous as to have no inter-textual relations of any kind? Why do we impose on photography such autonomous narrative preconditions when we do not impose these as rigidly on other kinds of texts, including the written or the spoken word? It seems to me that it is precisely because of its visuality that often unreasonable demands of narrativity are forced upon photography. Berger asserts that the explicability of a photograph may depend on the familiarity a person might have with events depicted in a photo prior to her/his encounter with the photo itself (Berger 2013: 19). This contextual relationship does not delegitimise the integrity of a photograph. It is precisely due to such preexisting knowledge that I am able to give voice to my family photographs in a way that younger members of the extended family simply might not. Even so, to make a photograph 'speak', one does not need to have a personal or familial affinity with what that photograph depicts. When I was first shown the large numbers of surviving negatives of photographs taken by the Ceylonese photographer Reg Van Cuylenburg[6] in the 1950s and early 1960s by my friend and his wife, Margaret Dodd, in Santa Barbara, California, in the mid-1980s, I could 'see' much information in the pictures. According to Dodd, many others in the US who had viewed these photographs and negatives before had not 'seen' what I had seen that easily. I could say where in Sri Lanka some images had been captured due to obvious geo-physical references, what the time period of some photographs were by looking at the clothing and hairstyles of people, while I remained clueless about many others. But this was merely after a cursory glance without specific training or research, simply on the basis of a preexisting life experience. Naturally, such a collection would narrate much more if it had the benefit of careful research. As such, any photograph is replete with multiple references to places, times, spaces, and many other reservoirs of meaning, which any researcher should be able to ascertain with reference to other sources of knowledge if s/he could make up their mind that carefully sourced photographs are useful forums of knowledge. As with social science knowledge production in general, the degree of accuracy in these interpretations can naturally vary, depending on numerous conditionalities.

Berger notes that all the objects recorded in any photograph carry the same value, weightage or conviction (Berger 2013: 19). He argues that what tends to vary 'is the intensity with which we are made aware of the poles of absence and presence', and for him, it is 'between these two poles that photography finds its proper meaning' (ibid.). It does not seem to me that Berger's assertion of the weightage of objects in a photograph makes much sense when viewed from the perspective of the photographer's intent. Why would a photograph's attention be focussed on a specific person or an object and not on others? Why would a photograph be framed with a very specific event in the centre, while others are sidelined or even beyond the frame?

While these can be accidental, they are more often deliberate efforts on the part of the photographer. In other words, these efforts inject a certain sense of politics and a hierarchy of choice into the photograph, which will remain intact as long as the photograph itself survives. So the objects recorded in a photograph are not of equal weight but of different weightage, depending on the conviction the photographer has invested in each object, person or event. This also means that the ability to read a photograph and mine the data it may contain would depend on a person's ability to read these choices made by the photographer and embedded in the photograph.

How is photography implicated in memory or memory in photography? Is photography a technical simulation of human memory? Sontag asserts that photographs are 'not so much an instrument of memory as an invention of it or a replacement' (Sontag 1977: 165). That is, for her, photographs are mere repositories of memory. But here, a cursory observation of Berger's also becomes useful. He notes that 'unlike memory, photographs do not in themselves preserve meaning' (Berger 2013: 52). That is, if memory is live, photographs are not. This static or 'non-live' nature of photographs is one of the most perennial issues its critics emphasise when discussing its ability to communicate. I would suggest that memory is implicated in photographs in a number of different ways, but this relationship has limitations which need to be overcome. True, photographs, unlike memory, do not reflect, do not have to recall, do not interpret, and do not erase. As such, a photograph is what it is as long as its physical sustainability is guaranteed. Its lifetime under the right circumstances is more tangible and can move beyond generations and time. In this sense, while memory is susceptible to the vagaries of time, photographs are less so. While memory creates meanings in the sense suggested by Berger, photographs do not go beyond what they present within their frames by themselves. In this scheme of things, my family photographs and others like them are incomplete without my memory and without the ability of someone to interpret and locate them in the sequence of appearances where they have been frozen. They are also triggers for my memory, in the sense that without reference to specific photographs, I will be unable to recall events or places that are very distant from the present and are no longer part of the day-to-day consciousness. Seen in this sense, photographs are neither an invention of memory nor its replacement. But they are scripts to reactivate memory and corpuses of visual evidence to vindicate memory. This explanation holds when photographs are closely linked to a person's biography and his time.

What are photography's implications of memory when it precedes a person's life and reaches into the distant past where that person's recallable memory does not have any reference? Here, what matters is not the personal memory of an individual or family when it comes to making a photograph narratable, but what other recorded sources of historical memory might offer to make the preserved appearances—in the Bergerian sense (2013: 52)—frozen in photographs find their voices. To do so, one will need to traverse from the realm of private memory to that of public, social, and formally recorded memories. Much of what I have to say in Chapters 2 and 3 will be based on this consideration.

A Brief Note on the Book: Structure and Politics

In the context outlined above, by focusing on the social and political histories of photography, anthropology, colonialism, lifestyle changes in the present, as well as my own memory and recollections with regard to the act of photography, this book—through the thematically different but intellectually related journeys sketched in each chapter—ponders over the basic fact that was already flagged at the very beginning of this Introduction. That is, given the importance of the 'captured' image of the camera as a possible freezing of history and time, why is it that photography has not been taken very seriously as a possible source of information in a methodological sense or as a core object of research in South Asia by practitioners of social anthropology or sociology?[7] Even in other parts of the world, despite the emergence of sub-disciplines such as visual anthropology and visual sociology, the focus on photography remains relatively marginal or occulted in the larger scheme of methodological and theoretical concerns in mainstream social anthropology and sociology. This is an issue I will explore in more detail in Chapters 6 and 9. More specifically, the book also attempts to address issues such as: What is the 'authenticity' or the 'truth' value of images captured in photographs, and why have anthropologists remained by and large sceptical of or disinterested in using photographs in their readings of society and culture, beyond their marginal use as a means of contextualisation or decoration? Is it because they are concerned that photos narrate only 'partial truths'? If so, how would such a 'partial truth' be any different from other 'partial truths' that have become a 'naturalised' part of the ethnographic enterprise, as scholars have argued since the 1980s (Clifford and Marcus 1986)? Or is it the case that social anthropology and sociology continue to be located in a relatively conservative mode of practice, which discourages practitioners from venturing into somewhat uncharted methodological domains such as photography, as well as research objects located in the midst of the visual, which by and large reside in the realm of the subjective?

To answer these questions, I think it is also essential to travel to the wider world beyond South Asia, where both photography and anthropology are practised and had their genesis. In doing so, I suggest that a number of themes should ideally be explored, which would link both photography and anthropology to the past as well as implicate their practice in the nuances of the present. It is this interlinked consideration that has nudged me to focus on the kind of themes presented in the chapters that follow. Early on in Chapter 2, I focus on the politics of image-making in the colonial period. This is not only because it was during this time that photography was introduced to South Asia, but also because this was the first time that the potential political and socio-cultural power of photography was clearly established and became a marker of things to come. Besides, colonial photographs, despite their many lapses, continue to inform us of the past. They remain one of the most important archives of the colonial past.

In Chapter 3, from the general implication of meaning-making in the colonial period via photography, I move on to reflect upon two specific histories—the history of anthropology and the history of photography. My interest here is to construct a historical base upon which to read photography's implication and non-implication in the social anthropology and sociology of the present. In fact, the first three chapters of the book are meant to collectively formulate an interconnected conceptual, theoretical, and historical foundation to explore how photography and social anthropology interact intellectually today.

From Chapter 4 onwards, my focus shifts from the past to the present. But in dealing with the present, I also turn constantly to the past to explore and reflect upon historical trajectories, continuities, and ruptures. In this context, in Chapter 4, I deal with the idea of the self, a core concern of social anthropology, through a close reading of the act of selfie-making, a thoroughly contemporary practice in photography. But what is contemporary is not the obsession with pictorially reconstructing the self, but doing so with the aid of very specific technologies and attitudes. Given these possibilities offered by the present-day photographic obsession with the self and its incarnations in the past, I am curious to understand why anthropology has not seriously explored the phenomenon of selfies despite its self-proclaimed interest in the self.

As we know, photography today—and in the past—has much to do with intimacy. That is, many genres of photography have attempted to capture and preserve moments of intimacy. In fact, photography has created ideals of intimacy as matters of performance when it comes to public interactions that may not have any linkages with photography. For instance, signs of intimacy as public performances during weddings, captured in wedding photography globally, have become standardised mostly as a result of the global reach of photography. In this process, some ideals associated with such moments, such as the smile, have been standardised to a large extent. In Chapter 5, I explore these ideals of intimacy by focusing on wedding photography, and the absence as well as the emergence of the smile as a defining feature in these kinds of photographs at different times.

In Chapters 6 and 7, I deal more directly with two methodological issues in anthropology and sociology where photography is implicated. In this sense, in Chapter 6, I deal with the emergence of visual anthropology and visual sociology from the mainstream of these two disciplines to specifically deal with visuality in general, including photography. My attempt is to comprehend why considerations of photography in particular were expelled to these sub-disciplinary realms from the centres of intellectual practice of mainstream anthropology and sociology. In Chapter 7, my focus is on the issue of ethics in situations where photography is used in research and writing. Unlike general research and writing ethics in the social sciences, photographic ethics in these contexts exist in what appears to be perpetual liminality. Rather than providing a prescriptive body of ethics, my attempt is to place in context the issues involved and the kind of ethical considerations that might be possible in social research involving photography in contemporary situations.

My focus in Chapter 8 is the kind of casual photography undertaken in today's circumstances, which appears to be a fleeting and unthinking practice. This is particularly so when compared to the investments, in terms of time and money, vested in photography until relatively recently. I attempt to make sense of this practice by locating such photography in the present socio-cultural realities, as well as in the radical transformations that have taken place in lifestyles and attitudes.

I conclude my thoughts in Chapter 9 by specifically pondering over the question of whether anthropology has a fear of the visual, when seen within its obsession on writing. I ask this question on the basis of the histories of colonialism, photography, anthropology, and sociology, as well as the exploration of other themes in the preceding chapters.

Collectively, these chapters are the signposts that provide the directions to my journey. These are themes that I consider important when attempting to understand the intellectual interrelations between photography and anthropology. Someone else, however, might see other themes and foci as more important in a similar reading. It is within the understanding of this effort as incomplete, fractured, fragmented, and interpretable that I have called this collection *The Fear of the Visual? Photography, Anthropology, and Anxieties of Seeing.* The seeing in this sense is fragmented because of the presence of my subjective self self-consciously crisscrossing across the chapters, deciding what should be explored and what should not. Seeing is also fractured in terms of time because I deal with different ways of seeing in the colonial and later times, seeing by individuals in the past and the present, and finally, my own ways of seeing. Each chapter, designed as an independent essay, is organised to clarify some of these issues in my own mind, and to see how these reflections might make sense in understanding photography's place in mainstream social anthropology and sociology in South Asia and beyond. Ultimately, however, everything I have written emanates from my location in South Asia, and the ways in which its sociologies and anthropologies have evolved. More specifically, these disciplines' collective institutional silences on photography's place, in the way their crafts are practised in the region, is what preoccupied me the most. But what I go on to describe is a global phenomenon, which also reflects on South Asia in the way we deal with the visual intellectually as well as in how we use the camera.

My entry into the thematic considerations covered in each chapter is often biographical. That is, what draws me initially into a given discussion is based on personal recollections and encounters that bind me to the specific kind of photography discussed in that chapter in some way. My theoretical interests as well as empirical explorations connected to each issue will be dictated by the parameters indicated by this entry point. Given that my personal entrenchment in photography in the realms of both leisure and research is an established fact, I cannot see any reason for erasing these personal entry points and reflections in the name of that much outdated notion of objectivity. These subjectivities, which I have ushered into the journey sketched in this book very self-consciously, reinforces the objectives as well as the objectivity of what has been undertaken. For me, autobiographical reflections and personal memories are a means to a series of conversations for which the book has provided a forum.

Besides, if the 'personal is political', as once famously argued by American feminist Carol Hanisch in 1970, then the personal, in the sense in which I have used my recollections in this collection of essays, is quite clearly sociological.

Notes

1. Sections of this chapter have been taken from my paper presented at the seminar, 'Knowing the Social World: Challenges and Responses', Indian Institute of Advanced Study, Shimla, 13–15 March 2013. An edited version of this presentation has since been published as 'Photography's Methodological Absence in Social Anthropology in South Asia' in Jayaram (2018).

2. Aaron Siskind. BrainyQuote.com, XploreInc, 2015. Available at http://www.brainyquote.com/quotes/quotes/a/aaronsiski141150.html (accessed 31 May 2015).

3. Nigel S. Roberts Photography. Available at http://www.nigel-roberts.info/photography.htm (accessed 31 May 2015).

4. The *pallu* is 'the loose end of a sari that is worn over the head and shoulder' (https://en.oxforddictionaries.com/definition/pallu [accessed 11 June 2017]).

5. Quoted by David Baldacci in his novel, *The Whole Truth* (Pan Books, 2008).

6. For information on Reg Van Cuylenburg's photography, please see Van Cuylenburg (1962), and his memoir, *The Green Stick: A Memoir* (2015).

7. The questions I pose are equally valid for other disciplines within social sciences and humanities, even though I frame my questions with a focus on social anthropology and sociology in the region. Moreover, I also do not find it particularly useful in contemporary practice to maintain a conceptual difference between sociology and social anthropology in terms of research objects or methodological concerns, and in this sense I agree with Pierre Bourdieu's observation that 'the distinction between ethnology [that is, social anthropology] and sociology is a perfect example of a spurious frontier' (Bourdieu 1995: 8–10). As such, in this chapter and elsewhere in the book, when I refer to social anthropology, I also mean sociology, and vice versa.

two

Imperial Power, Colonial Image-making and Photography

From today's vantage point, these popular images celebrating what was perceived as 'colonial achievement' reveal subtexts and meanings other than those intended by photographers and publishers or seen by viewers at the time. At the turn of the 20th century, pictures of ivory caravans and rubber production symbolized economic success; they now imply exploitation and harsh labor practices. An image of chained prisoners, then a metaphor for colonial control over defiant populations, now shows African resistance to often abusive practices and heavy punishment for minor infractions. Similarly, photographs of road and railroad construction have become testimony to forced labor rather than visual examples of what was seen as 'progress.'

In and Out of Focus[1]

T*here are three* things from the interior of my maternal grandfather's 200-year-old house that remain in my memory. One is the brownish, unpainted set of buckhorns mounted on a grey-painted, life-sized wooden buck's head with minutely hand-painted features and carved ears that hung in my grandfather's bedroom. He hung his shirts, sarongs (*lungis*), belts, and at times, his national dress on these horns. The next was an ellipse-shaped brown table, which had two large complete sets of buckhorns as its legs; this was in the right corner of the dining room near the border with the kitchen area, and was where extra food items were placed before being brought to the dining table when—and if—needed. Finally, in the attic, I remember seeing many stacks of buckhorns, still dutifully attached to the front skull plates of the hapless bucks who would have once proudly displayed them before being shot by some village hunter.

These animal parts were unusual items in a Buddhist household, given that they unambiguously symbolised the violent loss of life, violating one of the most fundamental Buddhist principles, which prohibits killing living beings. Besides, they were in significantly large numbers. My grandfather was not a hunter but a healer who had learned his *Ayurveda* craft in Calcutta in the early 1920s. The family lore held that these seeming trophies were given to him by some of his grateful patients from nearby villages who happened to be known hunters, in gratitude for his free medical services. His sense of ethics would not have allowed him to refuse these. So they remained in his house. The clothes hanger from my grandfather's bedroom and some of the unused horns from the attic ended up in my home and continue to collect dust, while the other items have disappeared from our family collections by now, but not from my memory. Often, when my parents took me to my grandfather's house for the local New Year in April, throughout the 1960s and up to the late 1970s, our elders told us that it was sinful to kill living creatures. The point of reference for this advice was always the buckhorns in the house.

On a few of these occasions, my grandfather showed me what I remember as old magazine prints or grainy sepia photographs of white men with guns displaying dead leopards and elephants. These were the trophies from their encounters with ritualised manliness in either Ceylon or other parts of colonial South Asia. I still recall these images quite well, along with some aspects of the stories I heard, I assume because they must have disturbed me at the time. The basic argument in these narratives, as far as I remember, was that the colonial rulers hunted animals for sport while locals did so for food, even though that necessity itself did not absolve them of the *karmic* repercussions of their act. We were told that the sporty hunting of colonial rulers had in some cases wiped out entire animal populations, such as the famed herd of wild elephants that once roamed free in the Horton Plains nestled amongst Sri Lanka's central hills.[2] While my grandfather's reference photos pointing to these colonial actions are no longer available to me (see Image 2.1 and 2.2 for similar photographs from

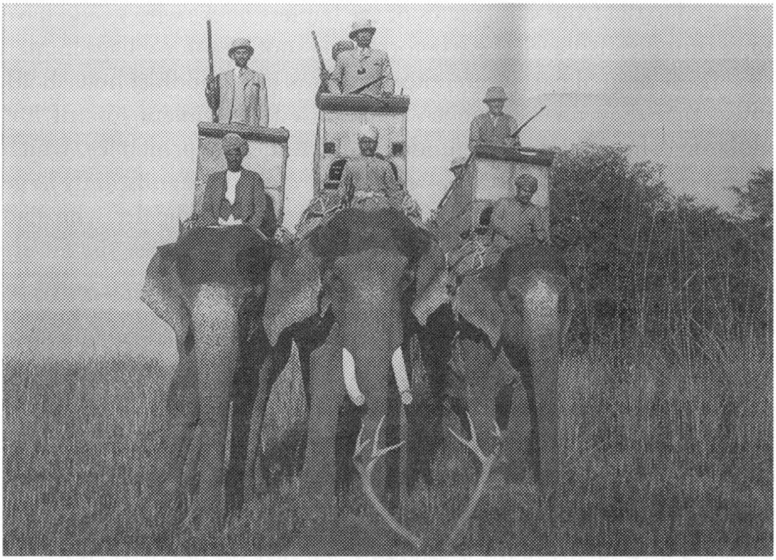

IMAGE 2.1 Maharaja Ganga Singh of Bikaner on a hunting expedition.
Photograph courtesy of: www.phillipsimages.in.

colonial India), I realised much later, what they depicted was a specific and very important genre of colonial photography—trophy photos squarely located within the colonial discourse of manly power and control, which were supposedly typified by the killing of ferocious or fast wild beasts, among other things. These photographs became a necessary part of the interiors of elite colonial households along with the kind of furniture my grandfather also owned, partially fitted with animal parts as well as stuffed animals, informed by the colonial traditions of taxidermy. All these—photos, furniture, and the stuffed animals—were essentially central triggers for conversations on power, control, heroism, manliness, intelligence, and so on at the height of colonial rule.

As I started to think about photography more seriously much later in life, I realised that these encounters in my grandfather's house in an almost forgotten childhood were simultaneously also encounters with the specific colonial practice of ritualised sports hunting, which

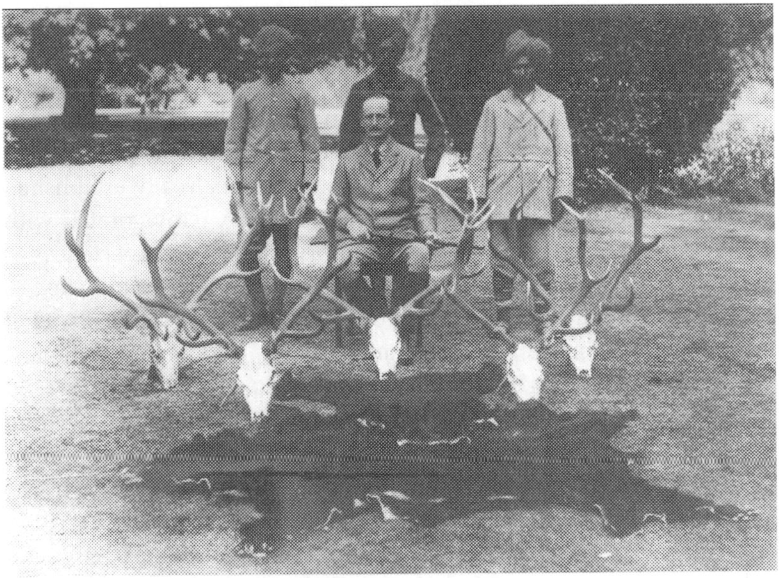

IMAGE 2.2 Lord Hardinger after a hunt in Kashmir.
Photograph courtesy of: www.phillipsimages.in.

had died out even at that time (the 1960s to early 1970s), while they were also my very first introduction to colonial photography. It seems to me that these memories offer a reasonable biographically nuanced entry into my discussion on photography in the colonial period.

Long before European colonial expansion over the rest of the world became a reality, Europe's imagination of the magical, the exotic, the strange, and the brutish in these distant lands was very much an active part of its articulation of these distant others and their places of living and culture, which would later become the colonised and the relentlessly experimented upon and transformed colonial landscape. Multi-headed men, flesh-consuming trees, giant 'Amazonian' women warriors, among others, were part of this imagination, which also established a pictorial tradition within the narrative texts on the unmet 'others' in the pre-colonial past. This tradition, where images were of central importance, was not based on what was seen or experienced, but on what was imagined and what was received via myth and folklore, yet often taken as fact.

As colonialism became a reality and was considered a crucial civilisational imperative for Europe and later the United States of America, narratives of conquest, conquered lands and peoples became an important genre of writing, within which the already established pictorial tradition of representing the 'other' was reinvigorated with an added sense of authenticity and authority, based on experiences of *actual encounters* as opposed to *imagined* or *mythologised* knowledge. Hence began the travel writings of colonial military officers, civil servants, missionaries, traders, adventurers, peripatetic 'scholars', armchair anthropologists, and many others.

One of the most intriguing early examples of this genre of writing is Robert Knox's book, *An Historical Relation of the Island Ceylon in the East Indies*, published initially in London in 1681, which was also well-illustrated with wood engravings. It was, however, written and published prior to the more complete expansion of European colonial intrusions into South Asia and the rest of the world, which were later colonised. Nevertheless, Knox's book is based on his observations, experiences, and biases accumulated during twenty years of open captivity (since 1659) by the Sri Lankan king of Kandy, Rajasinghe the Second. Early in the book, there are two interesting 'recommendations of its value in terms of "truth" and "integrity"'. In the first of these, Robert Blackbourne, Secretary of the Court of Committees for the East India Company, in a note dated 10 August 1681, writes: 'We Esteem Captain Knox Man of Truth and Integrity, and that his Relations and Accounts of the Island of Ceylon (which some of us have lately Perused in Manuscripts) are worth of credit, and therefore encourage him to make them public.'[3] In the second note, dated 8 August 1681, Christopher Wren writes the following recommendation to Richard Chiswell, Knox's publisher:

> I Perused Captain Knox's Description of the Isle of Ceylon, which seems to be written with great Truth and Integrity; and the subject being new, containing an Account of a People and Counterey little known to us; I conceive it may give great Satisfaction to the Curious, and may be well worth your publishing.[4]

The two recommendations assert the 'authenticity' of what is being said in terms of the narrative's 'truthfulness' and 'integrity' as coming from an eyewitness, which was not common at the time. The publisher and promoters of Knox's influential book needed to assert this claim to authenticity and 'factual integrity' as much of the literature that talked about the worlds of others at the time was based on hearsay. As an integral part of this assertion, the book came with a number of engravings allegedly depicting life in Ceylon at the time of Knox. The availability of print technology also helped this emerging process of narrating stories of the worlds beyond the known and the familiar. This is an early indication of the 'market of curiosity' to which this kind of text catered, which saw much more enhanced production once the colonial period had taken root.

The second edition of Emerson Tennent's two volumes, *Ceylon: An Account of the Island*, published in London in 1859, is an example of this genre of writing after colonialism was well-established. Tennent was knighted and appointed to the administrative service of colonial Ceylon in 1845 as Colonial Secretary for Ceylon. He was elected President of the Ceylon Branch of the Royal Asiatic Society in 1846, a year after the Society was established, and served until 1857.[5] It was based on the accumulated experiences that these positions offered him that he wrote his book, for which Andrew Nicholl provided the illustrations.[6] In actual terms, this meant thirty-one wood engravings in the first volume and fifty-nine in the second (Tennent 1859). Many other illustrators of the time, engaged in similar projects, created images to suit the narratives the authors of the books had penned. They also drew inspiration from other pictorial sources of the time. Compared to them, Nicholl was based in Colombo, where he was appointed as a teacher in landscape painting and drawing at the Colombo Academy, [7] the pioneering colonial school in the country and very much an integral part of the Empire's civilising mission for the colony. Given his location, one assumes that Nicholl must have 'seen' at least some of the scenes he painted for Tennent's book.

Despite the fact that Knox and Tennent's books were published 178 years apart, both were written on the basis of 'lived' experiences and based on what was perceivably 'seen' and 'heard' in local situations.

Both were also fed by the available literature, documents, ideologies, attitudes, and specific kinds of knowledge of the times. More importantly, in both cases and in many other texts belonging to these and related genres, the practice of presenting pictorial illustrations (including illustrated maps) as an essential accompaniment to the written descriptions was meant to take readers on a pictorial tour to distant and 'exotic' lands already 'experienced' by the writers, but not seen by the readers. It was also a matter of enhancing the 'truth-value' of what was seen by the privileged few and circulating what was seen without the curtailments introduced by filters of interpretation and imagination, which descriptions wholly dependent on written text might have necessitated. This was also an outcome of the limited European imagination of the time, coupled with that imagination's insistent demand for exotic visual objects as well as stories. This preexisting pictorial tradition depicting the non-European others and their worlds is of crucial importance in understanding colonial photography. For me, photography was an enhanced, technically reproducible, and a seemingly more 'authentic' and 'truthful' way of reiterating and continuing this same tradition.

These images were essentially integral companions to the written text. In this sense, what was written was incomplete if not for the images, which brings to mind Lewis Carroll's words in *Alice's Adventures in Wonderland*: '... what is the use of a book' 'without pictures or conversation?'[8] It is no accident that contemporary fictional narratives of travels in 'exotic lands', such as H. Rider Haggard's *King Solomon's Mines*, initially published in 1885, and early films focussed on 'natives' and their ways of life, created sentiments and visual tropes not too different from the anthropological texts and travel writings of the time. In the process, they created what MacDougal has called 'literary and theatrical savages' (MacDougal 1999 [1997]: 279).

In a similar sense, Daniel Defoe's famous novel *Robinson Crusoe*,[9] first published in 1719, Swiss clergyman Johann David Wyss' *The Swiss Family Robinson*,[10] first published in 1812, and the 24-volume *Tarzan* series written by American writer Edgar Rice Burroughs between 1912 and 1965 created through these texts a kind of European or American white superhero, who could deal with, 'understand', and subdue the 'savages' of these places. The 'literary and theatrical savages' who entered our consciousness through these fictional narratives continue to linger in our memories, and much of that memory is based on the visualisation of these characters and their adventures created by both written and pictorial texts. In these fictional accounts, the control of nature as well as the domestication of natives and their cultures in distant places was achieved through European ingenuity, superior intelligence, and a limited transfer of technology within the limits allowed by the storylines and prevailing ideological proclivities.

What is important is that these popular texts, along with their pictorial narratives, were fictional ideological statements that on the one hand justified and rationalised colonialism at a popular plain, and on the other, created in the European and North American imagination the kind of encounters, objects, and 'savages' that Euro-American readerships expected to see as travel narratives and images from the colonies began to circulate in Europe and North America. It was in such a context that Rice has observed, with particular reference to US colonial policy after the Spanish-American War, that 'colonialism can only be understood as part of the history of photography', in the context of which 'the legitimation of US colonial ambition relied on the effective use of photography to promote US interests' (Rice 2011: 1). There was obviously a very clear 'understanding' of the kind of images and photographs that made contextual sense in travel writing, fiction, early films, as well as anthropological and other early 'scholarly' works. Seen in this sense, none of these images or photographs created a discourse of innocence or leisurely curiosity devoid of a sense of politics; rather, they created one of power and ideological control. Photography, as it developed in the colonies, was essentially following the same trajectory that other image-makers had already established, but which it could do much more comprehensively. Biswas notes that after the opening of the Suez Canal in 1869, which made travel to Asia and East and Southern Africa much easier, European photographers began to 'seek out new professional avenues, following in the steps of early painters' (Biswas 2015: 52).

In this context, the specific construction of imagery and the way of understanding and using the visual were central considerations in the colonial discourse. Initially, Louis Jacque-Mande Daguerre invented photography through the daguerreotype technology in 1839. The arrival of this specific technology in South Asia was surprisingly rapid. The process of daguerreotype photography was explained in detail in Indian newspapers as early as December 1839, the same year its discovery was publicised in Europe (British Council 2000: 12). Available evidence suggests that the same technology was available in Ceylon by the mid-1840s (ibid.). An advertisement in the *Young Ceylon* (Vol. 1, 1850), a monthly publication focussed on arts and literature, attests to the prevalence and popularity of this process in the 1850s (Raheem 2015: 32). Almost from the beginning, photography became an essential technology of colonial expansion and expression. It started playing the role that other kinds of image-making had hitherto accomplished in documenting the pre-colonial other in the European imagination, as well as the objects of encounter in early colonialism. On the other hand, photography in this specific context was also a matter of locating and justifying the imperial presence and its political and social agenda in the colonies. As argued by Lanny Thompson, photography has to be understood as a core element in 'a comprehensive cultural process of establishing imperial hegemony; part of the practice of conceiving, creating, justifying, and governing a far-flung empire ...' (Thompson 2002: 4).

Malavika Karlekar, talking about the entry of the camera and the photographic studio into the colonial space with a focus on India, notes that nineteenth-century imperial politics necessitated the establishment of a number of new institutions and the introduction of specific innovations and different ways of life in the colonies (Karlekar 2013: xiv). In this context, 'the camera and the studio became necessary prostheses in this new arrangement between peoples', which 'recorded, classified, and docketed a subject people' (ibid.). In this new constellation of political power, ideology, and technology, she identifies two important ways in which photography established itself as a crucial cultural and political practice in the colonies.

First, at an official and formal level, 'the photograph assisted the imperial gaze' in setting up an 'intricate system of surveillance and control' (ibid.). One of the ways in which this was used very early in

South Asia was through the use of photographs to identify criminals and what was perceived to be categories of criminality. Anderson, in her book *Legible Bodies: Race, Criminality and Colonialism in South Asia*, explains convincingly how photographs of convicted criminals and tattoos on their bodies established the ability to keep tabs on these individuals over a long period of time, effectively making their criminal bodies legible in colonial law enforcement discourse and practice (Anderson 2004). More importantly, this also established the beginning of law enforcement's long-term association with photography in the process of criminal investigation and identity consolidation in the region. Photography's association with crime scenes, which came to be known much later as forensic photography, was also established in South Asia quite early on as part of the imperial expansion of this surveillance and control system in the region. Norman Chevers, in the context of his work in Calcutta, noted in 1856 that photographs of crime scenes and victims could help magistrates and civil surgeons who might be located at great distances away from the actual scenes of crime (Karlekar 2013: 10). That is, photography facilitated the creation of bodies of evidence that could be read later in the process of making judicial decisions.

Second, and at a more unofficial and informal level, the 'photographic gaze brought pleasure and excitement as it satisfied the proclivities to record, document, and immortalize' specific people and events (ibid.: xiv). This led to the emergence of both private and public collections of photographs. Some of these photographs also became an important aspect of formal and official publications. It is in the latter context that one can understand the power of photography-heavy books such as Arnold Wright's *Twentieth Century Impressions of Ceylon*[11] published in 1907, John Forbes Watson and John William Kaye's eight-volume tome, *The People of India*,[12] published between 1868–75 (with 468 photographs), Herbert Risley's *The People of India*,[13] initially published in 1908 (the second edition, edited by W. Crooke, was published in 1915 with thirty-six illustrations), and Dean Worcester's *The Philippine Islands and Their People*,[14] published in 1898, and many other such publications.

In the more informal and private realm, photography was not only a practice of the colonial rulers, European settlers in the colonies, and travellers, but also became a practice eagerly adopted by the colonised elites. As Pinney notes, 'the Indian elite's seduction by photography cannot be overstated' (Pinney 2015: 24). Many of the images they captured through photography at the time, such as the numerous portraits of Indian maharajahs and their families, today constitute an important component of colonial-era photographs. But photography in South Asia cannot be fully understood as a practice adopted and nurtured by the established elite alone. As Allana notes, by the last decade of the nineteenth century in the Indian context, photography, which had been patronised purely by the royalty, commercial enterprise, or the colonial government, became a practice that was also adopted by 'the emerging classes' (Allana 2013: 58). My reading of photography in the colonial period is undertaken through its implication in studio photography, science, commerce, and aesthetic and thematic politics of framing.

Studio Photography: Standardisation of Posturing and Equalising 'Public' Spaces

Early on, as the camera was invented and its practice progressed, one of the institutions that emerged with it was the 'photographic studio'. This was essentially a space in which experts ordered and situated people to be photographed according to a set of conventions, and then proceeded to photograph them. This was a matter of immortalising the self and her/his significant others in pictorial form, which was far easier to achieve than what was necessitated in portrait painting. This was due to photography's technical provenance, which allowed for a likeness to be manufactured more quickly than was possible with painting. At a very crucial level, studio photography emerged within the tradition of portraiture, which had already been established via painting. Barthes notes that 'the portrait-photograph is a closed field of forces' (Barthes 2000: 13). It is 'closed' because everything that is supposed to give the image meaning is restricted to within its frames, and has no direct reference to the worlds beyond pictorially. Within this field, four specific image-repertoires intersect, which simultaneously oppose and distort each other (ibid.). More specifically, 'in front of the lens, I am at the same time: the one I think I am, the one I want others to think I am, the one the photographer think I am, and the one he makes use of to exhibit his art' (ibid.). In this sense, the visual capture of a person in photographic form is not the simple memorialisation of a single manifestation of the self. It complicates how the person is represented in a single photo, which varies according to context as well as the intentions of the photographer and the sitter. In this scheme of things, as Barthes puts it, 'I am neither subject nor object but a subject who feels he is becoming an object: I then experience a micro-version of death' (ibid.: 14). That death, in the Barthesian sense, takes place when the portrait is captured in film, and when its repertoires of representation traverse beyond the control of the individual in the image.

In comparison, Pinney looks at portraiture more simply as 'the self-presentation of the body as "effigy"' (Pinney 2013: 12). That is, the portrait is simply a representation of the self or an effigy of the self constructed pictorially, in much the same way that portrait painting of the earlier era was understood. On the other hand, portrait is not only about the self. In the initial studio setting itself, the portrait was extended to include the significant others of the self, which created the group photo. The group photo was initially meant to be an extended image of the extended family, although it later expanded to include the photos of officers of military detachments, workforces of feudal lords, and entire 'communities' in terms of the colonial imagination of the ethno-cultural diversity of the colonies. Although there is a clear continuity between portraiture in painting and photography, in the sense that the traditions of the former informed the practices of the latter, the main claim of photographic portraits was its declaration of absolute authenticity in reproducing the likeness of the self, through technical means informed only by science. Unlike in portrait paintings, photographic portraits in the initial period under-emphasised the fallibilities and innovations brought in by photographers in preference to its perceived possibilities of absolute representation. A similar relationship exists between portraiture and figuration as well. While the primary goal of both is to construct representations of the self, their approaches vary at times. Citron has suggested 'that the primary goal of portraiture is to reveal a likeness of the sitter', while figuration 'may or may not include verisimilitude in its form as it explores physical and psychological aspects of the human condition' (Citron 2013: 32).

In the initial period, as portrait photography was inventing itself, portraits of individuals or groups produced in studios depended considerably on assorted accessories that were expected to add a sense of glamour as well as cultural and sartorial meaning to the photograph that was ultimately produced. These pre-photograph preparations with accessories were augmented later, after the photograph was actually taken, by retouching the print (Grundberg, et al. 2017).

A number of pioneering studio owners transited from this primary means of studio photography to engage in the same practice by introducing other elements, such as controlling light more creatively, changing the camera angles, and so on. One of the early success stories in this scheme of things were the works of Gaspard-Félix Tournachon, better known by his pseudonym, Nadar (ibid.). Tournachon began his studio photography in 1853 in Paris to make portraits of well-known Frenchmen of the time, in order to study their features and include these in a large caricature lithograph called the 'Panthéon Nadar' (ibid.). He made his sitters pose 'against plain backgrounds and bathed them with diffused daylight, which brought out every detail of their faces and dress' (ibid.). This technique was something that Tournachon innovated, even though he did not engage in photography himself, which was left to his assistants. His role, emanating from his preexisting career as a caricaturist, was to stage-manage and creatively visualise the entire studio setting.

Another pioneering and path-breaking studio-photographer was Julia Margaret Cameron, who was born in Calcutta in 1815 and died in Kalutara, Ceylon in 1879. Cameron, who started photography in 1863, insisted that her work must be considered 'art' (Higgins 2015). Her attempt was never to recreate any kind of perceivably externally existing reality within her studio space and claim a sense of authenticity over what she created, as was the case with much of colonial photography of the time, as we will see later in this chapter. Instead, she often created fantasies by reinventing historic or mythic characters through her photography. Her insistence that her work be understood as art thus becomes comprehensible. As noted by Higgins, 'from her housemaid to Alfred Tennyson', Cameron 'wrestled everybody into her studio, dressing them up as characters from Shakespeare and the Bible' (Higgins 2015). Laura Troubridge describes Cameron's insistent efforts to procure sitters for her work, which even extended to unknown tourists leisurely admiring the maritime views in her neighbourhood (ibid.). Such hapless tourists 'were liable to find themselves bidden in a way that brooked no denial into her studio, where, a few moments later, they would find themselves posing as Geraint, or Enid, Launcelot, or Guinevere...' (ibid.). But Cameron also created many regular portraits of well-known people in her signature style, in addition to the kind of reenactments referred to above.

Cameron's photography—whether recreations of mythical and historical characters or regular portraits of people—was typified by its soft-edged images, created by manoeuvring the lens to render some segments of the photographs blurry, giving them a kind of dreamy sensibility. In her own words,

> [M]y first successes in my out-of-focus pictures were a fluke. That is to say, that when focusing and coming to something which, to my eye, was very beautiful, I stopped there instead of screwing on the lens to the more definite focus which all other photographers insist upon. (Higgins 2015)

In this sense, Cameron was not only creating fantasies, but was also self-consciously experimenting with her photography.

Unlike many other studio photographers of their time, both Tournachon and Cameron brought into studio photography clear possibilities of experimentation and fantasy early in the development of the genre of portraiture within studio settings. The photographic studio, like the camera itself, came to South Asia as a result of colonial intrusions into the area. In the Indian context, members of the middle classes began patronising studios from about the end of the 1850s onwards (Karlekar 2013: xvi). Other major cities in the region show a similar trend. Initially, only men were allowed to be photographed in studios, even though women followed soon after. In India, after the commercial success of the early studios frequented by the social elites of the time was quickly established, many studios were set up in different parts of the country, initially in the three presidencies, and then in the princely states and in cities like Hyderabad and Lucknow (ibid.: 85–86). One can see a similar trend in other parts of South Asia, such as colonial Ceylon with well-known studios not only in Colombo, but also in Kandy and later in the southern town of Matara and the northern town of Jaffna. Not only studio photography, but photography in general also spread soon, from the higher social strata to other socially powerful and upwardly mobile classes.

Looking specifically at the Indian experience, Karlekar identifies the studio as a 'performative space', within which 'the "sitters" often catapulted into the role of unwitting actors' who had to perform in front of a number of possible backdrops and other accompaniments, which were expected to make the resultant photograph 'perfect' (ibid.: 19). It was also 'an environment of consent, and closeness' as well as 'alienation', depending on the way individual photographers opted to map out their subjects (Allana 2013: 60). So early studios, despite the anticipated gratification of the final product, were also stressful places in which one required considerable discipline, time, energy, and a positive frame of mind (Karlekar 2013: 19–21). These conditionalities emanated from the nature of the technology available, the need to sit still for considerable periods of time due to slow shutter speeds of cameras, and so on. The items that were needed to create the anticipated ambience and make the performance successful included 'vellum-bound tomes, a variety of exotic potted plants, a selection of object d'art, and ottomans, divans, ornate chairs, footstools', etc. (ibid.: 19). While the exact nature of these objects changed with the affluence of specific studios, their location, and their clientele, there was nevertheless a certain standardisation of the type of objects and the overall settings. As a result, this led to a relative homogenisation of atmosphere and backgrounds across the colonial world, which is very evident in South Asia as well.

However, backdrops and accessories did not always make their presence felt in some genres of portraits that emerged in South Asian studios. Instead, the entire focus of these images was the person himself, while the background remained under-defined or blurred, much like many of Cameron's well-known portraits of people such as Alfred Lord Tennyson, Henry Thoby Prinsep, Sir John Herschel, Julia Prinsep Jackson, and many others (see Image 2.3 for an example of this kind of portrait from India). In the words of Pinney, this was often a matter of privileging 'formality and frontality' (Pinney 2013: 12).

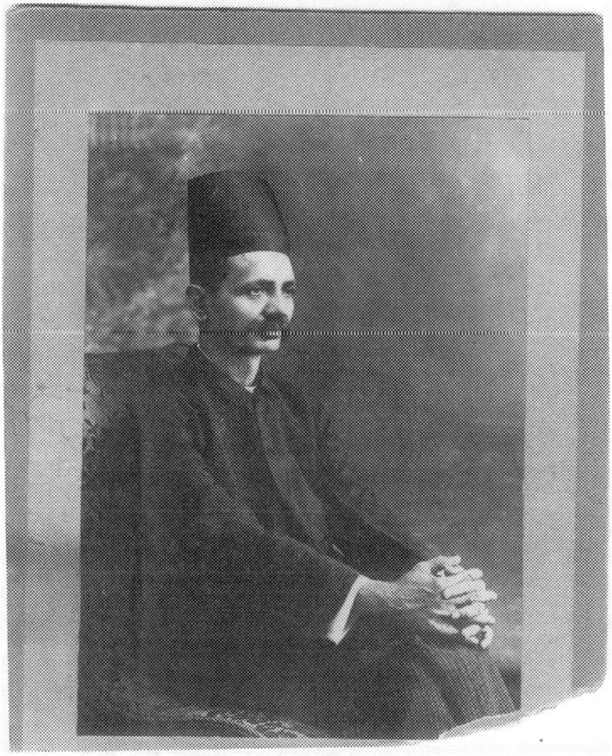

IMAGE 2.3 Portrait of a Parsi man with a blurred and under-emphasised wallpaper with floral design. Perhaps circa 1930s, studio and photographer unknown.

Photograph courtesy of: Author's research collection.

The photographic capture of persons and the popularisation of portraits nudge us to ponder over how the self and its visual re-creation as well as figuration in general was understood in South Asia, and to see if these ideas had an impact on portrait composition in the region. The practice of figuration in South Asia, as seen in its multiple traditions of painting and sculpture, is quite old, even though portraiture itself as we understand it today was introduced in the Mughal period in India via European influence (Citron 2013: 32). In South Asian art, the history of dealing with the figure is 'layered', and 'spans from Mohenjo Daro to Mumbai, sacred and secular forms, and every imaginable artistic medium and moment' (ibid.: 30). Coomaraswamy, in his essay 'The Traditional Conceptions of Ideal Portraiture', notes the existence of votive bronze statuettes in the Indian tradition, which were specifically meant to be 'portraits' of different donors (Coomaraswamy 1956: 117). Similarly, at times Sri Lankan Buddhist temple paintings also depicted the figures of kings and regional rulers who had contributed to the construction of specific temples. And in the colonial period, it was also quite normal to find the painted portrait of Queen Victoria above the main doorways in major temples, in recognition of her political sway over the island. But in the South Asian tradition understood in this sense, these portraits 'cannot be distinguished, or scarcely distinguished, from divine Images' (ibid.). Even so, 'the intention to represent a human being is evident' in this tradition (ibid.). As Coomaraswamy further elaborates, in these local renditions of portraiture, 'facial expression is altogether of a type, without individual peculiarities' (ibid.). What is present is the idea of representation of the self or a specific other. However, in this case, identity was not established by facial or other such clearly defined physical identity features in the manner that photography later claimed to do. Instead, this was done in symbolised form and by various associations, including sartorial codes, politically and culturally defined insignia carried by painted figures, and so on. But again, according to Coomaraswamy, the region's dramatic literature provides numerous and detailed references to a 'secular art of portraiture in which a real likeness to the living subject was essential to the social, and largely erotic, purpose of the work' (ibid.).

In this sense, the extent to which a likeness of the subject was maintained in the traditional South Asian conception of portraiture was contextual, and based on the exact purpose for which the portrait was being made. This was also partly related to the two main types of portraiture in the Indian tradition that Coomaraswamy refers to (ibid.: 117–18), which I think can be broadly extended to much of pre-colonial South Asia's understandings of portraiture. One of these was the 'posthumous, hieratic, and ideal' conception of portraiture, while the other was 'taken from life, profane, and sentimental' (ibid.). This categorisation is also linked to two other appearances of the self, as referred to in a number of Indic texts such as *Lankavatara Sutra* and *Chandogya Upanisad* (ibid.: 118). This distinction is between the 'appearance of the man' as he is outwardly seen to the naked eye, and 'the interior image' of that same man, 'invisible to the physical eye but accessible to the eye of contemplation' (ibid.). *Lankavatara Sutra* refers to this latter perception of the self as 'the picture that is not in colours'[15] (quoted in ibid.). These understandings of the self and their replication in pictorial form are deeply rooted in the region's religious and cognitive-intellectual traditions. Even so, as Coomaraswamy himself notes, similar positions of ideal portraiture also existed in European traditions (ibid.).

My intention behind this diversion into a brief reflection on the conventional South Asian understanding of portraiture outlined above was to explore whether the kind of photographic portrait we have inherited from the colonial archive is based on a continuity of this older tradition. Pinney notes that the ancient Indian practice described by Coomaraswamy and others 'could be easily transposed to a 19th century colonial context in which photographers working directly or indirectly or even the British colonial state presented anonymised "typical" specimens of the peoples of India' (Pinney 2013: 62). But can the transmission of aspects of local tradition in painting and sculpture to colonial period photography be seamlessly and so easily accomplished? It is true that some specific nuances of local tastes, cultural sensibilities, and aesthetics were creatively, and at times directly, adapted to painting and photographic practices imported from Europe. It is in such a context that we can see examples of Rajput and Mughal aesthetics in the framing of some Indian photographs of the nineteenth century (Citron 2013: 30). But these are only in very specific and highly contextual examples, and did not necessarily form the norm of period photography, even in India. There is also no substantial evidence in the form of written articulations of the time, or any actual and consistent practice of photographers self-consciously adopting pre-existing local practices in their work, as opposed to what was imported. What is more visible in practices such as studio photography in general and studio-based portrait photography in particular is the ready adoption of conventions established in Europe, which were available at the time photography and its associated practices initially emerged, and were imported to the rest of the world as a set of codified practices. But there is no doubt that embellishment of these practices based on local conditions and tastes did take place at times. This is what is also evident in South Asia more generally. Given the power of aesthetics in the colonial period, it is likely that the early portrait photographers in South Asia were far more familiar with these European-derived traditions rather than with the finer points of local conventions. It is a different matter that these practices coincided with some local aesthetics and structures of taste, which were then incorporated into contemporary practice under very specific circumstances.

Except in the case of local royalty, who sometimes demanded elaborate backdrops for their portraits, the most commonly available surviving studio efforts in South Asia did not create the kind of fantasies associated with some of Cameron's best-known works, despite the performative nature of these spaces. While what was created in early South Asian studios also had many elements of constructedness and make-believe, they were essentially photos of individuals or groups in recognisable settings. For instance, ordinary people were not transformed into fairies or gods, as one can deduce from many surviving portraits. Instead, they were immortalised in seemingly respectable poses, often with regalia indicating the sitters' social and political power, while being foregrounded in broadly accepted settings. Although the kind of things people wore depended on ethno-culturally and politically derived sartorial codes mandated by existing traditions as well as conventions in transition under colonial influence, what they sat on, how they stood, the personal space between people, accessories in place, backdrops, and so on show a remarkable degree of routinisation and standardisation (see Images 2.4 and 2.5 for representative examples from Sri Lanka and India).

Nevertheless, the studio in South Asia as a 'theatrical set-up' manned by experts, studio sets (such as what can be seen in Images 2.4 and 2.5, as well as much more elaborate accessories in more affluent studios), and specialised lighting systems became a norm as the studio evolved as an institution (Karlekar 2013: 20). All of these gave such spaces the 'impression of a stage, a place where the client had often to play-act as to appear "real"' (ibid.). But 'real' in this sense can only be ascertained in comparison to absolute fantasy, as nothing in these portraits was 'normal'. Rather, they were hyped to create a heightened sense of reality or normalcy, which itself was unreal.

In this context, as Karlekar notes with regard to India, clients very quickly adopted and adapted studio codes from the West in their quest to acquire studio portraits (ibid.). At one level, these included what was available in terms of props and services to make the final photograph as perfect as possible. For instance, Raja Deen Dayal's studios in Bombay, Indore, and Secundabad, which invested heavily in props, were not very different from the London studios of the time (ibid.). However, on another level, these studio codes went much beyond adopting props and services from Western models to include a set of protocols on how and where to place them, where sitters should sit and the angles of the cameras, and so on. In this sense, the entire studio exercise was a matter of using a set of Western-derived codes to order the interior of the studio and the bodies of sitters according to similarly adopted conventions, to make a portrait that had local iconic value. What differed or what was adapted were the sartorial practices, which were influenced by local trends and regional cultural identities as well as colonialism's hybrid impact on the one hand, and the affluence of a specific studio and its clientele on the other. But the entire exercise of going to a studio and getting a portrait made was also a matter of establishing that one had acquired a specific kind of taste, which hopefully placed them on par with their colonial masters.

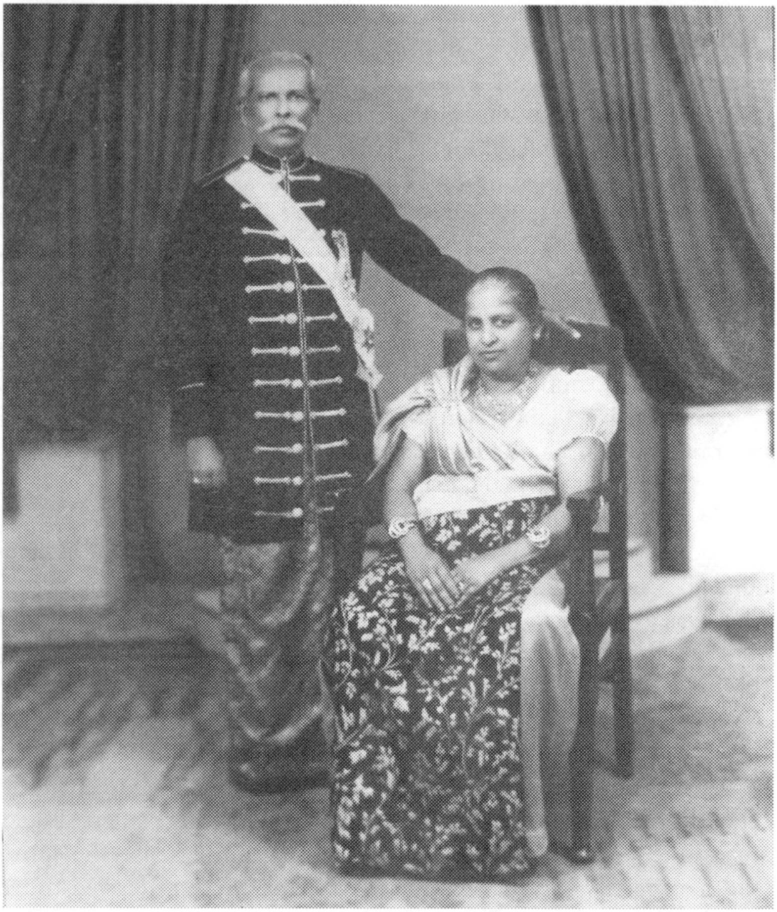

IMAGE 2.4 Don Phillip Rajapakse and Seelawathi Rajapakse, circa 1950s; Broadway Studio, Matara, Sri Lanka.

Note the simple draped backdrop (studios in Colombo at the time would have offered something far more complex), faded carpet, and posturing, in terms of the man standing while the woman is seated. In situations where both men and women were involved, women were almost never standing while men were seated. Also note the man's sense of authority, based on sartorial coding. He is wearing an 'official' jacket denoting recognition from the colonial government, which many recipients continued to wear well into Independence as a status symbol.

Photograph courtesy of: Author's family collection.

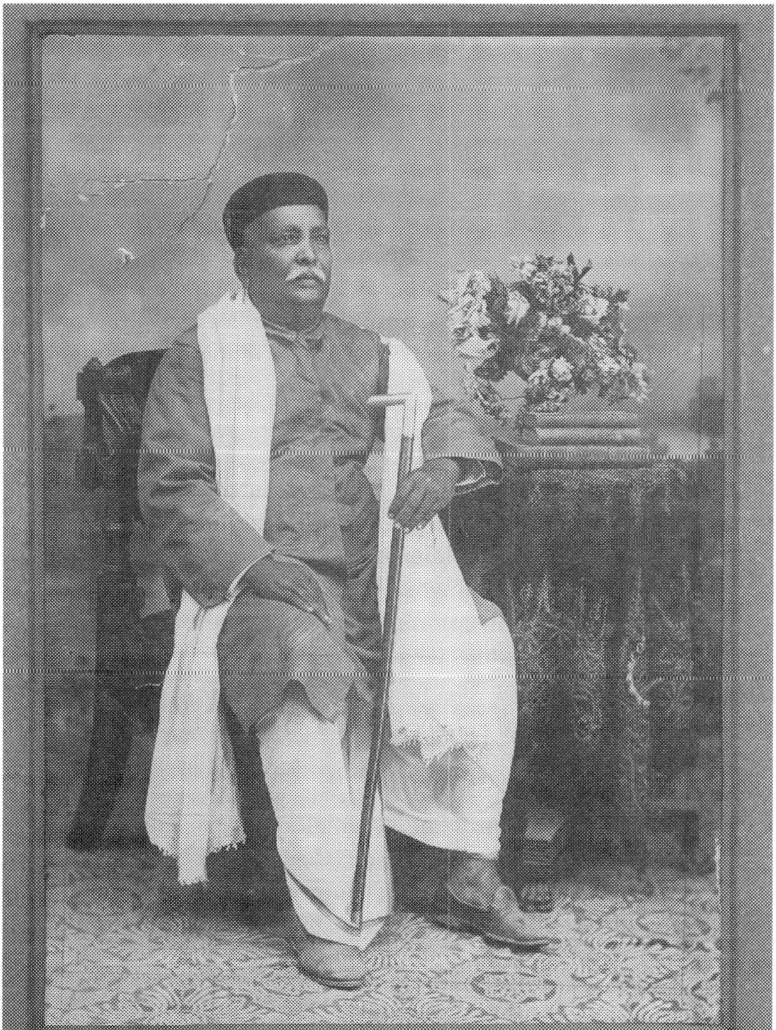

IMAGE 2.5 Unidentified sitter, circa 1940s; studio unknown, India.

Note: Note the blurred backdrop, carpet, and the uncomplicated accessories, indicating a regional studio. Also note the seating arrangement, offering the man a sense of authority based on sartorial coding.

Photograph courtesy of: Author's research collection.

In a very different context, with reference to aboriginal portrait photographs from nineteenth-century Australia, Michael Aird suggests that through these photographs, the aboriginal people who commissioned them 'felt a very real need to tell their successes in the European community to ensure protection from the oppressive "protection" policies' (Aird 1993: vii). In the specific history of Australia's relationship with its native people, photographs in this sense offered a kind of protection against the division of families based on what was known as protection policies. That is, children deemed neglected by their parents could be removed from their families and communities, ostensibly for their own benefit, while adults requesting government assistance could be resettled in aboriginal stations specifically set up for that purpose far away from their original locations (Aird 1993). In these very specific circumstances, according to Aird, photographs of assumed aboriginal success in European terms were expected to protect them from the intrusive and disruptive actions of the State (ibid.). That is, photos became 'evidence' of the aboriginals' adoption of the practices and tastes of white middle-class respectability.

While the situation in colonial South Asia where studio practices expanded was nothing like what Aird describes for Australia, the broader implications of the adoption of studio photography by the middle classes across regional and ethno-cultural boundaries in the region shows a similar tendency in terms of the adoption of what was considered 'respectable', 'upscale', and 'measures of success' within the prevailing dominant, colonial European cultural norms. For the locals, this was a civilising practice while for the colonial elite, it was an indication of the relative cultural success of the colonial-imperial project. It is precisely this urge that ensured that even in the initial period of studio photography in India, it was not just the first generation of Anglicised professionals who ventured into the studios. This experimental journey was also undertaken by native princes and the landed elite (Karlekar 2013: 86). As such, what mattered was not merely one's proximity to the powers that be in social and cultural terms, but one's local social and cultural status as well as affluence. But it took much more time for the studios to become places where very ordinary people could also get their portraits done.

Although clearly a very mediated product, studio photography has offered a very distinct genre of photographs of both the colonial world in general and colonial South Asia in particular, which narrates sedate and structured stories of cultural difference, dynamics of taste acquisition, social power, sartorial variations based on regional and ethno-cultural considerations, and so on (see Images 2.6, 2.7, and 2.8 for studio portraits from colonial India and Ceylon depicting clear sartorial differences based on variations in class, regional, and cultural identities).

When it comes to portrait photography and studio photography in particular, 'painted photographs', which emerged from about the 1860s onwards, stand out as an important genre throughout South Asia. At a fundamental level, a painted photograph is a black-and-white photo on which paint has been applied manually. Dewan (2012) notes that paint on a photograph of this kind may be applied through retouching, hand-colouring, tinting, or through any other method. Effectively, then, this was a matter of bringing together two different types of pictorial expression on a single surface, that is, photography and painting. The difference between these two forms, as evident in the early justification for the 'scientific' nature of photography outlined earlier in this chapter, was that photographs offered an 'immediacy and transparency of depiction', which paintings never could (Van Gelder and Westgeest 2011: 14). This is despite the latter's claims to authenticity in the representation of objects in realist painting traditions and in the skills of artists.

However, the idea behind making this colour intrusion into the black-and-white surface is to enhance the sense of 'realism' it is supposed to present. That is, in order to make the photo seem more real, its original structure is self-consciously manipulated, making it far from real. But the idea was to bring into the photographs the actual colour of the clothes, jewellery, and ornaments worn by the sitters, and in some instances, to make them look 'better'. It is in this context that Dewan (2012) has suggested that Indian painted photographs need to be understood within the broader practices of photo manipulation. Obviously, this understanding goes much beyond Indian painted photography to embrace this genre of photography everywhere.

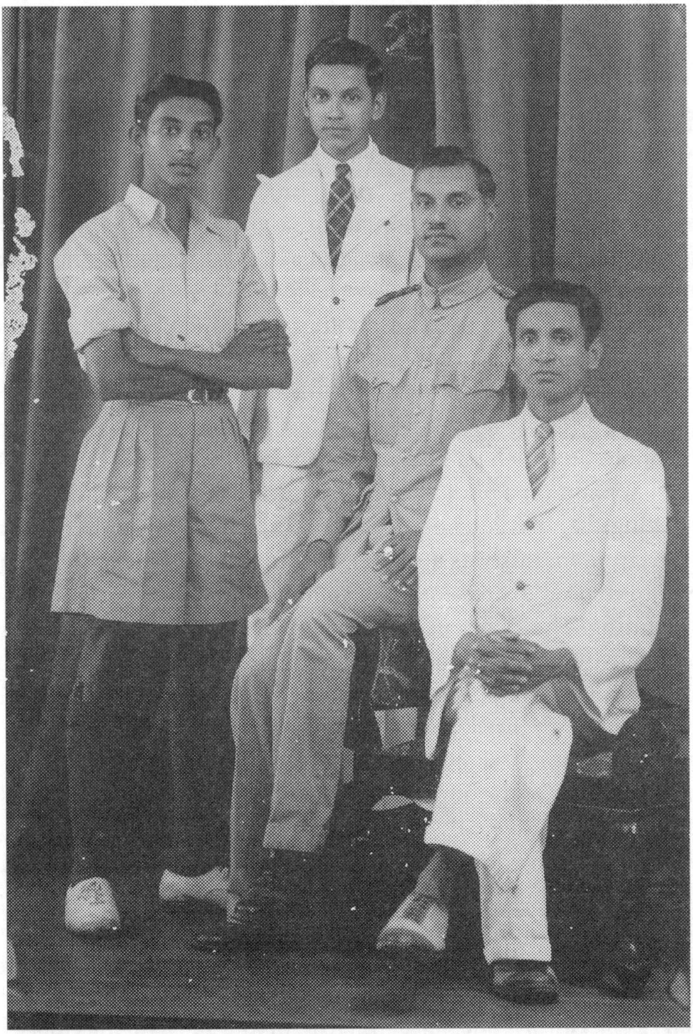

IMAGE 2.6 A group of brothers in Ceylon in the late 1940s, photographed in an unknown Colombo studio.

Their clothes indicate their clear adoption of colonial sartorial preferences, which transgressed beyond Independence in 1948. One of the costumes is a uniform, indicating government service (see the second man from right).

Photograph courtesy of: Author's family collection.

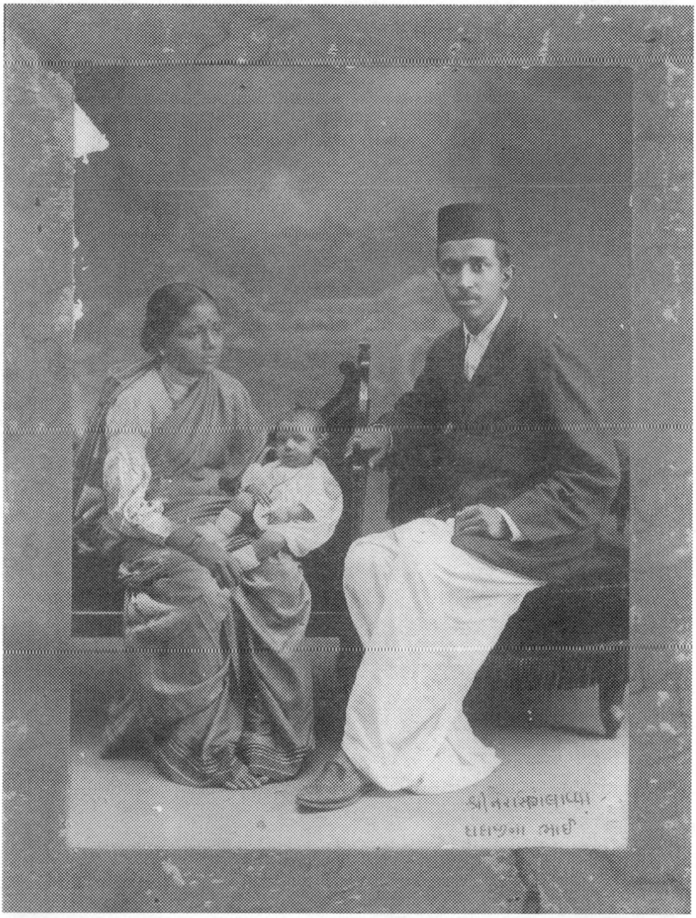

IMAGE 2.7 A mother, a father, and a child in the 1930s in India. Studio unknown.

The father's jacket indicates a limited adoption of what was available from colonial sartorial practices to invent a hybrid local code. This photo, like many others in the period, indicates an interest to photograph the nuclear family in studio settings, evident in India post-the 1870s, despite the fact that most people lived within extended family conditions. But Karlekar notes that the trend of photographing married couples on their own indicates a 'more compact domestic arrangement, a shift from the joint family norm' (Karlekar 2013: 88).

Photograph courtesy of: Author's research collection.

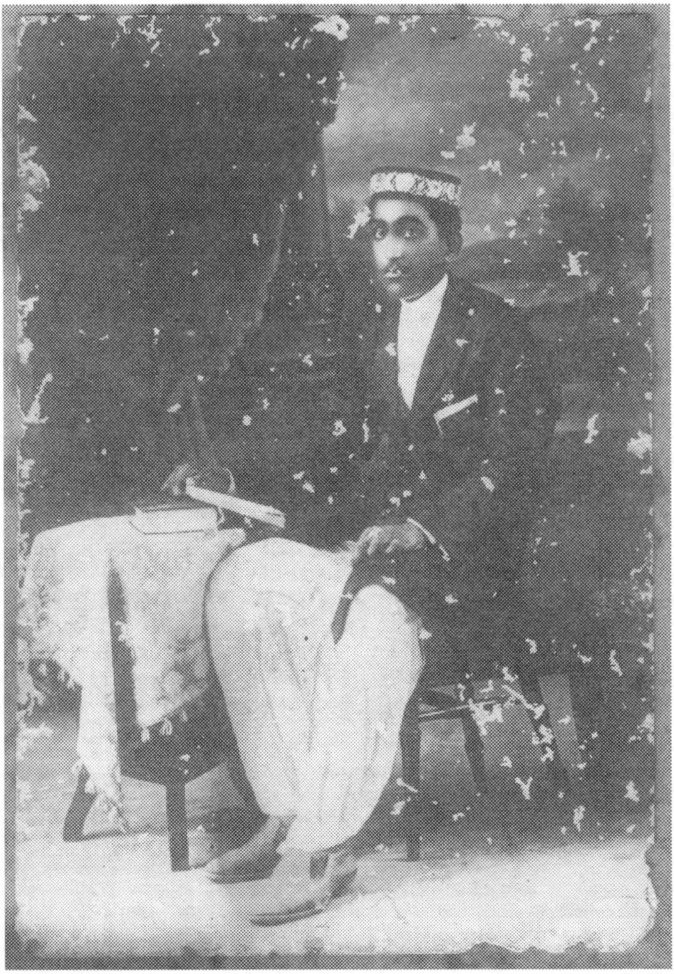

IMAGE 2.8 A studio portrait of a young man in the 1920s in India. Studio unknown.

As in the case of the man in Image 2.7, the jacket indicates a limited sartorial innovation by combining colonial practices and local conditions. The right hand resting on books on a side table, a common posture at the time, most probably suggests that the man in the photo was educated in the colonial system of schooling.

Photograph courtesy of: Author's research collection.

Although, like the camera and the act of photography itself, the colouring of a black-and-white photograph as a technique was borrowed from the West, the nature of comprehending colours within a local structure of taste as well as preexisting traditions of painting impacted the way painted photographs were executed. This was very visible when it came to the traditions of portraiture already mastered by Mughal courts, whose compositions were borrowed by painted photographs. In India and in South Asia more generally, rather than built structures or landscapes, the preferred subjects of paintings were portraits. As a result, throughout the colonial period, painted photographs developed in the region as mostly individual or group portraits. As in the case of photography more generally, painted photographs too initially developed as an elite practice.[16] Much of the base photographs needed for painted photographs were either taken in studios, or in studio-like set-ups created in the households of elite patrons from royal families, and upper-class individuals. They were also the ones who initially adopted the practice.

But particularly in South Asia, with its intense degrees of social and cultural segregation and hierarchies, studios interestingly became equalising spaces to which Maharajas as well as local merchants, traders, and government servants would go to get their portraits done, as long as they had the ability to pay for the services. As noted by Karlekar, 'the unsegregated photographic studio clearly went against the principle of difference so carefully maintained in railway compartments, clubs, and even parks' (Karlekar 2013: 21). This does not, however, mean that the studio's social experimentation percolated down to the broader society. Instead, it was a liminal space which offered respectability and fantasy to everyone while they were in the studio, even though people from differing social or cultural backgrounds were not necessarily photographed together. It was a sequential enterprise, in which the same space became the stage for differing people to perform at different times by themselves. Institutionalised differences beyond the studio continued until much later times.

Clearly, the kinds of images presented in this discussion (for example, Images 2.3–2.8) are no longer merely visual tropes that ended up in people's personal albums or framed and hung on the walls of their homes. But this was the primary reason for undertaking the effort, because they were considered 'precious objects' and 'important markers of the cultural milieu still in the process of defining itself' (Karlekar 2013: 88). Today, these photos are also pointers to a bygone era, even though some of their personal and emotional information might have been lost over time. As such, I am unaware of the family details of the individuals whose photos have moved from their original personal albums and homes to my research collection, in the context of which the personal dimension has been ruptured. This is true to some extent about the portraits and other photographs in my family collection as well, even though some personal details can still be compiled with an effort. Despite these lapses and gaps, it is still possible to at least partially narrate through these images an incomplete but telling cultural history of the late nineteenth century, and the first half of the twentieth century. The partial information suggested in the captions of these photographs is indicative of these narrative possibilities. In this sense, as Tagg has noted, portrait constitutes of 'a sign of whose purpose is both the description of an individual and inscription of social identity' (Tagg 1988: 37).

Colonialism, 'Science', and the Implication of Photography

As colonialism expanded, it created in its wake an intellectual climate where social Darwinism had considerable influence. It is in this context that Maxwell notes that 'no less than the botanical and zoological specimens that preoccupied Victorian scientists, colonized peoples were exposed to hierarchical systems of classification' as a means to explain the emerging evolutionary theories of human origins (Maxwell 1999: 2). It is also in the same context that the first British Viceroy to India, Lord Canning, gave instructions in an official circular in 1861 to compile 'photographic likenesses of characteristic specimens of the more remarkable tribes of India', which he wanted reproduced in a large enough size to 'exhibit the chief physical peculiarities and distinctive costume of each race' (quoted in Karlekar

2013: 11). In this situation, colonial anthropology, zoology, and botany became influential not simply as 'sciences', but as a corpus of knowledge that had a direct implication on the colonial and imperial projects of expansion and domination. Photography became an essential tool in this scheme of knowledge and power.

This intellectual environment, fed directly by the successful expansion of colonies and the growing demand for a sustained gaze upon the 'uncivilised others' within the imperial metropolises, meant that the visual appearance of 'exotic people' or 'savages' as live exhibits in European and North American cities, and in the form of photographs in written texts as well as in exhibitions, became not only an established practice, but also an essential and anticipated one. Between 1863 and 1865 alone, Canning's instructions referred to above ensured the production of over 100,000 prints ostensibly depicting the 'various divisions of the Asian family' (Karlekar 2013: 11). These practices were catering to two needs: the need for what was considered scientific knowledge in post-industrialised Europe and North America within a discourse of enlightenment, and the need to satisfy curiosity at a more popular level. It is in this expanding and complex context that a group of Kwakiutl people were displayed live as part of the World's Columbian Exposition in Chicago in 1893, while 'imported' Senegalese swam in Parisian fountains to add a sense of African 'authenticity' and colour to the Exposition Ethnographique de l'Afrique Occidentale in 1895 (MacDougal 1999 [1997]: 276). These people, forcibly removed from their habitats, had no option but to utilise their performative power to enact in no uncertain terms the all-encompassing manner in which the empires held sway across their colonies. In a sense, on these occasions people from colonised lands had become very similar to performing animals in circuses and zoological gardens.

Even so, live performances were not always possible. Objects from the cultural repertoire of these peoples as well as photographs of them allegedly in their natural habitats, displayed at these exhibitions and at similar events, also helped to provide a sense of authenticity to these kinds of displays. It was in a similar vein that the Spanish government organised an exposition of 'Filipino Culture' in Madrid in 1887, which, in the words of historian Luis Angel Sanchez Gomez, was officially meant to increase 'commercial and economic relations between the archipelago and the metropolis' (quoted in Rice 2011: 2–3). At the same time, it also had the 'objective of showcasing' the Philippines' 'indigenous population to the Spaniards' (ibid.). Raheem has referred to a series of such expositions, some of which took place regularly in locations such as London (1861, 1871), Paris (1867, 1878, 1889, 1900), St. Louis (1904), and Sydney and Melbourne (1880) (Raheem 2015: 36). In all such exhibitions, the colonial gaze and the demands to visually consume the 'native' and 'savage' others were centrally implicated.

Collectively, beyond mere public consumption, these live and photographic expressions of 'difference' offered a sense of scientific respectability and validity not only to practices such as public exhibitions, but also to colonialism more generally. After all, many of these were undertaken within a discourse of expanding knowledge about the world and the human species. This scheme of things also helped to situate the displayed 'natives' on a scale between the 'civilized man and animal' (MacDougal 1999 [1997]: 279). In effect, it was this location that made it possible for such newly encountered people and their material culture as well as structures of belief to be understood within a discourse of primitive curiosity. Such visual aids were also tools of political intrusion, which attempted to justify the continued colonisation of these distant lands and their peoples for the ostensible goal of their future development and civilisation. One of the forms in which this alleged proximity of 'native' people to nature was documented and communicated was through photographs that focussed on the physical features of these peoples, their abundant use of animal products, and so on (ibid.). For instance, the 'primitive photos' exhibited in the 1887 Madrid exposition were seen and interpreted as those of 'savages' by most of the public at the time (Rice 2011: 3). Sanchez Gomez notes that contemporary liberal and more conservative Spaniards collectively believed that the reason for the 'low' quality of the material objects from the Philippines presented at the exposition was the 'consequence of the inherent abilities of the

Filipinos', which were ultimately attributed to their perceived racial inferiority (quoted in ibid.).

American zoologist, photographer, and ardent supporter of US imperialism, Dean Worcester, was an accomplished photographer who used his images—in the name of science—to promote specific ideological, political, and 'scientific' positions. Historian Alfred McCoy notes that Worcester was one of the most vociferous supporters of US imperialism, particularly in the Philippines, 'who believed firmly in racial evolution' and informed the students in his University of Michigan zoology classes that 'Filipino tribal "savages"' were the 'lowest of living men', the first step in man's cultural evolution from 'the gorilla and the orang-utan' (quoted in Rice 2011: 8). As outlined by McCoy, Worcester used photography to directly promote his political and scientific positions, in the context of which he posed himself, 'frame stiffly erect, body fully covered in colonial costume—towering above diminutive forest Negritos, their dark, wiry frames clad only in loincloths' (quoted in ibid.: 8–9). As he wrote in his well-known book illustrated with his own photographs, *The Philippine Islands and Their People* (initially published in 1898),[17] 'there are good reasons for believing them [that is, the Negritos] to be incapable of civilization; but this is of little importance, as they are rapidly disappearing, and seem destined to speedy extinction' (quoted in ibid.: 9). But in his thinking, the spread of colonialism had nothing to do with this state of affairs. Instead, the natives' 'supposed unfitness for survival in the modern world' was the cause for their own anticipated extinction (ibid.).

In this sense, in public displays and contemporary colonial documentation, there was a direct correlation between the exhibition of material objects on the one hand and live or photographed 'natives' on the other, which established a 'scientific' linkage between culture and mental abilities. Photographs in these cases heightened the sense of orientalist anxieties, bewilderment, adventure, and 'enlightenment' that the written text had already established as a tradition, which exhibitions further enhanced.

Commerce of Photography in Colonial Times

In the colonial period, photographs were not simply tools of scientific or political expression. From very early times, they also acquired a certain business legitimacy that was located in the colonial centres' appetite for exoticised knowledge of the colonised lands and their people. Betao's studio photos of aspects of Burmese society, Matzene's depiction of Nepali royalty, and Herzog's composition of the numerous families of the Rana clan indicate clearly their understanding of the 'growing private and public interest in viewing images from the East' (Allana 2013: 56). That is, these nineteenth-century photographers practising in South Asia had a realistic grasp of what their market demanded, and this was predominantly a market in Europe. In fact, a considerable proportion of what remains today as archives of colonial period photographs are the products of commercial or commissioned work. Enhanced technology available by the late nineteenth century, which led to the possibility of mass-production, ushered in a 'proliferation of stock images', which brought the 'enthralling world of printed images within reach' of anyone who wished to have them (ibid.). In the case of South Asia, Skeen and Company and Plate in Ceylon and Bourne and Shepard in undivided India are among the best-known companies—in addition to many individual photographers—that ensured the two territories were widely photographed as an integral part of a profitable commercial enterprise. One of the ways by which period photographers gained global recognition was through their participation in the kind of major expositions referred to earlier. With reference to colonial Ceylon, Raheem notes that resident photographers in the country were encouraged to take part in national and international exhibitions, which offered participants 'wide publicity, which generated new markets and hence, wider clientele' (Raheem 2015: 36). At the time, how photographs were framed and presented helped to make careers. For instance, Worcester's *Philippine Island and Their People* was printed four times within the first five months of its publication in October 1898, and captured the attention of American consumers and 'propelled its relatively young and unknown author to a career of fame, power, and fortune' (Rice 2011: 5).

But such popular demand for the consumption of photographs from colonised places also meant that the images had to be presented in a way that was easy to digest. That is, more than any sustained scientific knowledge, what was popularly demanded was a generalised and palatable sense of information about, and visually sensationalised images of, the colonised. But this was demanded in the name of authenticity even as the gaze of the market was being significantly standardised, often creating a considerable distance between what was 'real' and what was actually photographed. But period photographers generally claimed that their work was the result of 'a close encounter with a distant culture', with photography believed to be the 'ideal tool to capture the "real" hinterland' (Allana 2013: 58). In this context, Appadurai notes in his essay, *Colonial Backdrop* (1997), that 'colonial photographic practices, at least where human subjects were involved, allowed the documentary realism of the token (the particular person or group being photographed) to be absorbed into the fiction of the general "type," most often an ethnological type' (Appadurai 1997: 4). In this process, individuals and their specific locations in terms of culture and geography often lost their sense of identity and agency, and became exemplars of specific types. Allana notes how specific group portraits, often taken in outdoor locations, become 'a community image of ethnographic interest (as in the case of "Tea Planters" from Ceylon and "Todas" from India), or community occupation (as in the case of "Parched Grain Seller" or "The Prawn Seller")' (Allana 2013: 50). As Appadurai notes, 'the original captions for many nineteenth-century photographs capture this ambivalence in the choice of a definite article before the noun when referring to the subject of the photograph (Indian water-carrier; the Oriental harem; a Civil War Soldier)' (Appadurai 1997: 4). That is, the 'original captions are part of the photo backdrop (which can itself be understood as a component of the overall context of the photograph)' (ibid.).

This practice was overtly evident in *Twentieth Century Impressions of Ceylon* (1907), *The People of India* (1868), *The Philippine Islands and Their People* (1898), and many other period publications belonging to the same genre. This meant that the distinctiveness of places and people mattered less as opposed to their ability to be categorised and ordered as a specific and generalised type. This was partly the outcome of the demand for palatable visuals for mass public consumption. At the same time, this was also a matter of presenting visuals to a public that demanded the exotic as a general object, but not the specifics in a defined intellectual sense. This was particularly evident in collections of photographs and books with photographs produced for mass circulation. As a result, 'despite the fact that the settings are themselves highly distinctive, these images effectively "typicalize" the subject, even as they represent individuals more realistically' (Appadurai 1997: 4). In this context, 'early colonial photography contains, from the start, an ambivalence about its documentary authority, since it simultaneously seeks to capture individual subjects both as tokens and as types' (ibid.). However, the drop in this authority and the resultant ambivalence, which was at least partly a marketing device to make these images more palatable to the general public, was not an issue in the increasing popularity of these images. In fact, one of the main reasons for the intense popularity of such photographs in the colonial period was this lack of specificity, making such photographs viable commercial objects that adhered to a generalised sense of taste.

It is in this specific context that one can understand the rapid development in the demand for picture postcards and stereographs in the first decade of the twentieth century. The former—in different incarnations—continues well into the present. This demand grew and the supply of images expanded, based on two preconditions: (*i*) the almost complete expansion of colonialism throughout the world; and (*ii*) the resultant curiosity for visual records of its conquests that emerged in colonial centres, and more importantly, the ability of the technology of the time to cater to these demands. Take, for instance, the Keystone *Stereoscopic Encyclopedia*, published in 1906. Its first collection of 600 'views' or images comes with 154 references to race, location, and other 'cultural' details of people from across the world as understood at the time (MacDougal 1997: 279). In other words, these were not simply pictures of people and their socio-cultural contexts. More significantly, they were visual narratives of the world's ethno-cultural variation, accompanied by perceivably authoritative explanations within the limits of contemporary knowledge and ideological positions, which legitimised what these images sought to convey. In this situation, the photographs presented in the *Stereoscopic Encyclopedia* worked both as general objects of curiosity for those who wanted this, and also as more 'informed' visual objects via the written documentation for those inclined towards additional information. Thus, the way these images were presented ensured that they catered to both dominant structures of taste and demand for photographs from the colonies that were in place at the time.

Similarly, by 1907, H.C. White Company alone was able to produce 15,000 stereo view cards each day, while in the UK itself, 866 million picture postcards were produced between 1909 and 1910 (MacDougal 1997: 279). This shows the nature of the demand for visuals at the time; a very popular genre of such cards carried images of indigenous people in their local dress or in the nude (ibid.). Interestingly, many of these cards had borrowed from the photographic systems initially developed by scientists such as T.H. Huxley, John Lamprey, and others, and presented these images in a 'self-consciously "anthropometric" style' (ibid.). Again, the correlations between the Euro-American demand for 'exotic' visuals from the colonised world, the role of early anthropology in creating a specific anthropometric style of photography which lasted over the years, and the location of these images in fictional, scientific, and travel literature as well as in the business world of image production—as in the picture postcard business—should be self-evident.

Aesthetic and 'Subject' Politics of Colonial Photography

Colonial period photography was not merely a matter of science, colonial politics, and commerce. Intertwined with these primary concerns were three other important preoccupations, which dictated the way these photographs were framed during the period as well as what was considered worthy of photographing. These three preoccupations were: (*i*) iconic natural and architectural features within a broader understanding of 'landscape'; (*ii*) picturing people within a discourse of local cultural variety—often 'dramatised' for an added sense of the exotic; and (*iii*) scenes of 'development' and 'progress' brought about by the colonial masters. In this sense, photography in the colonial period—or, for that matter, in any period—cannot be assumed to consist of an over-encompassing and complete capture of the multiple realities of the time in a specific place. Self-consciously photographing the socio-cultural and geographic variety of a place in its complexity was hardly the concern of photographers. Given the fact that colonial photography by and large survived on commercial viability or official sponsorship, much of what was photographed and presented depended on the kinds of visual objects for which there was a demand, and how that demand could be aesthetically constructed. The photographic decisions taken also depended on subjective choices and the tastes of individuals, which invariably carried the social imprint of the time as well. In this situation, compared to photographs that fell within the three preoccupations referred to above, not too many opted to capture the realities of war, famine, or other kinds of misfortunes brought upon by colonialism itself. In this sense, one can argue that the colonial gaze, captured and preserved as above, was to a large extent thematically standardised and sanitised.

At the same time, there was also an obvious degree of aesthetic homogenisation at the time. What was photographed—particularly landscapes and ancient sites—was framed within an aesthetic sensibility that was familiar to the photographers as well as the consumers of their photographs in the metropolises. With regard to photography in colonial Ceylon, Biswas has noted that

> following artists and engravers of the earlier era, photographers had adopted a similar Victorian pictorial convention as a powerful framing device for representing natural beauty and the crumbling architecture to satisfy the demands of European artful manner, and frame ideas around their own land and culture. (Biswas 2015: 59)

Similarly, Montrescu-Mayes notes with regard to early photographic compositions in India that the '"archetype" style guide' was 'eighteenth and nineteenth century English paintings' (Montrescu-Mayes 2015: 94). She further notes that the works of William Hodges (1774–97),

Thomas Daniell (1749–1840), and William Daniell (1769–1837) worked as the 'main points of reference in their portrayal of romantic, sublime, picturesque, and exotic(ised) landscape' (ibid.). In this sense, while the objects photographed might have been 'local', they were framed and presented in terms of prevailing European, and later American, aesthetic sensibilities, thereby visually colonising, standardising, and ordering what was allowed to be seen.

Within this scheme of things, there were very specific aesthetic preoccupations that led to images being framed very similarly in different geographic and cultural locations in approximately comparable circumstances. With a focus on the history of photography in India, Pinney notes that 'the archetypal location of photography in the mid-nineteenth century was the foothills of the Himalayas', while 'in the 1920s and the 1930s it was the street' (Pinney 2015: 24). Referring to the strikingly similar framing of the Kandy Lake and surrounding areas, buildings, and foliage in central Sri Lanka and the Royal Lagoon and its vicinity in Rangoon in the late 1880s within a discourse of 'oriental' landscapes, Biswas points to the 'uniformity in the depiction of a landscape, establishing common "circuits of aesthetic forms", in order to render unfamiliar places into a consumable visual idiom' (Biswas 2015: 64). Seen in this sense, what was photographed commercially in the colonial period was, at one level, the exotic in the popular Euro-American imagination. At another level, as a result of consistency and repetition, such photographed objects and contents were also made more palatable as a familiar aesthetic form. It is in this context that Mitchell referred to images frozen in colonial photographs 'as something like the "dream work" of imperialism', which might 'disclose both utopian fantasies of the perfected imperial prospect and fractured images of unresolved ambivalence and unsuppressed resistance' (Mitchell 2002, quoted in ibid.).

However, in the colonial period itself, 'unsuppressed resistance' is not something that captured much attention, except in specific circumstances. In this situation, the framing of photos also depended on the cost and technologies involved. Referring to the photographic practice of Samuel Bourne, who worked in northern India in the 1860s, Pinney notes that Bourne needed up to thirty labourers to carry his equipment, in addition to the cooperation of many colonial government agencies and corporate interests to facilitate his travel and accommodation (Pinney 2015: 24). In many such cases, these very interests were also the sponsors of these expensive and time-consuming expeditions. The nature of this obvious interdependence and its structures of patronage directly impacted the framing of photographs and their aesthetic consistency. That is, what is to be photographed, how, and where were often by and large predetermined and meant to serve a number of vested interests, which in most cases were those of the colonial regimes and colonial commercial interests. It is in this context that one can understand the carefully selected framing and sometimes very dramatic ordering and choreographed sense that early colonial photographs expressed, from which realms of unhappiness, gloom, and misfortune had often been expelled.

This structure of interrelationships and aesthetic sensibilities only began to change somewhat since the early twentieth century as photographic equipment became smaller and, by that very token, more mobile (Pinney 2015: 24). As such, under these newer circumstances, photography was no longer as dependent 'on the kinds of official support or financial investment that was so central to earlier photographers' (ibid.). More mobile and less cumbersome photographic technology allowed interested photographers to 'document chaotic public spaces on which colonial hegemony appeared increasingly fragile' (ibid.).

In the final analysis, until the early twentieth century (and even well into the twentieth century in the case of much mainstream photographic practices), what mostly mattered was packaging the wilderness, local peoples, and ancient sites within an orientalist idiom tempered by Victorian aesthetics, which made sense in the prevailing political circumstances and within the existing dominant structures of taste. As such, many things that did not fit into these sensibilities and preoccupations were likely to be missed, not framed, and therefore not recorded in photographs. The conditions allowing for these lapses, and how they might also explain obvious absences in the photographic record, need to be kept in mind when the past is fathomed via photographs of the period.

What is to be Remembered?

These dominant preoccupations in the framing and presenting of photographs in the colonial period—including the hyping up of reality and normalcy in studio photographs—and the resultant absences within the frames have to be taken as a necessary lens through which colonial photographs must be viewed today. It is also clear that they bring their own biases and subjectivities into the discourse they help to create. In this overall scheme of things, does it mean that they are no longer legitimate as visual objects when we look at the past, taking as our point of departure the post-colonial circumstances of the present?

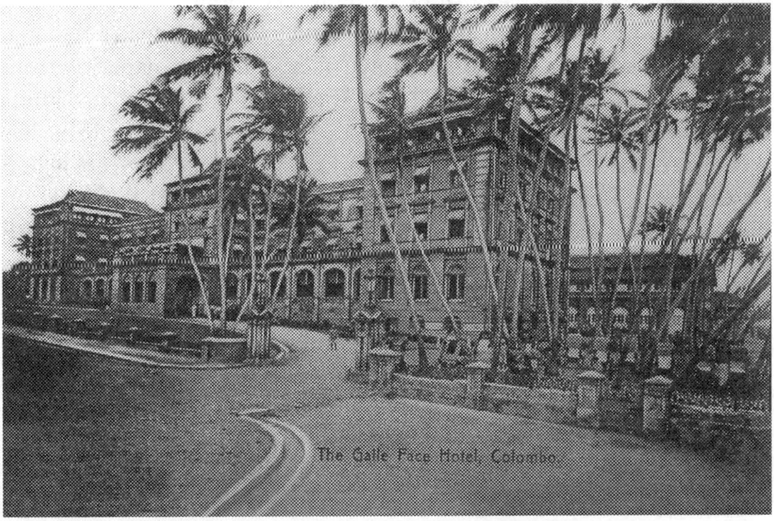

Image 2.9 Galle Face Hotel, Colombo, Ceylon, 1890.
As one of the first purpose-built hotels in the island, the Galle Face Hotel indicated one example of not only the institutionalisation of colonial commerce, but also Ceylon's clear entry into what would become global tourism.
Photograph courtesy of: Plâté Limited, Colombo 3, Sri Lanka.

In a sense, this cluster of doubts is what the quotation I presented at the very beginning of this chapter from *In and Out of Focus* partly alluded to. It noted that images of the past presenting 'colonial achievement' 'reveal subtexts and meanings other than those intended by photographers and publishers or seen by viewers at the time'.[18] Images of ivory trade and rubber production, which supposedly typified the benefits of modernisation and economic advancements that colonialism allegedly introduced, might today 'imply exploitation and harsh labor practices'.[19] In the same vein, photographs of the colonial period often present large archives of images, which depict the construction of transport networks in the colonies as well as the imposing structures of colonial buildings (see Image 2.9). These were supposed to epitomise both progress on the one hand and the reach of colonial power on the other. But instead of symbols of 'progress', these images are seen today as examples of 'forced labor'.[20] In the case of Sri Lanka in particular, the system of service to the king and regional rulers empowered by the king, known as *rājākariya*, emanating from the country's pre-colonial feudal past, was meant to address two kinds of service: 'public works, such as road and bridge building or, in earlier days, the construction of irrigation works', and 'special services elicited on the basis of a person's caste-related occupation'.[21] The word itself literally means 'obligatory duties'. The British Governor Fredrick North banned the practice in 1802 in areas under British control, thirteen years before the country was completely subjugated in 1815, as it was deemed akin to 'slavery', and was replaced by a new tax. However, *rājākariya* was reintroduced soon after, until it was banned again more comprehensively in 1832.[22] Crucially, its reintroduction in this interim period was mainly for the purpose of using the free or cheap labour it opened up for road construction and other 'public' works projects of the colonial government. In Sri Lanka and elsewhere in South Asia, most public construction projects undertaken to enhance the power and stability of colonial regimes were sustained by local labour under the most trying circumstances.

Particularly in India and Sri Lanka, these road construction projects have been widely documented by photographers, and continue to offer certain glimpses into the past. However, the mere fact of under-emphasising or not emphasising specific subtexts of hard work and negative work conditions in preference to the grand narratives the colonial regimes and photographers intended to articulate at the time does not negate the overall narrative capacity of these photographs. These are, like most other documents or political texts, open to interpretation. After all, it is possible to at least partly resurrect the subtexts that were initially drowned in these photos precisely because these photographs are available, and can be read with other documents today to unravel these absences. Besides, while some of these photographs are carefully choreographed, ordered, and posed, many others are not, which seem to have been framed in situations of routine activity. Large festivals, which simply could not have been ordered as wished by a photographer, or even road construction activities and routine street scenes captured from a distance, might be considered within this category (see Images 2.10 and 2.11 on the Perahera procession in Kandy and a Hindu festival in Colombo, Ceylon, from a distance. Also see Image 2.12 for a street scene from a distance).

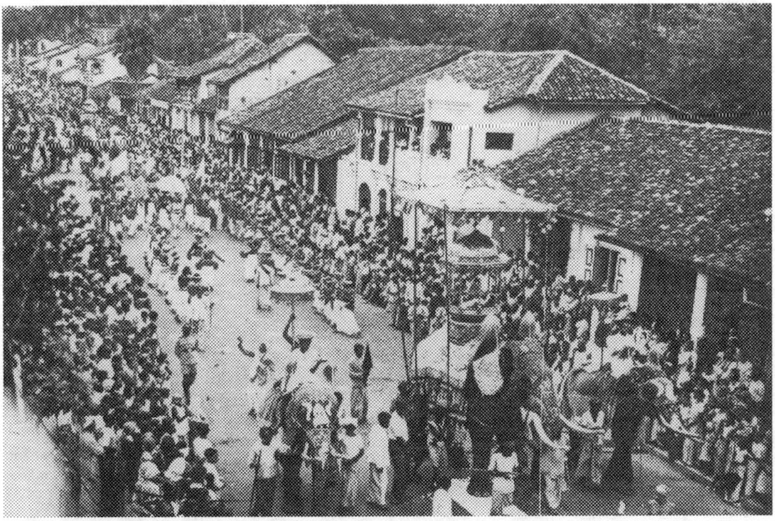

IMAGE 2.10 Perahera Procession, Kandy, Ceylon, 1900.
Photograph courtesy of: Plâté Limited, Colombo 3, Sri Lanka.

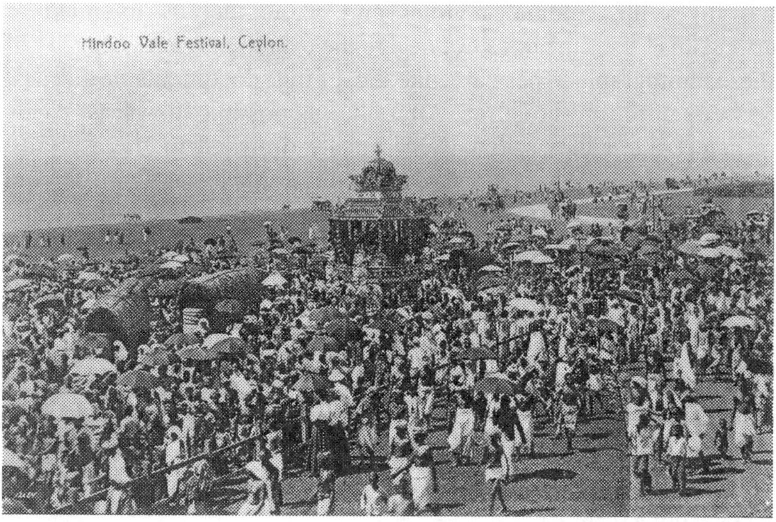

IMAGE 2.11 The Hindu Vel Festival, Galle Face Green, Colombo, Ceylon, 1900.

Photograph courtesy of: Plâté Limited, Colombo 3, Sri Lanka.

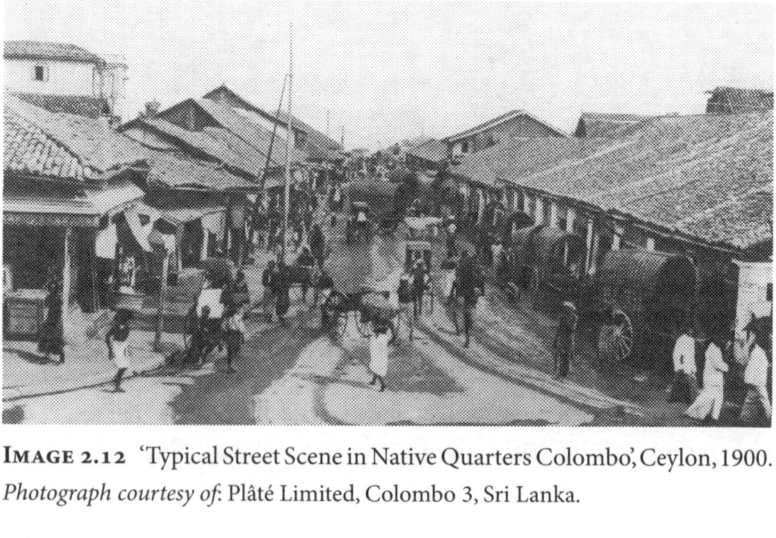

IMAGE 2.12 'Typical Street Scene in Native Quarters Colombo', Ceylon, 1900.

Photograph courtesy of: Plâté Limited, Colombo 3, Sri Lanka.

Today, these kinds of photographs allow for at least two broader narratives, both of which are valid from their own political perspectives and circumstances within which they were constructed.

(*i*) The first perspective is that of the colonial regime and the photographers at the time the photographs were commissioned. This perspective brings to us a very specific interpretation that can only be located and understood in the contexts in which the images were made, and the political circumstances that gave meaning to these interpretations;

(*ii*) The second perspective is that of contemporary researchers, which allows for these same photographs to be unlocked emotionally and intellectually by reading them against the grain in a more nuanced manner today, thereby making audible the references embedded in them, which were once inaudible or alluded to via a series of obvious absences.

On the other hand, colonial photographs of particular places such as ancient ruins offer the present a very clear vision of what they looked like before they were renovated, looted or, in some cases, razed to the ground. Of course, the very act of photographing these sites at the time was to pictorially articulate the sense of 'discovery' and 'adventure' that the colonial regime ushered in. They were also a signpost to the kind of orientalist historiography of local places that colonialism allowed. Nevertheless, these are important archeological and architectural references to the built-environment of a bygone era, documented long before they were impacted by the changes of the last two centuries (see Images 2.13 and 2.14 for examples of framing ruins in Ceylon). Referring to colonial-period photographs of Sri Lanka's ancient ruins in the North Central Province, Biswas notes that they 'not only captured the magnificence and scale of the architecture but also conveyed a silence and desolation, devoid of human presence' (Biswas 2015: 64). What to photograph and how to frame was based on a combination of personal choice and prevailing aesthetic conventions. This means that such photographs may not have captured some of these structures in full or with reference to specific features that were considered more crucial by the local people.

Nevertheless, they created an important archive of these buildings before significant transformations befell them later.

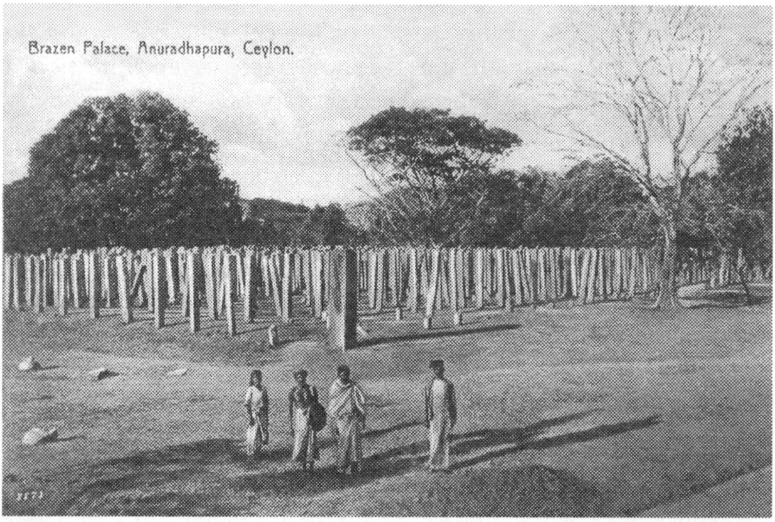

IMAGE 2.13 Lowamahapaya or the Brazen Palace, Anuradhapura, Ceylon, 1900.

Photograph courtesy of: Plâté Limited, Colombo 3, Sri Lanka.

However, when it comes to early colonial-period portrait photos of socially underprivileged people[23]—whether in studios or in seemingly 'natural' habitats—this situation changes considerably. It is in these contexts that the violence of ordering and choreographing was most evident, because it was in such settings that the ability to control was most manifestly available to photographers. In all colonial situations, portraits of local people were popular objects of consumption, and they also helped to create specific psuedo-ethnological categories of people in visual form. This was not only a matter of how a person or groups were idealised, categorised, and photographed in their 'typical' regalia or in the nude, and often claimed to be in their 'natural' surroundings, but also how these people were categorised as what Appadurai calls 'the fiction of the general

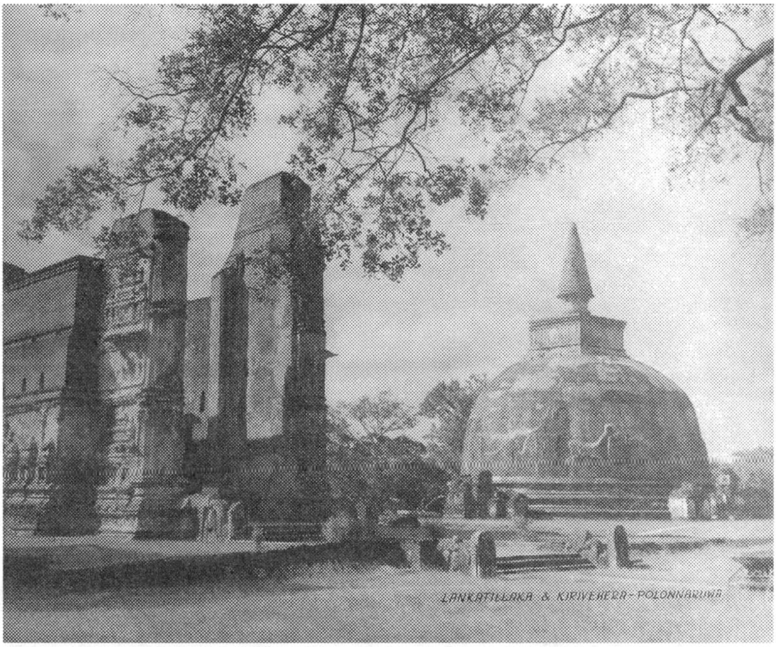

IMAGE 2.14 Lankatilake and Kiri Vehera Temples, Polonnaruwa, Ceylon, 1900.

Photograph courtesy of: Plâté Limited, Colombo 3, Sri Lanka.

"type"', or more often as 'an ethnological type' (Appadurai 1997: 4). This is what created categories such as 'Malay Man', 'Rodiya Girl' (see Image 2.15), 'Veddhas (or 'Wild Men', in some colonial usages; see Image 2.16), etc., in the Ceylonese context, and 'Malabar Peasant', 'Hindoo Brahmin', 'Mahomedan Minstrels', etc., in the Indian context. That is, ethnological and cultural identities were imposed upon the people who were photographed, even though they were quite likely choreographed in ways that made aesthetic sense to the photographer and his audiences rather than in the sense of any clear ethnographic category or cultural identity as these terms are understood today, or as they were understood by the people who were photographed.

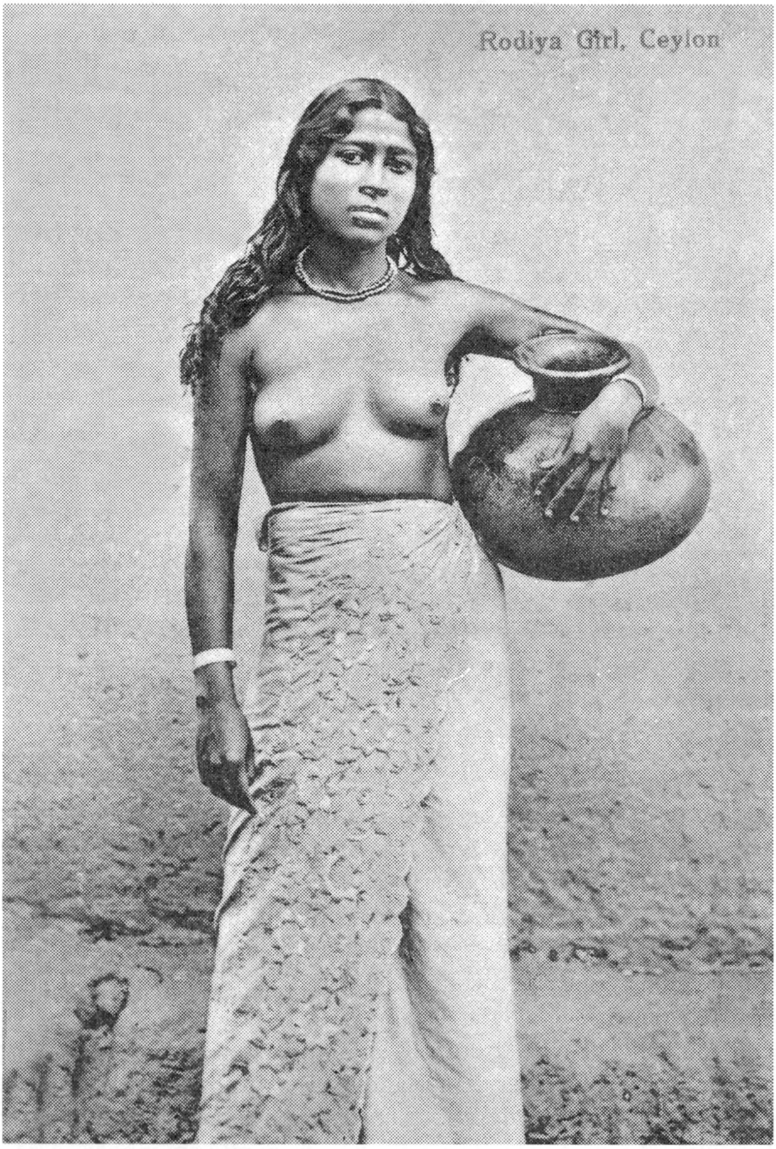

IMAGE 2.15 Rodiya Girl, Ceylon, 1900.
Photograph courtesy of: Plâté Limited, Colombo 3, Sri Lanka.

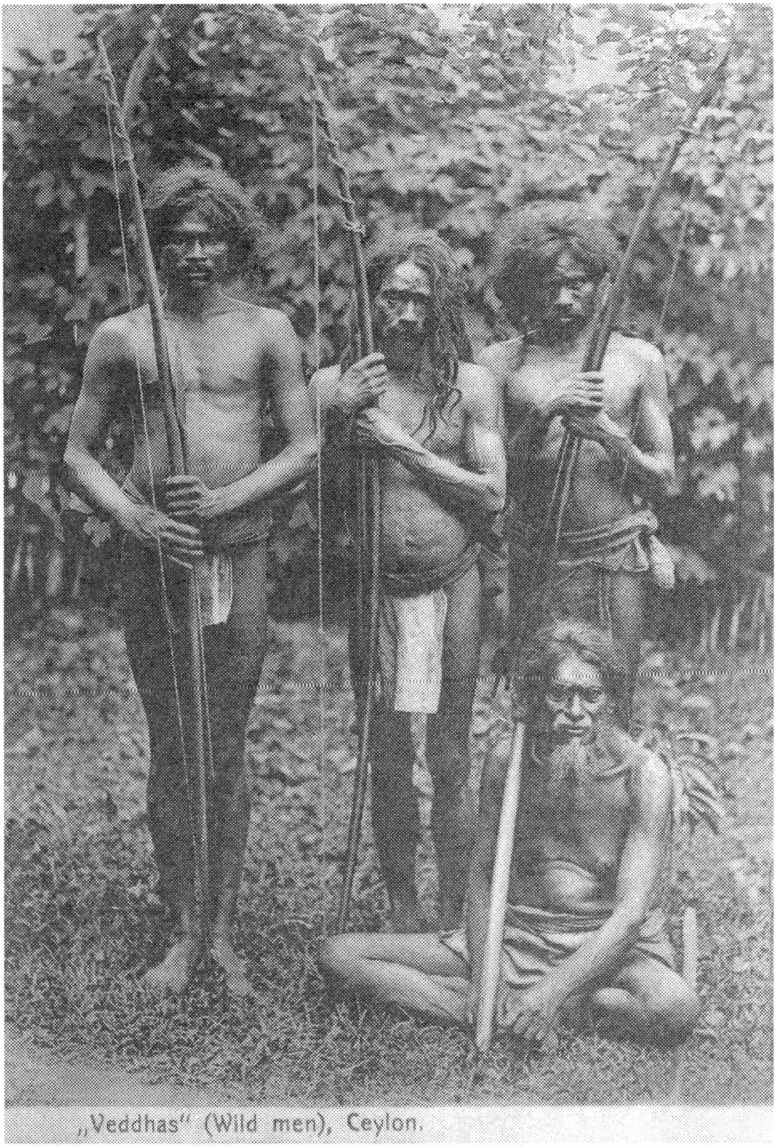

IMAGE 2.16 Veddhas (Wild men), Ceylon, 1890.
Photograph courtesy of: Plâté Limited, Colombo 3, Sri Lanka.

These categorisations were based on the colonial knowledge systems that emerged at the time, along with census activities as a necessary part of governance and control. It is in such a context that Matthan notes, with reference to portrait photographs of Rodiya women in Ceylon in the 1880s, that 'one is taken up by the ease at which they posed for the camera' (Matthan 2015: 74). This observation also brings to mind Pinney's comment that the nineteenth-century photographs from South Asia presented at the 2013 exhibition, *Allegory and Illusion*, is 'evidence of a self-representation by South Asians when confronted with the camera' (Pinney 2013: 12). It seems to me, however, that the issue here is not about the seeming 'ease' with which local people collaborated in these circumstances, or whether the surviving photographs from the colonial period are examples of willing and self-conscious 'self-representation' by South Asians. The crucial issue at play here is how the power relations under which this kind of photography took place actually worked on the ground. In these conditions, due either to the money or limited material benefits that were offered to local people, which were difficult to refuse in the prevailing economic conditions, or due to the inherent power of the photographer in the prevailing political and social circumstances, or due to a combination of both, what was photographed and how it was photographed cannot be understood within a simple idiom of volunteerism or as a matter of self-representation. Nevertheless, the result is the exhaustive archive of portraiture photographed inside studios, inside homes, or in open settings that we have today (see Image 2.17 for a representative photograph of an outdoor group portrait from Ceylon, and Image 2.18 for a group portrait in the interior of a home, also from Ceylon).

However, there is a fundamental difference between the two photographs (Images 2.17 and 2.18). The former is a photograph of migratory pearl fishermen whose social status in local conditions was not very different from the Veddhas or the Rodiyas. As such, it was not too difficult to order them to suit the colonial sense of aesthetics. The people in the latter photograph are some of the decedents of the traditional elite of the Kandy Court of Ceylon, which was dismantled

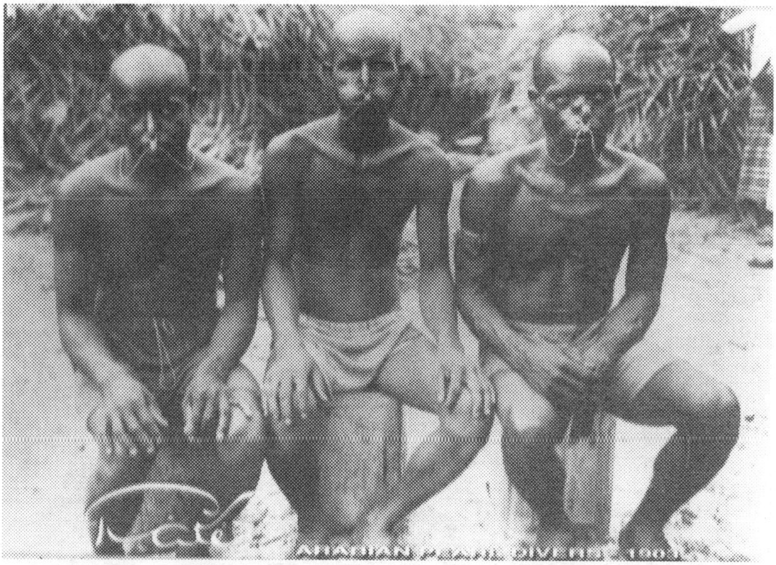

IMAGE 2.17 'Arabian Pearl Divers' in Ceylon, 1903.
Photograph courtesy of: Plâté Limited, Colombo 3, Sri Lanka.

in 1815. But even at the time the photo was taken in 1900, they wielded considerable recognition in local social circumstances as well as in the colonial hierarchy. So the conditions of ordering this photograph were undertaken under very diffident power relations than the previous one.

In the contexts outlined above, the issue that arises in reading colonial-period photographs is not merely a matter of their partiality or inequality in power relations, which made them possible. These circumstances do not make them illegitimate as sources of information or objects of study. However, any reading of these photographs needs to keep in mind both the limitations brought about by these power relationships and the nature of colonial knowledge and the sense of aesthetics, which were predicated upon the framing of these images.

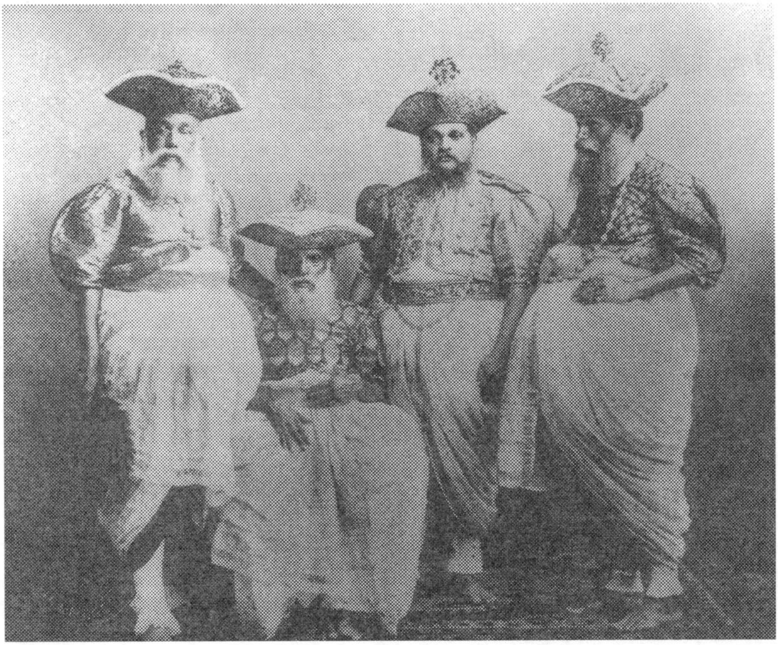

IMAGE 2.18 Kandyan Chiefs, Ceylon, 1900.
Photograph courtesy of: Plâté Limited, Colombo 3, Sri Lanka.

NOTES

1. https://africa.si.edu/exhibits/focus/colonial.html (accessed 18 June 2016).

2. For information on colonial period hunting and some illustrations, one can refer to Samuel Baker's *The Rifle and the Hound in Ceylon* (1854). Available at https://archive.org/details/riflehoundinceyl00inbake.

3. https://books.google.co.in/books?id=LBcuz37GrLQC&pg=PA75&source=gbs_selected_pages&cad=3#v=onepage&q&f=false (accessed 21 June 2017).

4. https://books.google.co.in/books?id=LBcuz37GrLQC&pg=PA75&source=gbs_selected_pages&cad=3#v=onepage&q&f=false (accessed 21 June 2017).

5. http://www.royalasiaticsociety.lk/about-2/past-presidents/ (accessed 21 June 2017).

6. http://www.stephenongpin.com/NICHOLL-Andrew-DesktopDefault.aspx?tabid=45&tabindex=44&artistid=196408 (accessed 21 June 2017).

7. http://www.stephenongpin.com/NICHOLL-Andrew-DesktopDefault.aspx?tabid=45&tabindex=44&artistid=196408 (accessed 21 June 2017).

8. http://www.goodreads.com/quotes/22528-and-what-is-the-use-of-a-book-thought-alice (accessed 9 July 2017).

9. The title of the original 1719 publication was: *The Life and Strange Surprizing Adventures of Robinson Crusoe, Of York, Mariner: Who lived Eight and Twenty Years, all alone in an un-inhabited Island on the Coast of America, near the Mouth of the Great River of Oroonoque; Having been cast on Shore by Shipwreck, wherein all the Men perished but himself. With An Account how he was at last as strangely deliver'd by Pyrates.* Available at https://archive.org/details/afv8235.0001.002.umich.edu (accessed 21 June 2015). Many believe that Defoe's novel was based on Robert Knox's *An Historical Relation of the Island Ceylon in the East Indies*, published thirty-eight years earlier in 1681.

10. The original German version was called *Der Schweizerische Robinson.* Available at http://gutenberg.spiegel.de/buch/der-schweizerische-robinson-833/1 (accessed 21 June 2015).

11. For the digitised version of the book, see https://archive.org/details/in.ernet.dli.2015.22966 (accessed 27 June 2017).

12. For the digitised version of the book, see https://archive.org/details/peopleofindiaser02greauoft (accessed 27 June 2017).

13. For the digitised version of the book, see https://archive.org/details/cu31924024114773 (accessed 27 June 2017).

14. For the digitised version of the book, see https://archive.org/details/philippineisland00worciala (accessed 27 June 2017).

15. For a detailed description of Coomaraswamy's ideas, refer to his essay, 'The Traditional Conceptions of Ideal Portraiture' (1956: 117–29).

16. For more information and discussion on painted photographs in India, please refer to Allana and Kumar (2008).

17. The digitised version of *The Philippine Islands and Their People* can be accessed via the following link: https://archive.org/details/philippineisland00worciala.

18. https://africa.si.edu/exhibits/focus/colonial.html (accessed 29 June 2017).

19. Ibid..

20. Ibid.

21. https://www.britannica.com/topic/rajakariya (accessed 29 June 2017).

22. Ibid.

23. This should not be confused with the voluntary studio photography of middle-class and privileged people, discussed earlier in this chapter.

three

The Shadows of Two Histories
Anthropology and Photography[1]

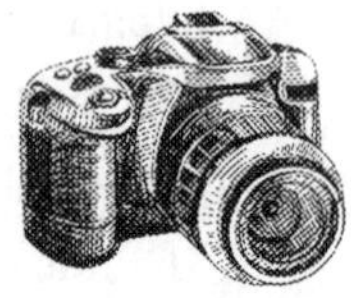

The photograph contains and constrains within its own boundaries, excluding all else, a microcosmic analogue of the framing of space, which is knowledge. As such it becomes a metaphor of power, having the ability to appropriate and decontextualize time and space and those who exist within it.

Edwards (1992: 7)

My first encounter with what I might now call 'anthropological photography' was in the mid-1970s. In my father's office in our house, there was a wooden trunk, which was always locked with an old padlock. Given this enforced out-of-bounds-ness of the box, I often wondered what could be in its protected interior. Once, I got my chance when my father had mistakenly left the key in the lock. Despite the anticipation, much of what I saw was uninteresting for a child of twelve or thirteen years of age. There were stacks of files containing plans for the lands my father had surveyed all over the country, handwritten documents in English, which I could not read at the time, and bottles of red, green, and black ink, which I think must have been essential raw material for his plans. But two things captured my interest. One was a stack of about ten thick cards with old sepia photographs of nude women erotically posed, but with no heads. In retrospect, rather than pornography, I think what I saw were somewhat artistically posed portraits of female nudes. But they failed to capture my interest beyond a point. I think this might be due to their being faceless; I could not connect with them on some tangible human or sexual level. The way light and shadow had been used to make the photos appear mysterious (as I vaguely recall them now) meant nothing to me at the time. In retrospect, I think the reason for the facelessness in the framing of these photos was perhaps the unknown photographer's sense of ethics, and an attempt to blur out the identity of the models.

But another set of black-and-white photographs immediately captured my interest, and remains etched in my memory in reasonable detail. These were part of a local magazine (I think a supplement of the *Sunday Observer*, published in Colombo in the 1950s) with a series of young Rodiya women, all of them featured bare-breasted. I think the images captured my attention not only due to their partial nudity, but also because they had faces, expressions, smiles, and therefore a sense of identity with which I could identify. I have no recollection of what the accompanying English-language essay said; I could hardly read English at the time, anyway. But most of the images remained in my mind. The loss of memory with regard to the writing and the retention of memory with regard to photographic content are quite indicative of the communicative power of the photos I saw.

As I learned much later, while looking through colonial-period photographs of Ceylon in my dual personality as anthropologist and photography enthusiast, these were most likely photographed in the last two decades of the nineteenth century or the first decade of the twentieth, when European photographers had considerable power to photograph almost anything they wished. Many similar portraits claiming to be of Rodiyas that I have seen since then belong to this time period (see Image 2.15 for an example of the kind of photo I saw in the 1970s). In a sense, more than any other genre of photographs, it was the genre of onsite or studio portraits of local people, ordered in the way the photographer wanted them to be—attired or naked—that displayed the power colonial photographers routinely wielded to create the kind of pictorial reality they deemed fit, and which continues to impact the way we look at the past, particularly at the popular level. Portraits of bare-breasted Rodiya women from this period exemplify, more than many other such Sri Lankan examples that I have seen, the practices of extreme ordering via culturally highly unusual poses, given the times.[2] It appears that the Rodiyas' low social esteem, emanating from their unenviable location outside the structure of the Sinhala caste hierarchy as a kind of 'untouchable' social group, allowed for this level of exploitation of their bodies in the photographic pursuits of colonial photographers. This tendency is evident in colonial photography of the same genre in other parts of South Asia as well. Many studio-portraits of individuals, families or other similar on-location portraits in later colonial times tended to be taken on a voluntary basis. Comparatively, the kind of images I have referred to above, of tribal peoples or other local peoples allegedly in their 'natural' habitats, were not voluntary photographs in the strictest sense, even though they have contributed to the creation of the large body of work that came to be known as 'anthropological photographs'.

Crucially, such photography was justified on the basis of science and often in the name of anthropology rather than as the result of simple voyeurism. Once photographed, these images were meant not only for the consumption of anthropologists or other scholars more generally, but also became an instant commodity in the broader colonial market for pictorial memorabilia from faraway lands. It is in this broader market context that one has to understand the massive demand for and popularity of the larger body of photographs from the colonies during the colonial period. While I will have more to say about this kind of photography as the chapter evolves, it is against the backdrop of the childhood encounter recalled above that I would like to enter my discussion on colonial photography.

Photography in Early Anthropology

Even if a cursory exploration of the history of photography were undertaken, it would become apparent that anthropology has conventionally had an interest in the visual. As Chapter 2 has partially indicated, the history of colonial photography is at least to some extent also a history of anthropological photography, or the kind of photography that was motivated by anthropological knowledge production, which emerged during colonialism. As such, photos have historically been present from almost the initial beginnings of anthropology. This is clearly evident in its early textual tradition, although it has waned in recent times. To begin with, let me briefly survey this initial presence and its more recent evolutions to place in context their core markers.

The use of photos in early anthropology is a direct simulation of the extensive use of images (mostly engravings, drawings, and paintings) in eighteenth and nineteenth-century travel literature, as discussed in Chapter 2. Early anthropological tradition was very much located within the practices of the desk-bound amateur 'anthropologist', commentating upon what he had not actually seen. Instead, he articulated his descriptions of, and ideas and thoughts on what others who had visited 'exotic' places in the rapidly expanding colonies had seen and recorded. These were literally distant commentaries laced with interpretations and over-interpretations, based on the descriptions of others and the dominant imaginaries of the time. In this context, photographs became an important aid in making what was seen by a few manifest pictorially in the written texts, ostensibly for the reading and viewing pleasure of many others. But soon, particularly as the nineteenth century drew to a close and with the advent of the twentieth century, these descriptions were increasingly provided by anthropologists themselves, who had actually visited the places they were describing. And in some cases—as we will see later—the accompanying photographs were authored by these anthropologists as well. It is in this context that Edwards notes that photographs taken in field situations comprised an integral aspect of early British ethnographic practice (Edwards 1992). Referring to the same period, Pinney suggests that the 'anthropological potentiality of photography was defined' partly in the context of early anthropologists' anxieties about the truth-value of the verbal communications of 'natives' (Pinney 2011: 14). Often, lacking the required language skills to comprehend local contexts and suspicious of the ability or the interest of natives to describe their circumstances 'accurately', many early anthropologists assumed that information gathered from such contexts would be irrelevant or false (ibid.). This was essentially a trust issue with regard to the locals, rooted in both the Eurocentric race theories of the time and the dominant logic of anthropology, both of which situated many local cultures, civilisations, people, and their intellectual capacities in lower hierarchical positions compared to their 'Western' counterparts.

On the other hand, as colonialism expanded, one could also see the simultaneous growth of a certain curiosity to 'know' more about the colonised and exoticised people, along with their cultural paraphernalia. As we have already seen in Chapter 2, these items were widely exhibited in events such as The World's Columbian Exposition in Chicago in 1893, the Exposition Ethnographique de l'Afrique Occidentale in 1893, and similar events that verged on spectacles (MacDougal 1999 [1997]: 276). This amalgamation of phenomena also coincided with the early development of anthropology itself. What is obvious is that considerable visibility was provided to satisfy the emerging European and North American curiosity about the strange and the exotic from distant lands, to which much of the 'scientific' legitimacy was offered by contemporary anthropology. Nevertheless, it was not possible to duplicate the 'live performances' by native people at these spectacles or the elaborate museum exhibits within the pages of early anthropological texts. In this context, the most logical solution was to insert images of these people, their artefacts, and practices as the technology of photography had also become available to enable this practice. Moreover, by the beginning of the twentieth century, early film was also making this viewing more dramatic by virtue of the 'magic' offered by moving images. It was in this new visual context that Sir Walter Baldwin Spence observed in the early twentieth century with regard to the purpose of his own documentary films, 'what I would like to show would be the real native' (quoted in ibid.). In this scheme of things, it would have been far more 'authentic' and appealing—given the popular and scientific tastes of the time—to *photograph* the 'real' native than to draw or sketch him, as had been done in earlier times. But, as we will see later in this chapter, this notion of 'real' was often rendered unstable in the way colonial photography evolved, with its inbuilt dynamics of ordering and choreographing. This realisation, however, comes only with hindsight, and was not a prerogative of the dominant thinking at the time.

Within this context, photography offered a kind of 'irrefutable' record of 'facts' whose authority was seemingly established; they were bound by time and place, and were captured in real time by someone who was 'right there', as opposed to paintings or engravings that might have been done after an event or on the basis of hearsay. In these circumstances, in the practice of early anthropology, photography was conceived as an important tool in recording and disseminating 'facts'. It is in this context in 1869 that the *British Journal of Photography* made reference to two specific uses of photographs, which made sense in terms of the anthropology of the time: to formulate 'a record as complete as it can be made ... of the present state of the world', and at the same time, to offer 'valuable documents' for future research (Wright 1991: 43). In other words, photographs were seen in a purely evidential sense as purveyors of the truth of the present, which would also become an accurate archive of the past in the future. This perceived clinical validity as a method (although the word 'method' was itself not used) or as sources of irrefutable information bestowed on photography has to be understood with reference to four closely interrelated contexts, which can be summarised as follows.

First, as already noted, this resulted from early anthropologists' pronounced suspicion about the natives' capacity to present factual information about themselves, due to their perceivably inherent civilisational lapses. That is, something 'scientific' that could transcend this perceived duplicity of natives had to be found for the sake of the advancement of science. Photography effectively fulfilled this requirement. That is why E.H. Man noted in his 1886 essay, 'A Brief Account of the Nicobar Islands', that 'more correct information can be obtained from photography than from any verbal description' (quoted in Pinney 2011: 14–15). It is important to note that Man expressed this uncertainty about the spoken language's ability to communicate accurately, despite his competence in the languages of the Nicobar and Andaman Islands, where he worked (ibid.: 14). This, of course, is not an issue of language as such, but an anxiety over the expressive capabilities of the languages of so-called 'primitive' people, and the perceived backward intellect of these peoples. In such a context, photography was considered the means that could record 'facts' without the fallibilities of the colonised people getting in the way.

Second, photography emerged in a situation where careful in-field observation, compilation of case studies, and interviews were not yet established as acceptably 'scientific' methods of research, even though anthropologists and some of their non-professional predecessors had been conversing with the natives they encountered over a considerable period of time. It is in such a context, and with reference to the practice of observation in anthropology, that Andrew Lang rhetorically asked in his 1896 book, *The Making of Religion*: 'How can you pretend to raise a science on such foundations, especially as the savage informants wish to please or mystify the inquirers, or they answer at random, or deliberately conceal their most sacred institutions?' (quoted in ibid.: 25, 156). That is, conversations with natives were not a viable means of collecting information in the context of which something as technically 'accurate' and 'scientific' as photography would make contextual sense.

Third, and related to the two issues outlined above, photography was considered inherently scientific due to its scientific-technical provenance and its perceived ability to freeze time in moments believed to be authentic states. Also, in the wider contexts of post-enlightenment and post-industrialisation intellectual curiosity, within which anthropology first emerged and later developed, the actual chemical processes involved in making photography work entrenched its sense and claims of being scientific. As such, with regard to early anthropology, C.H. Read noted that photography was considered capable of capturing and presenting information 'about which there is no question' (quoted in Pinney 2011: 15). In this sense, photography in the anthropological enterprise of the early period was beyond reproach. No wonder, then, that by the late 1870s, the British Association for the Advancement of Science had formed a committee for the expressed purpose of gathering, preserving, and registering photographs that were of anthropological relevance (Wright 1991: 43).

Fourth, the influence of photography in nineteenth-century anthropology also emanated from its relationship with documenting the human body. Long before social anthropology was accepted as a legitimate domain of intellectual practice, much of anthropology in the nineteenth century was focussed on the human body. This is what later evolved into physical anthropology. In this context, for most practitioners, nineteenth-century anthropology was almost a matter of 'comparative anatomy' (Pinney 2011: 15). As such, the visual was vested with the task of organising societies by types, and in this context, photography offered a new way to create human models that could also be later compared with other samples (MacDougal 1999 [1997]: 280). More specifically, at this historical juncture, photography was seen as a technically reliable tool that could record the complexities in human body types. There was a felt need to accurately describe each physical characteristic. Anatomist E.R.A. Serres published a series of brief observations in 1844 on the usefulness of photography in the study of race (Pinney 2011: 18).

In the same overall intellectual context, *A Manual of Ethnological Inquiry* (1854), meant as a guide for late nineteenth-century anthropologists, advised, 'it is desirable to obtain individual likeness by means of some photographic process' (quoted in ibid.: 21, 156). In 1856, Ernest Lacan talked of the comparative possibilities of studying humankind via photographic portraits of Indians, Africans, and Russians (ibid.: 18). Similarly, J.H. Lamprey's insistent proposal in 1869 that anthropologists photograph their subjects against a background grid of 2-inch squares placed upon a wooden frame was meant to standardise the comparative study of human types (ibid.: 28). It added a further, seemingly scientific dimension to the practice of anthropological photography. As he noted, 'by means of such photographs, the anatomical structure of a good academy figure or model of six feet can be compared with a Malay of four feet eight in height' (ibid.: 29). Of course, the ideal point of reference in this comparison, a 'good academy figure or model of six feet', was based upon the visualisation of an idealised European male body-type. As Pinney notes, Lamprey's interest was to 'assimilate bodies as data in a vast system of comparison', as for him, 'individual variation was an obstacle' in the creation of a comprehensive visual understanding of the human body (ibid.). Despite the serious lapses inherent in these ways of measuring and classifying, which significantly restricted the path to knowledge at this time, they nevertheless 'had the satisfying look of knowledge' (MacDougal 1999 [1997]: 281) under the prevailing intellectual conditions. As noted by Edwards, the focus on 'objective' photographs of body types and shapes centrally implicated in early anthropological photography tended to support theories consistent with colonial ideology, such as Social Darwinism, that now stand rejected (Edwards 1992).

Photography in Social Anthropology

In these circumstances, as social anthropology emerged on the intellectual horizon in the late nineteenth century by transforming itself from an informal, non-professional armchair practice, augmented by the descriptions provided by colonial adventurers and travellers, into a formal academic discipline, photography as a method of reliable data-capture and comparison was already well-accepted. In 1896, Maurice Portman, in his essay 'Photography for Anthropologists', based on his work in the Andaman Islands, wrote how photography could be used with a certain degree of 'accuracy' and 'clarity' in anthropology. His text was meant to be an instructive guide in which he insisted that native bodies must be naked for them to be of anthropological value in terms of photography, and that all sensibilities of aesthetics should be removed from photographs (Pinney 2015: 23). For him, the demand for nudity was an essential prerequisite to ensure scientific accuracy in the study of human types and anatomy, while in the same vein, the anti-aesthetic demand stemmed from viewing aesthetic considerations as a series of lenses enforcing multiple layers of filtering, which in the end curtailed accuracy. Interestingly, however, for Portman, the people thus photographed could not be trusted with the equipment that relentlessly 'copied' their bodies and material culture through the act of photography. So, in his series of instructions was a demand to 'lock up all apparatus from savages and others' (quoted in ibid.).

It is no wonder then that E.B. Tylor, one of the most influential figures in early social anthropology, was moved to suggest that 'the science of anthropology owes not a little to the art of photography' (quoted in ibid.: 29). It is interesting, however, that he uses the word 'science' for anthropology and 'art' for photography in the same sentence, which for many would have posed an insurmountable contradiction. He was also convinced of photography's relative accuracy in recording details such as human physical features when he observed, 'most engravings of race-types to be found in books [are] worthless—now-a-days little ethnographical value is attached to any but photographic portraits' (quoted in ibid.: 30). Tylor's words clearly underlie the sense of finality in scientific and truth terms that photography had acquired in the anthropological discourse. In a similar vein, in 1892, Everard Ferdinand im Thurn's address to the Anthropological Institute was focussed on the 'Anthropological Uses of the Camera' (Wright 1991: 43). One of the uses he referred to was 'the accurate record, not of the mere bodies of primitive folk ... but of these folk regarded as living beings' (ibid.). im Thurn had taken the possibilities of photography in anthropology much beyond the recording of body types to the broader enterprise of recording cultural practices and life-ways. So by this time, within the practices of evolving late nineteenth and early twentieth-century anthropology, photography was already in the process of displacing engravings and other kinds of visual accompaniments that had been such an important aspect of colonial travel literature as well as of early anthropological texts.

In this sense, in addition to the perceived reliability of photography as a source of irrefutable 'facts', its popularity in social anthropology by the late nineteenth and early twentieth century also grew from its ability to enhance the *ethnographic authority of the work* presented by professional anthropologists, just as much as it had offered similar authenticating power to travellers, colonial officers, missionaries, and traders previously. To be more precise, photographs extended a pictorial validity to the narratives these scholars were presenting about 'strange' and 'exotic' places and their inhabitants. This was a matter of reporting 'facts' within a paradigm of 'authenticity'. But this explanation needs qualification. In early anthropology, much of the photos were not taken by the scholars in the 'field', but came from other sources such as colonial officers, professional photographers, missionaries, and so on. They were selected as 'illustrations' for their texts by the earlier generation of armchair 'anthropologists', who perceived these images as 'facts'. Besides, for such 'researchers sitting at their desks in museums without the chance of making direct observation, photography was a wonderful and indispensible medium to help compensate for this lack of mobility' (Wolbert 2000: 323). None of the best-known early anthropologists undertook any serious fieldwork, as we understand the practice today. As noted by Herdt, many of these scholars were 'proud of their lack of contact with their subjects' (Herdt 1998: xxii). As they understood it, their craft could be perfected without getting their hands muddied. When American psychologist William James requested James Frazer—best known for his multi-volume classic, *The Golden Bough* (1911–15), focussed on religious practices around the world—to describe the natives he had met in the course of his studies, his shocked response was, 'But God forbid!' (ibid.).

'Anthropological' texts accompanied by an abundance of photographs as a specific kind of illustrated writing continued well into the mid-twentieth century as professional social anthropology evolved into a mainstream academic enterprise. MacDougal points out that photographs remained a prominent feature of anthropological writings until the 1930s, but became less obvious in later times (MacDougal 1999: 281). In making this generalisation, one needs to take into account the work of both amateur and professional anthropologists. C.W. Hattersley's *The Baganda at Home* claims in its subtitle: 'With One Hundred Pictures of Life and Work in Uganda'[3] (1908). Hattersley, who was a missionary as well as an established amateur photographer, manages through these photographs to offer a graphic image of what life among the Baganda was like from his own perspective. That is, he took the decision to present what was important to be seen, which ranged from agricultural practices, local royalty in their regalia, various local people engaged in different kinds of work, house types, the introduction of train services and allied technologies, evidence of the impact Europeans had brought in, and so on (Hattersley 1908). That is, the pictorial narrative is about what Hattersley saw, what he could choreograph, and what he thought was important enough to be seen by others. *Baganda at Home* was a sequel to his earlier work, *Uganda by Pen and Camera* (1906). Professionally, he played a crucial role in providing an education to the sons of Ugandan chiefs, and later became the headmaster of the Church Missionary Society School on Mengo Hill, Kampala.[4] He also served as 'the official photographer to the Ugandan Court and the Church'.[5] Given the crucial social and political power accruing from these positions, Hattersley had enhanced access to different segments of society at the time, which varied from Ugandan royalty to colonial elites on the one hand, to regular people on the other. His ability to not only photograph cross-sections of the geo-political and cultural terrains he traversed through, but to also do so quite profusely and proximately is visible in both books.

Similarly, Henry A. Junod's *The Life of a South African Tribe* (1913) presented 112 black-and-white photographs,[6] offering a clear pictorial description of what captured his attention. Junod was a Swiss missionary and an anthropologist, and photo credits indicate that he as well as a number of others contributed photographs to the book (a few of whom are not credited). Seen in the context of his detailed descriptions of what he saw, one can understand his conviction that for an ethnographic study to be considered 'scientific', it was necessary to focus observation on a single tribe in a single geographic area,[7] and *The Life of a South African Tribe* is the result of this conviction. It was within this conviction and his concerns about the scientific validity of ethnography that his interest in photography can also be located.

Charles Seligmann and Brenda Seligmann's book, *The Veddas*,[8] published in 1911, also falls within the same category of text accompanied by about 112 photographs, in addition to numerous maps and drawings. Charles Seligmann, who was at the time a Lecturer in Ethnology at the University of London, was studying the Veddas with his wife Brenda Seligmann at the invitation of the colonial government of Ceylon, and they were hoping to document the Veddas' rituals, aspects of material culture, and social life before the group 'disappeared' (Seligmann and Seligmann 1911). Many anthropologists shared this theme of urgency at the time, based on the impact of colonial expansion and the resultant culture change evident among many social groups. As they note in the *Preface*,

> not only was the work urgently needed on account of its scientific importance, but it was known that the Veddas were a numerically small people verging on extinction, and so affected by contact with Tamils and Sinhalese that if they were not studied promptly there was every possibility that it would soon be too late to study them at all. (ibid.: vi)

Before the arrival of the Seligmanns, the Veddas had been widely photographed as part of the photography of curiosity, which expanded in the colonial period referred to in Chapter 2 and earlier in this chapter. Pinney notes that the Seligmanns were hoping to find a typical hunter-gatherer society in the form of the Veddas, as presented in the commercial photography of 'Ceylonese studios such as W.H.L. Skeen, Scowen, Plâté and Colombo Apothecaries' (Pinney 2011: 93–94). The Seligmanns soon came face to face with the gap between what was allowed to manifest in colonial commercial photography and the ethnographic reality on the ground. Despite their search for the elusive hunter-gatherers, Charles Seligmann notes, 'indeed, with all my efforts I was able to meet only four families, and hear of two more, who I believe had never practiced cultivation' (Seligmann and Seligmann 1911: vi). In his opinion, even at this early age, the Veddas had already become 'professional primitive' men, in the context of which, 'they are commonly fetched to be interviewed by travellers at the nearest rest house, where they appear clad only in the traditional scanty Vedda garment, whereas, when not on show, they dress very much as the neighbouring peasant Sinhalese (ibid.).

Despite this considerable social and cultural change that the Veddas had already undergone, the Seligmanns were still keen to add a certain tangible ethnographic depth to their published work. In addition to their thick description of what was seen and what was going on among the Veddas they had met, the profusion of photographs was expected to add to this sense of depth. In fact, the photos published in *The Veddas* are among the first to emerge of the group in non-commercial photography. Nevertheless, we can see that many of these photos were carefully posed for the colonial anthropologists, while others had to be 'touched up' to give them the necessary presence and dramatic effect. But Charles Seligmann openly accepts this difficulty in the *Preface*:

> [W]ith regard to the dances photographed, those witnessed at Sitala Vanniya and Bandaraduwa were performed in the depth of the jungle under circumstances which necessitated underexposure in spite of the use of the most rapid plates. Hence a number of the photographs reproduced in Chapter IX have been more or less 'faked,' the detail being painted in on bromide prints and fresh negatives prepared. Probably no one will have any difficulty in recognising the photographs which have been treated in this way, but in order to avoid any possibility of a mistake, those plates which have been touched up are indicated by an asterisk. (Seligmann and Seligmann 1911: vii)

Here is a rather unusual and candid acknowledgement of the doctoring of a set of anthropological photographs to ensure that they were adequately 'authentic' in visual terms. Charles Seligmann's explanation emanated from his belief that photographs needed to be treated as a serious source of information, and hence, what was 'touched up' had to be clearly identified to ensure that their overall methodological validity was not undermined. But of course, he and other anthropologists of his generation were generally silent on the politics ushered in by making people pose for such photographs, and also by often controlling or ordering the backgrounds. This was another kind of 'touching up' of the objects that were to be photographed, which nevertheless took place before the photograph was taken.

R.S. Rattray's *Ashanti* (1923) can also be seen as a book belonging to the same genre as those of Hattersley, Junod, and the Seligmanns. It contained 143 black-and-white photos (MacDougal 1999 [1997]: 281). The most obvious feature in these books, and in those of many others in this generation, is the profusion of photographs, which are nevertheless not inherently linked to the written text. Instead, the photos along with their captions weave a secondary but complementary narrative to what is presented in writing. Photos provide a broader pictorial contextualisation and rooting to what was observed and written. In other words, this kind of writing could have worked reasonably well on the basis of their descriptions alone. Seen as a particular kind of anthropology, which typified the discipline's knowledge production at the time, these photo-heavy books were meant to enhance the intellectual personality of the writer, given his location in the midst of distant and strange lands from where he was reporting. This was not the armchair practice of the mid to late nineteenth-century anthropology. Arguably, these people were speaking from the 'field', and the most acceptable way to establish their presence in the field was to embed the text with the photos captured during work or in related contexts, either by themselves or by others. And in some cases, some of these photos also embedded the writer himself within their frames, to stress his presence in the place the stories were emanating from.

However, the mere availability of photographic technology and its service to anthropology did not always make its use sensible or clearly conceived in either anthropological, or even in an aesthetics sense. Diamond Jenness' early photographs, and how they did or did not inform his own anthropology is a case in point. His best-known collection of photographs, taken during fieldwork in the D'Entrecasteaux Archipelago, Papua, between 1911–12, is now part of the photographic collection in the Pitt Rivers Museum at the University of Oxford. The collection consists of 576 photographs (Wright 1991: 42). *The Northern D'Entrecasteaux*, published in 1920 as a collaboration between Jenness and his fieldwork partner, Andrew Ballantyne, contained many of these images.[9] But Jenness was not an accomplished photographer. The letters exchanged between him and his supervisor, Robert Ranulph Marett, shows that Jenness practised photography in a number of places on his way to his field site. Writing from his home in New Zealand prior to the expedition on 7 November 1911, Jenness notes: 'I have taken some photos of some of our curios, & shall take prints of them with me' (ibid.: 45). He was not merely practising the act of photography, but wanted to have the photos as references to framing. Then, in another letter written on 16 December 1911 from Samarai, he notes that he took with him 'some notebooks & my anatomical instruments, as well as a camera & 2 or 3 dozen plates' (ibid.). The letters also indicate that Jenness experimented with his photography upon a group of local patients in a hospital, which Wright describes as an opportunity 'to cut his photographic teeth' (ibid.). Beyond this seemingly amateurish 'self-training', there is not much evidence to show that Jenness intended to use photography in his research or subsequent publications. In fact, compared to this silence, he seems to have taken better care to suggest that in case of death, his camera and other equipment should be given to the Oxford Committee for Anthropology (ibid.).

In these circumstances, it is hardly surprising that his photos are not particularly inspiring, leading Wright to describe them as 'dull and uninspired', which 'closely follow the prescribed routines of nineteenth-century ethnography' (Wright 1991: 45). In a sense, this description is valid for most anthropological photographs of the time, which were expected to simply be a record of people, events, and things. In this scheme of things, his intention in photography was merely to 'obtain "scientifically valid" information' (ibid.). Wright's argument is that in this early stage of Jenness' fieldwork and career, his entire approach to fieldwork was so clearly amateurish that it 'did not enable him to make the most of the photographic possibilities' that were available (ibid.).

Given these circumstances, notwithstanding the somewhat large collection of photographs this expedition generated and despite the fact that *The Northern D'Entrecasteaux* carried many of these images within its pages, it is not surprising that only a passing reference is made to photography in the book itself: 'Once when we had run out of tobacco we engaged a native to carry the camera and its outfit two or three miles, promising him a stick of tobacco the following day. We never saw him again for a month' (Jenness and Ballantyne 1920: 207). This is hardly a reference to the methodological or even decorative use of photography in the study or in the book. In fact, it is a passing comment, whose main purpose is to explain via an example the 'honesty' of 'natives' rather than anything about photography. With reference to the absence of a discussion on photography in *The Northern D'Entrecasteaux*, and particularly to this passing sentence that barely mentions the camera, Wright notes that 'some may consider that this in itself is telling with regard to his approach to ethnology and equally, perhaps, to photography' (Wright 1991: 43). As Wright further notes, 'that Jenness, in particular, makes few comments about his approach to photography is tantalizing, yet hardly surprising: general commentary about the use of photography in fieldwork has been seriously neglected by anthropologists' (ibid.). In this sense, this is not merely an issue with Jenness, but of anthropology of the time. That is, photography has been used in the public expression of the discipline ever since it was available, merely as a matter of setting the required mood of the place or context 'accurately' or in a 'scientific' manner. However, it was not seen as a methodological approach with its own parameters.

Bronislaw Malinowski is also well-known for the photographic record he made of his own fieldwork. His work in the Trobriand Islands came about three years after Jenness' work, and approximately in the same geographical area. Yet, compared to what appears to be Jenness' 'point and shoot' attitude towards photography, Malinowski has established himself as a more accomplished photographer, while he was also decidedly more conscious about photography as a craft. Wright describes his photos as 'an active gathering of information, through which he evolved his own style and line of enquiry' (Wright 1991: 42). For Wright, Malinowski's attempts at photography went beyond the mere supply of information, which extended 'beyond the scope of the text' (ibid.: 49). At the same time, Malinowski's photographs, 'though impressionistic and at times self-critical, are informative in their embellishment of the text' (ibid.: 53).

Malinowski's diary entries[10] suggest that he was quite conscious of photography's purpose in his work. This primarily emanated from two preoccupations—an ethnographic recording of what he saw in the field on the one hand, and perceiving photos as his own individual point of contact with the world beyond on the other (Wright 1991: 50). He also took pride in 'the marvellous photos I have taken along' (quoted in ibid.). For him, photography was not merely a matter of recording, but a self-conscious act that involved a degree of passion, to which he gave importance. This is why a number of photographs in his collection, obviously taken by others (in some cases, by Billy Hancock), show him in the act of photographing (ibid.). But such photographs would only have become possible through his own intervention and due to his perception of photography's value in his work. In other words, he wanted to be known not only as an ethnographer, but also as an ethnographer with a camera. Malinowski's diaries also indicate that he regularly consulted the *Notes and Queries on Anthropology* published by the British Anthropological Association during his fieldwork, for tips on the ethnographic practice in general as well as on photography. He notes at one point, 'read some more N & Q and loaded my camera' (quoted in ibid.: 55). As Wright suggested, 'Malinowski would compare his photographs to the recommendations of *Notes and Queries*, which in turn, appears to have inspired his photography' (ibid.).

It is an established fact that *Notes and Queries on Anthropology* had a considerable impact on the development of methods in fieldwork in late nineteenth and early twentieth-century British anthropology. In this context, it is hardly surprising that both Malinowski and Jenness referred to different editions of the book as a manual during their separate stints of fieldwork (Wright 1991: 55). Even so, it would be too simplistic to assume that Malinowski's more successful encounter with fieldwork photography can be directly traced to guidance from *Notes and Queries on Anthropology*. His photography as a specific corpus suggests that while he consulted this period text for possible guidance, the actual framing and composition were not always in keeping with the more conventional advice given by it (ibid.).

The differences as well as the more pronounced use of photography in Malinowski's work possibly come from two different sources. One has to do with his self-conscious understanding of photography as an integral method in fieldwork. It is also clear that such clarity about what photographs meant for research must also have made an impression on him of their importance in writing and publishing. As he notes at one point in his diary entries, one 'looked around, noticing things to photograph', which indicates a sense of planning with regard to what was to be photographed (quoted in Wright 1991: 52). It is also clear that he set aside considerable time for photography, as indicated in his observations: 'I worked honestly for 3 hours, with camera and notebook, and learned a great deal, lots of concrete details' (ibid.). Equally importantly, he also assessed his photographs in the field itself. He was at times 'mortified by the poor results' of his efforts, while at other times, he noted with satisfaction of 'photographs which are a success!' (ibid.). The second reason for his producing relatively interesting photographs has to do with his ability to visualise situations, which manifest from his use of language itself. Many of these visually evocative descriptions have emerged with reference to what he saw in nature. He notes at one point in his dairy that the 'subtle thin line of the horizon breaks up, grows thicker, as though drawn with a blunt pencil' (ibid.: 51). At another moment, he makes the very visually-conscious observation: 'the damp velvety sheen of vegetation, the marvellously deep shadows, the freshness of the stones darkened by the rain, the outline of the mountains through the curtains of rain, like shadows of reality projected on the screen of appearances' (ibid.). These are the words of a man capable of seeing things visually, which was not the case with Jenness.

With the development of a field research-based and more theoretically informed social anthropology by the first decades of the twentieth century (in which Malnowski played a crucial part), one could see some of these anthropologists more consistently opting to take their own photographs rather than depending on images produced by others. These people were operating with a more clearly defined understating of the discipline as well as its research methods within the limitations of their times. The Seligmanns were clear examples of this trend, even though Malinowski is a better example of a more conscious and disciplined photographer. What made this transition possible was the transformation in technology, which made cameras more mobile and easier to use. But these scholars were no longer merely interested in tangible aspects of material culture, but also in 'forms of political rule, kinship and marriage systems', or what was generally 'invisible' (Wolbert 2000: 323). That is, they were interested in issues that could not be photographed as well. This change in photographic technology, combined with the emerging theoretical orientations in anthropology, allowed for a different relationship with photos and the written text. As opposed to the simple indexical and illustrative nature of photography in early anthropology, the newer orientation allowed for a closer relationship between the two. According to Wolbert, 'while photographs previously had been accompanied merely by brief information as to the place, date, and subject, now text and picture began to develop a new connection with each other', paving the way for the emergence of 'illustrated text' from 'commented picture' (ibid.).

E. E. Evans-Pritchard's celebrated ethnography, *The Nuer: A Description of the Modes of Livelihood and Political Institutions of a Nilotic People*, published in 1940, was one of the first texts to mark this change more clearly. Evans-Pritchard's book only contained forty-one photographs, compared to the earlier body of more profusely illustrated books. Nevertheless, *The Nuer* took its readers visually to those parts of Sudan where Evans-Pritchard had conducted his fieldwork. While thirty-one of the photos were his own, Evans-Pritchard also used images produced by others. He specifically thanked F. D. Corfield 'for the interest he has shown in my work and for his generosity in allowing me to use many of his fine photographs' (Evans-Pritchard 1940: vii). He also acknowledged the contributions others had made with regard to photographs, as well as diagrams and maps (ibid.: viii). Clifford Geertz has referred to Evans-Pritchard's writing as 'optical', in the sense that his 'being there' adds a certain sense of enhanced visuality to what he writes (Geertz 1988: 65). Although Geertz was talking about how Evans-Pritchard's way of writing brings what he describes to life and makes them visual metaphorically, this visuality is more literally enhanced as a result of the photos embedded in the text as well.

Wolbert has argued that anthropologists of Evans-Pritchard's generation, despite their role in the professionalisation of the discipline, were often not competent in the language of their selected site of study (Wolbert 2000: 324). Although this changed as the twentieth century advanced, these researchers needed acceptable methods to enhance the credibility of the ethnographies they wrote (ibid.). In methodological and experiential terms, prolonged fieldwork itself added to the ethnographic authority of the texts, as well as to the authority of the anthropologists who wrote them. This also marks the time when ethnography as a specific form of writing with its own literary merit took root. This later led to the 'writing culture' debate. At the same time, photographs taken by these field anthropologists in the context of specifically designed research activities further added to this sense of authority. These were not amateurs writing about a strange place from a distance. They were formally trained in the discipline and were investing considerable time in person in the places they were supposed to study, creating the foundations for what came to be known later in anthropological parlance as 'participant observation'. And the photographs they captured *themselves* in the midst of their work—and, on occasion, by others—which embedded the participant observers squarely within their 'field', helped to enhance their ethnographic and professional authority as the discipline developed. With reference to *The Nuer*, this is what Wolbert identifies as the '*visual* construction of ethnographic authority' (ibid.).

The presence of the anthropologist in the field and the nature of his gaze were established more subtly by Evans-Pritchard in his photograph titled 'August Shower' in *The Nuer* (1940; illustration 56). Here, a herd of cattle and a cluster of local huts are to be seen in the distance through the rain, photographed from what appears to be a tent with its flap open. Although the photographer/anthropologist is not physically present in the image itself, his presence manifests itself when the gaze of the camera from the protective environs of the tent in the midst of rain is taken into account. 'August Shower' is an intriguing and imaginative photograph, which ensures that the physical presence of the outsider, the anthropologist with the camera, is clearly established in the pictorial record itself.

Fieldwork is, by definition, an intrusive process. As a result of this, a stranger hovers around people he does not know well for considerable periods of time, in the name of research. The intrusive nature of this fieldwork relationship is further compounded if the researcher is carrying a camera with the expressed intent of photographing the people he is studying. It is with reference to such situations that Wolbert observes that an '"anthropologist as photographer" is both an amateur and professional', and 'as a rule, anthropologists are not trained photographers' (Wolbert 2000: 321). But what is more crucial is that 'even when they photograph without training—they do make photos in a professional context' (ibid.). As a result, the photos they capture in field situations become 'delicate documents of the anthropologist's transgression of intimate boundaries and temporary participation in the lives of others' (ibid.: 321–22). My own photographic intrusion into the lives of others in the context of research and that of another researcher is captured in Image 3.1. Here, my role was that of the anthropologist with the camera, documenting a specific ritual of the indigenous group, the Veddas, known as the Vedi Perahera, in the Buddhist temple Mahiyangana Raja Maha Viharya in 2009. The frame, which shows a participant in the ritual preparing himself by sticking blobs of cotton on to his body with honey, also shows another researcher with a video camera at work. While I am not in the frame, this particular image came into existence simply due to my presence in that location with my camera.

Although I had taken permission for my visual intrusions from the chieftain of the group, I have always found such a situation discomforting in my own work in Sri Lanka, Nepal, Japan, and India when it involved micro-situations, when my lens was likely to capture close-ups of people. In these conditions, I have always asked for permission to photograph, and interestingly, in over twenty-five years of fieldwork, I have never been told *not to*. But due to the rather cumbersome nature of this relationship, I do not have too many photographs captured by me that centrally focus on individuals in my collection, as opposed to photos that focus on objects, events, and groups of people from a 'comfortable' distance. Given this perennial truth with regard to fieldwork photos, what Wolbert notes of Evans-Pritchard's photographs in *The Nuer* is important. According to her, 'collectively, the photographs of the Nuers' day-to-day interaction with their cattle give the impression that we see the Nuers' daily life, as if when no anthropologist is present!' (Wolbert 2000: 325). That is, these images seem to show 'Evans-Pritchard as the perfect fieldworker', within which 'he was so much a participant that he succeeded in performing the ultimate trick in making himself invisible as an observer!' (ibid.) But since his time, one can also see a relative demise of photography's presence in ethnography, as the written form of anthropological work acquired much greater power.

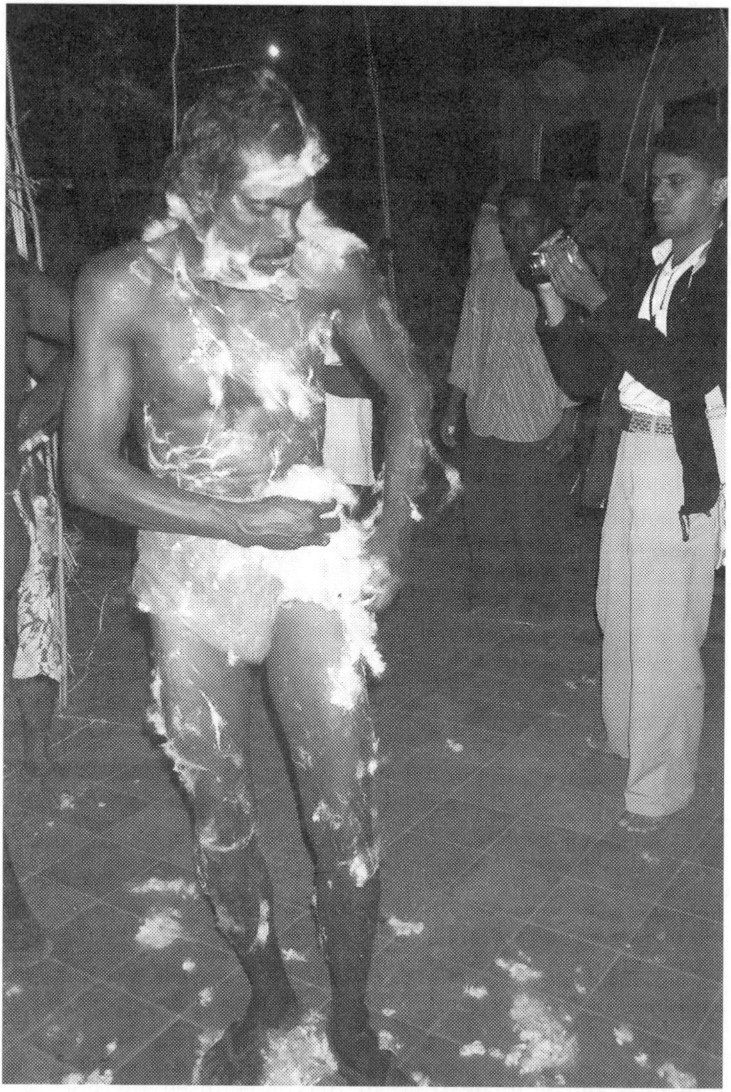

IMAGE 3.1 Preparing for Vedi Perahera in the presence of two cameras, one within the frame and one outside, Mahiyangana Raja Maha Viharaya, Sri Lanka, 2009.

Photograph courtesy of: Author's research collection.

As the practice of anthropology expanded in European and American academia in the first half of the twentieth century, one of the most ardent supporters of using visual methods in anthropology was Margaret Mead, in the context of her efforts to promote the visual more generally in social science research using both photography and film. She called passionately for the enhanced use of images in anthropology, which she derided as a 'discipline' or 'science of words' (Mead 1995: 3, 5). Although she wrote with a focus on film, her ideas outlined in the essay, 'Visual Anthropology in a Discipline of Words' (1995), makes sense with regard to photography too. She critiques anthropology's resistance to visual methods as a matter of 'clinging to verbal descriptions when so many better ways of recording aspects of culture have become available' (ibid.: 5). Here, 'so many better ways of recording' includes both photography and film. She argues that 'ethnographic enquiries came to depend upon words, words and words, during the period that anthropology was maturing as a science' (ibid.). Obviously, Mead's understanding of photography and film is mostly based on an assumption that these are essentially methodological devices rather than the object of research or a broader kind of discourse, which is nevertheless different from the written text. Within this understanding, for Mead, film and photography represented 'a reliable, reproducible, reanalyzable corpus' (ibid.: 8–9). She criticised those opposed to photography and film in anthropology for their 'demand for "scientific" work', as people who have been 'least willing to use instruments that would do for anthropology what instrumentation has done for other sciences—refine and expand the areas of accurate observation' (ibid.: 10). In this sense, Mead's arguments in support of visual methods in anthropology resonate with proponents' support for photography in anthropology in the initial period, when photography made its first concerted inroads into anthropology in the late nineteenth century.

Her support for photography in anthropology emanated from another felt anxiety, in continuation with a similar anxiety among some members of the previous generation of anthropologists. This had to do with the rapid disappearance of specific human groups and the perceived need to record their presence in some form.

As we have seen earlier, this was one of the stated objectives in the Seligmanns' study of the Veddas. With reference to radical cultural and demographic change, Mead notes that it was necessary to 'unequivocally recognize that because these are disappearing types of behavior, we need to preserve them in forms that not only will permit decedents to repossess their cultural heritage (and, indeed, will permit present generations to incorporate it into their emerging styles)' (Mead 1995: 8). In such a context, photography was naturally seen as one of the best means to ensure this 'preservation'. In the general context of this structure of argument, one can also think of Edward Curtis' work, which has become well-known for attempting to 'stage manage' a romantic representation of 'dying native American culture' (Pinney 2011: 90–92).

Mead's approach, developed with Gregory Bateson in their work in Bali, had a significant impact on the later development of visual anthropology and sociology (Pink 2003: 182). Nevertheless, Mead's use of the 'observational method' in social research during her time, influenced by the 'ways of seeing' perspective in anthropology, makes little sense in today's contexts where the craft of anthropology is employed (ibid.). The observational method assumed a photograph to be an objective fact emerging from scientific research, very much in line with the thinking that had made photography an important aspect of anthropology much earlier. But today, many anthropologists as well as other social researchers would agree that ethnographic research is the outcome of a 'relationship and negotiations between the researcher and informants rather than of the former's objective observation of the latter' (ibid.). As such, photographs cannot simply be used as objective scientific facts today, but need to be situated in the larger context of discourse.

Since the 1980s, one can also see some limited support for photographic input in the anthropological discourse in the writings of scholars such as Wilbert Norman (1991) and Albert Piette (1993). For scholars like Knappet, photos are not lifeless images, but captured moments that 'come alive' (quoted in Edwards 2012: 223). A.C. Haden was convinced that the film camera was 'an indispensible piece of anthropological apparatus' (MacDougal 1999 [1997]: 282). However, such intermittent support has not allowed photography to become an integral component of contemporary mainstream anthropology, either as a research method or as a focus of research.

Critiques of Photography in Anthropology

Despite the seal of scientific authenticity given to photography in early anthropology, only a few of these photographs offered a sense of movement or dynamism with regard to rituals or other social events. Photographs of people in distant lands gazing at readers from the pages of early anthropological texts were often posed, with the people in question dressed in a manner that was supposed to contribute an aura of cultural authenticity and presented to the world. Pierre and Marie-Claire Bourdieu, in their work on the practice of photography among the French peasantry in the 1960s, suggest that the 'posed photograph, which only grasps and fixes figures who are settled, motionless, in the immutability of the plane, loses its power of corrosion' (Bourdieu and Bourdieu 2004: 612). In other words, for them, such posed and controlled photos are incapable of facilitating interpretation. But one can also argue that a certain kind of photographic authority can emanate from this sense of immobility and silence linked to photographs posed under specific situations. This, however, has also created a somewhat obvious relationship between photography and death (Metz 1985: 81). Pinney has suggested that the 'stillness' and 'suspension' embedded in photographs are similar to 'the glance in childhood which fixes the fetish' (Pinney 1990: 43). Within this larger context, visual imagery appeared 'disquieting', in the sense that 'they appeared to show everything and yet, like the physical body, remained annoyingly mute' (MacDougal 1999 [1997]: 276). As such, for many, 'the stasis upon which acuity depended was itself increasingly seen as a betrayal of the anthropological study of cultural praxis in motion' (Pinney 2011: 154). One can argue that it is in this cluster of concerns and anxieties about photography that its critique in anthropology itself is located.

Claude Levi-Strauss offers an interesting early professional critique of photography from within anthropology. His *Tristes Tropiques*, initially published in French in 1955 as a memoir, is essentially based upon his travels in Brazil, including Sao Paulo, and among Amerindian groups such as the Caduvevo, the Bororo, and the Namikawara in the 1930s. But in his reflections, he refers to many other places as well. It enigmatically begins with the words, 'travel and travellers are two things I loathe and yet here I am, all set to tell the story of my expeditions' (Levi-Strauss 1962: 17). Although formally presented as a travelogue, Levi-Strauss' anthropological and philosophical sensibilities are closely intertwined within the text, which takes the reader on a fascinating journey via intersections marked by anthropology, music, history, and literature. More importantly, his reflections are tempered by a series of black-and-white photographs captured by Levi-Strauss himself, indicating both his skill as a photographer and his ability to embed these photos within his written text to give the book the character and cult status it received, particularly after its English translation was published in 1962. Right at the beginning, the book informs its readers that it is 'illustrated with 48 pages of photographs' (Levi-Strauss 1962). If one takes this specific posturing into account, it appears that Levi-Strauss was experimenting with the possibilities of photography in anthropologically informed writing quite some time after anthropology's more engaged infatuation with photography had begun to wane. In a 2015 reflection, Rob McSweeney referred to *Tristes Tropiques* as 'melancholy anthropology', written by an anthropologist who 'took notes' and 'rather beautiful photographs'.[11]

However, notwithstanding the fact that *Tristes Tropiques* was formally called a memoir, Levi-Strauss was quite critical of the role of photography and film in academic discourse. At one point, he notes that 'travel-books, expeditionary records, and photograph-albums abound', and 'they are written or compiled with an eye mainly for effect', within which 'the reader has no means of estimating their value' (Levi-Strauss 1962: 17–18). Although he is not talking about anthropological texts *per se* and their use of photography, his anxieties clearly reflect on anthropological writings as well. His concern over this kind of writing and the photographs they carry had to do with the possibility that they were meant to titillate rather than to advance knowledge. At the time of his travels in the 1930s and even when

Tristes Tropiques was first published in 1955, many anthropological texts came very close to 'expeditionary records'. They were often about 'discovery' and 'exploration'. It is in this context that he further laments, 'exploration has become a profession; not, as one might suppose, that it is a matter of unearthing new facts in the course of several years of laborious study ...' (ibid.: 18). He was concerned that these kinds of writings had become ends in themselves via superficial efforts, rather than resulting from robust work. In such a context, photographs would seem to be an 'excuse' or a 'camouflage' for this superficiality. And then he reasserted his critique of photography more clearly, juxtaposed with this kind of 'exploration':

> Mere mileage is the thing; and anyone who has been far enough, and collected the right number of pictures (still or moving, but for preference in colour), will be able to lecture to packed houses for several days running. Platitudes take shape as revelations once the audience is assured that the speaker has sanctified them by travelling to the other side of the globe. (ibid.)

It is clear that Levi-Strauss was critical of the kind of anthropology as well as travel writing that typified the colonial period, where the valorisation of the writer as reporting from a distant place was crucial.

Levi-Strauss' displeasure with photography also emanates from what he believes to have been its role in glossing over the disruptions that colonial expansion had introduced into the tribal social formations he had become familiar with in his travels. As he notes, 'today the savages of the Amazonian forests are caught, like game birds, in the trap of our mechanistic civilization' (Levi-Strauss 1962: 18). He accepts this state of affairs as 'inevitable'; nevertheless, he asserts that he 'will not be deceived by' 'the black magic' in the form of 'an album in full colour' presented to eagerly awaiting audiences (ibid.). For him, the last straw is: 'now that the Indians' masks have been destroyed, these albums have taken their place' (ibid.). In the overall context outlined in *Tristes Tropiques,* it is clear that Levi-Strauss viewed photography emanating from places where social upheaval had been introduced by colonialism as mere excuses to bypass colonialism's excesses and destructions. More than an issue with anthropology as such, this is a frustration that had its genesis in the visible consequences of colonialism. But the political and cultural circumstances of his unhappiness precluded Levi-Strauss from reflecting on the broader possibilities of photography in anthropology, particularly in post-colonial situations.

In 1994, approximately sixty years after he took his photographs and forty years after *Tristes Tropiques* was first published, Levi-Strauss' antipathy towards photography in the specific context outlined above had become more dispersed to include more clearly his doubts about the utility of photographs in narrativising anthropology. In his *Saudades do Brazil: A Photographic Memoir*, Levi-Strauss rejected his own photographs as useless, and viewed them simply as suggestive of 'a void, a lack of something that the lens is inherently unable to capture' (Levi-Strauss 1995: 9). For him, they were merely 'silent images' lacking a sense of 'perfume' of the time and place that he thought his field notes still contained, albeit faintly, all these years later (Levi-Strauss 1995).

Kirsten Hastrup, although writing with reference to film rather than photography, notes that 'words and stories may transform places into spaces or vice versa, the picture remains a motionless image of a place' (Hastrup 1993: 11). For her, images tend to be consumed in a single glance, while reading a written text has more discursive potential, similar to a journey (ibid.: 18–19). Clearly, static images like photographs have less of a sense of motion than the moving images offered by film. However, Hastrup's concern is that visual tropes like photography and film freeze an event or an object at a specific moment, and therefore 'remains motionless' (ibid.: 11). She also asserts that film is 'thin' description compared to anthropological writing (ibid.). Similarly, Maurice Bloch has suggested that anthropologists who dedicate too much time to film do so because they have 'lost confidence in their own ideas' (quoted in MacDougal 1999 [1997]: 282). Although Hastrup and Bloch's criticisms have focussed on film, there is very little difference between film and photography in visual terms in anthropology. As such, these criticisms of film with regard to anthropology can be levelled against photography, too, with much greater vigour. But then, a written description of the same event or object also freezes what is described within the temporal moment in which it was observed, not too unlike a photograph or an ethnographic film. That is, what is written about as well as what is filmed or photographed does not constitute an eternally evolving sequence of events. Instead, they only refer to a specific moment bound by both time and space. However, given the nature of language, it offers more discursive possibilities of interpretation and description even if the image of the event or object might not be pictorially present; it is nevertheless engraved in the minds of readers via the way the writing is crafted. This is what Geertz would call the 'optical' in writing (Geertz 1988: 65). In this sense, it seems to me that within limits, a photograph may be more 'truthful' of a moment than the multiple interpretations that could commence from writing. In any case, Hastrup and Bloch's arguments are emblematic of the privilege writing has acquired in the social sciences in general, and in anthropology in particular since the 1970s.

No wonder, then, that photography's romance with professional anthropology was so doomed as the twentieth century progressed, given the nature of sustained criticisms such as the above from influential sections of the community. Compared to early anthropology's affinity with photography in its ethnographic production, by 1965, when Spencer's *The Samburu* was published, it only contained four photos while his *Maasai of Matapato*, published in 1988, contained no images at all (MacDougal 1999 [1997]: 281). Closer home in South Asia, the plight of photography in ethnographies has faced similarly reducing numbers, but a few crucial works have retained some interest in having photos within their pages. Gananath Obeyesekere's seminal work, *The Cult of the Goddess Pattini* (1984), has one black-and-white photo and twenty-five captioned colour images depicting various aspects of the Pattini rituals. In Plate 1, identified as 'ritual specialists eating the consecrated rice', one can also see the seemingly tired anthropologist eating the same rice, adding what one may call a very ordinary picture of the anthropologist in the 'field'. Similarly, James Brow's work, *Demons and Development: The Struggle for Community in a Sri Lankan Village* (1996), carries eight captioned black-and-white photos. In both cases, based on research in Sri Lanka, while the photographs add a sense of place and context to the overall narrative, one cannot argue that they are inherently embedded within the narrative. In other words, the stories both scholars weave are already told well without needing recourse to the images. Comparatively, Sharika Thiranagama's *In My Mother's House: Civil War in Sri Lanka* (2013) carries no images at all. In her text, Thiranagama deals with living in conditions of war, and having access to photographs of such trying times and difficult family circumstances is understandably not easy. Amita Baviskar's *In the Belly of the River: Tribal Conflicts over Development in the Narmada Valley* (2011) does pay some conscious attention to images, in that she incorporates a number of illustrations by Orijit Sen as well as sixteen uncaptioned black-and-white photographs by Rahul N. Ram within the text. Comparatively, Ankur Datta's *On Uncertain Ground: Displaced Kashmiri Pandits in Jammu and Kashmir* (2017) carries five captioned black-and-white photographs taken by the author himself.

In these two works based on research in India, the attention paid to photographs/visuals is very different. Baviskar had self-consciously commissioned an artist to conjure a number of illustrations of objects directly related to the people she is talking about, while the photographs she has used provide a sense of the place she has seen and been to. Comparatively, Datta's five photographs suggest no indication of such conscious effort, even though they also offer a sense of his field site. But both Baviskar and Datta's books—like Obeyesekere and Brow's works referred to above—also manage to carry their narratives on their own merit, rather than due to any inherent conversation between the photos and the written text. Mathew Hull's 2012 work, *Government of Paper: The Materiality of Bureaucracy in Pakistan*, carries twenty captioned black-and-white photographs, out of which twelve are images of maps or documents captured off specific folders. As such, only about eight actually refer to the urban life within which much of the narrative is located. Nevertheless, all the images are far more effectively woven into the written text than the other South Asia-based research briefly considered above.

Seen in this sense, although the life of photographs in some ethnographies such as those discussed above, based on research in South Asia, seems marginally better-off than in many other global examples, the relative diminishing of photographs in such texts is obvious when compared to the period before the 1950s. Rather than being an amalgamation of accidents, the relative non-interest in photography in these and many other important works shows a clear trend and is the result of conscious decisions, which marks the relative avoidance or expulsion of photographs from ethnographies as well as anthropological writing more generally.

Notes

1. Sections of this chapter have been taken from my paper presented at the seminar, 'Knowing the Social World: Challenges and Responses', held at the Indian Institute of Advanced Study, Shimla, 13–15 March 2013. The paper has since been published as 'Photography's Methodological Absence in Social Anthropology in South Asia. Some Preliminary Thoughts for Consideration', in Jayaram (2017).

2. Intriguingly, except in groups, Rodiya men did not capture the attention of period photographers as subjects of portraits. Perhaps male partial nudity was not as 'interesting' as female nudity—partial or otherwise—for them. I have not seen many portraits of Rodiya men.

3. The digitised version of Hattersley's book, along with its images, are available at https://archive.org/details/bagandaathome00cwha (accessed 18 July 2017).

4. https://www.wdl.org/en/item/7772/ (accessed 19 July 2017).

5. Ibid.

6. The digitised version of Junod's book, along with its images, are available at https://archive.org/details/lifeofsouthafric02junouoft (accessed 18 July 2017).

7. https://www.britannica.com/biography/Henri-Alexandre-Junod (accessed 23 July 2017).

8. The digitised version of the Seligmanns' book, along with its images, are available at https://archive.org/details/veddas__00seliuoft (accessed 23 July 2017).

9. *The Northern D'Entrecasteaux* (1920), by Jenness and Ballantyne, is available at https://archive.org/details/northerndentreca00jennuoft (accessed 13 February 2018).

10. Malinowski's diary entries were published in 1967 in London by Routledge & Kegan Paul as *A Diary in the Strict Sense of the Term*. The complete text is available at https://monoskop.org/images/f/ff/Malinowski_

Bronislaw_A_Diary_in_the_Strict_Sense_of_the_Term_2nd_ed_1989.pdf (accessed 17 February 2018).

11. https://www.theguardian.com/books/booksblog/2015/aug/17/tristes-tropiques-by-claude-levi-strauss-melancholy-anthropology (accessed 23 July 2017).

four

'Selfies' and the Meanings of the Self[1]

In its digital state, the self-portrait is complex and full of visual and computational nuances as it is layered with information we have yet to decode or understand. The use of the smartphone and the presence of the network influences how we engage with and create our selfies. Filters and hashtags add new data to our selfies, which make them more than average self-portraits.

Brooke Wendt (2014: 10)

Biography of a Personal Interest in 'Selfies'

Unlike many others today, I don't take selfies, flippantly and casually manoeuvring a smartphone. But clearly, it is a ubiquitous activity, which I see wherever I travel in the world. And that too, in such varied and mundane places, ranging from the private spaces of people's homes to public spaces such as malls, airports, parks, streets, and so on (see Image 4.1 for a representative example of a casual selfie capture in progress).

Clearly, it is an important global social practice with its own notions of social and cultural capital, which have been largely homogenised across the world, and for which various paraphernalia have by now been manufactured and marketed. Today, most popular mobile phones are not advertised for their efficiency in verbal communication, but for the power of their inbuilt cameras, their ability to capture 'high quality' selfies and other photographs, to store such images in the phone itself, and finally, their ability to instantly edit and share these images online. Together, these are the prime

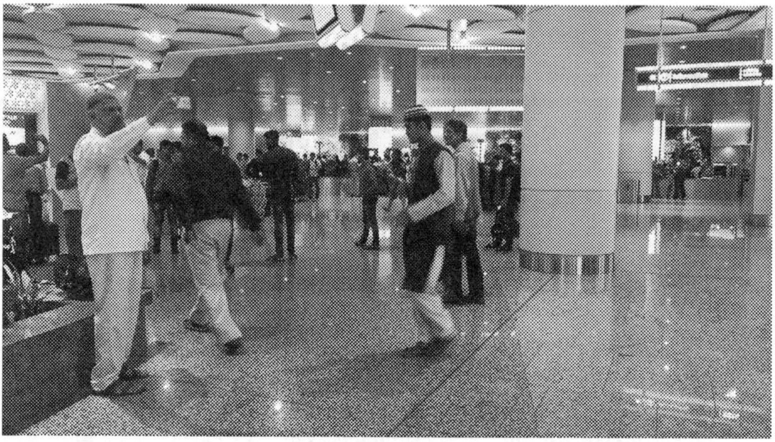

IMAGE 4.1 A quick selfie by a passenger against the backdrop of a luxury car (not in the frame) at the Chhatrapati Shivaji International Airport, Mumbai. Towards the left (partially in the frame), another passenger is also seen taking a selfie with the same backdrop, but from another angle.

Photograph courtesy of: Anoli Perera, 16 July 2017.

factors driving the selfie fad. For instance, Oppo mobile phones—particularly models F3 and F3 Plus—present themselves as the 'Selfie Expert' with a 'Dual Selfie Camera'.[2]

As a practice, selfie-taking has its own discourse, its own fans, supporters, detractors, courses, and research groups such as 'The Selfie Researchers Network'.[3] As part of all this, it has generated thousands of opinions. But what does the overall practice mean in social and cultural terms? How can it be historically located? Or is it a practice that can only be understood in terms of twenty-first century technology and twenty-first century structures of taste, located well within the realm of the general and popular practice of photography? Should such a reading not be located within humanity's relentless obsession with the self in general? But what happens to the self when it becomes a constantly and instantly reproduced, edited, crafted, shared, and deleted technical practice and product of the digital age? And why do people attempt to capture such images so obsessively, and at times at extreme risk to the self itself? These were the kind of questions that generated my interest in selfies since about 2015 within my broader interest in photography, as I also started to read about deaths related to selfies.

Despite my lack of personal interest in the present form of selfies, I have not been a stranger to processes of capturing self-images in technological forms. When I was a young man of seventeen, my parents packed me off to a place in New South Wales, Australia known as Orange, which I had never heard of until that time. I thought the name itself quite strange, as it had no reference to either the colour or the fruit bearing that name, as suggested by my incomplete command of English language training at that time. This travel came about because I was the recipient of a 'travel' and 'living abroad' scholarship offered by the American Field Service or AFS. Taking a cue from AFS' noted propensity at the time for leisure and adventure of sorts as opposed to scholarship as such, the more mischievous of the recipients referred to AFS simply as 'alcohol, fun and sex'. When I left the shores of Sri Lanka for the first time in my life in 1978, and quite anxiously boarded a Swiss Air flight to Singapore to hop onto my connecting Qantas flight to Sydney, my main concern was my obvious lack of a camera. I was wondering how I would document my travels; momentous moments, which I anticipated would beckon me as life progressed in that distant and unknown place. How could I ever 'prove' I was 'there'? And how could I stake a claim for my own presence in well-known places such as the Sydney Opera House, which I had only vaguely heard of at the time? How could I embed myself on Kodak or Fuji photo prints with famous landmarks in the backdrop and festoon my family album with images from 'abroad', where no one in my immediate family had been before? What is the point of the great steel 'wave' of the Sydney Harbor Bridge or the sail-like exterior of the Opera House without me in the foreground? How could I make a claim for my ordinary presence in the flow of a very ordinary history, which was nevertheless personally momentous?

Although I had neither the terminology nor an accurate conceptual framework to describe my state of anxiety at the time, my concerns clearly emanated from my obvious inability to conjure 'selfies' due to the simple lack of a camera. My family still owned the Kodak Brownie Box camera, which I referred to earlier in the Introduction and which had by the late 1970s become a family heirloom, although it still worked. But it neither suited the times nor offered the convenience of use to merit accompanying me on my maiden trans-oceanic voyage of discovery so far away from home and country. Besides, I knew quite well that its technology had become obsolete—with no timer to enable selfies. But of course, the word 'selfie' did not exist at that time. Besides, the value of this old camera in terms of social prestige had plummeted in the two-and-a-half decades it had been in my home. That was another crucial reason why this camera could not be taken to Australia. The bottomline was that my family simply could not afford a new camera.

But my host parents, Alfred and Grace Brown, resolved my difficulty within weeks of my arrival in Orange. For one, they bought me a 110 mm Kodak Fixed Focus Camera with which I could document my circumstances at will, which I naturally did. But with this camera, I could not even think of selfies, as it did not have the facility to automatically control the shutter release with a timer. But many people did offer to take my portrait at different places—with traffic signs of kangaroo crossings on some highways in the background, or koalas in my arms in theme parks, and so on. This generosity of strangers, as well as people I got to know, allowed me to own a series of colour prints that were portraits of myself, but were not self-portraits. That is, I did not author these images myself. Nevertheless, a month after my arrival in Australia, one of the family members, Ross Brown, loaned me a second camera he owned, some version of a Fuji semi-automatic camera with a timer-enabled shutter-release. This allowed me to author a series of often badly and strangely framed 'selfies' by setting the camera on tables, chairs, rocks, boxes, piles of books, or any other suitable surfaces readily available in a given location, setting the aperture-release and the distance from the object correctly, and then running to a pre-designated spot before the timer did the rest. I mastered the use of the camera and the art of selfie-capture in a short time, albeit with some serious framing issues. But I was never missing from the frame, although at times I was too much to the left or the right, and at times the head was missing beyond the top frame. My four albums from February 1978 to January 1979 present a collection of colour photos outlining an incomplete narrative of what I saw, where I went, and more importantly, evidence of my own teenage obsession with myself in places I thought of at the time as 'cool'. In other words, these were selfies from a different time, using different techniques and technologies requiring considerable planning, experimentation, and effort. But I cannot remember it being an obsession or a flippant activity, casually and thoughtlessly engaged in by myself, or by others I knew at the time.

I presented this autobiographic sketch to make a simple point, which I think is important to take note of when we enter a discourse on selfies. That is, as an idea, what we refer to as 'selfies' in the digital age of today is nothing new. The urge or the fad to capture one's own image pictorially has pre-existed. What is new is what appears to be people's obsession with endlessly replicating images of themselves, mostly due to the wide availability of affordable and readily accessible technology, and the availability of good cameras in mobile phones, which can be manipulated easily by ordinary people, including very young children. Taking into account this constellation of circumstances, Kaufmann notes, 'selfies arise out of social conditions of our lives: the technology and cheap labor that make wallet-size cameras readily available, the hi-tech innovations that allow us to upload pictures in an instant, and the increasing norm and emerging forms of social media' (Kaufmann 2014). In other words, this very availability of technology, material, and a conducive collective frame of mind have fed and recreated humanity's long-term obsession with replicating the image of the self in pictorial form. And the ability to digitally store and edit these images and widely share them online via multiple social media platforms has added to this massive expansion of interest in obsessively capturing images of the self.

An Incomplete Pre-history of Selfies

As I noted at the beginning, the contemporary practice of capturing selfies needs to be partly located in a specific historical context and within a specific genealogy of obsession. In the European tradition of painting, over a considerable period of time, self-portraits were a very specific genre which many artists engaged in as a matter of routine. Among the best known in this tradition are Leonardo da Vinci's self-portrait in red chalk, executed in 1512 and presently held in the collection of Biblioteca Reale in Turin,[4] as well as the numerous self-portraits by Vincent Van Gogh at different times in his career. This is what Ben Dreyfuss refers to when he mentions selfies as having a 'noble heritage in high art' (Dreyfuss 2014). He specifically talks of Rembrandt's compilation of over sixty self-portraits (ibid.). This painterly tradition was introduced to South Asia through colonialism as a necessary part of the Empire's colonising and civilising project targeting the 'natives'. As a practice, this was a matter of constructing a sense of perpetuity for one's self. That is, self-portraits, or commissioned paintings of one's self, ensured under certain circumstances that a likeness of the self in pictorial form would survive over time, even after the corporeal self had ceased to exist. These would in turn become points of reference to familial and social histories and memories of a place, depending on the social and political worth of the individuals concerned. At the same time, there have been traditions of painting in South Asia as well, which were also partly influenced by the traditions of European portraiture introduced to the region via the expansion of the Empire. But these traditions were also necessitated by local conditions of power, in the context of which individuals with means were keen to get their portraits painted. As such, in India, during the Mughal period, many of the better-known Mughal rulers commissioned their portraits, a practice also seen among many Maharajahs, and this tradition expanded during the British colonial period. This was often a practice focussed not merely on the individual, but on extended members of the royal family as well. But despite the obvious interest in the self and the extended networks of individuals socially or politically related to the self in these portraits, these were not self-portraits. But they too indicated very clearly the emphasis on the self in the broader practices of personal image-making.

Tifentale and Manovich note that at times, the term selfie is imposed retroactively to include the photographic self-portraits made in the nineteenth and early twentieth century (Tifentale and Manovich 2014: 8). In this revisionist history, they refer to Robert Cornelius' 'daguerreotype self-portrait made in 1839' and Hippolyte Bayard's dramatically staged '*Self-portrait of a Drowned Man* made in 1840' (ibid.). These examples suggest that the shift from self-portraits via paintings to early photographic self-portraits were already enabled by the 1840s. What becomes obvious in this brief history is the considerable interest in creating self-images among individuals who could afford it, who had the required social taste for it, and also had access to the necessary cultural practices. As a trend, this has evolved and has been maintained over a long period of time. It is in this context that Berger notes, 'digital cameras, photo sharing websites and camera phones do not fundamentally alter snapshot photography; they simply amplify an already existing tradition' (Berger 2011: 184). Berger is not talking about selfies as such, but snapshot photography more generally. Nevertheless, selfies need to be understood as a category of snapshot photography. As such, Berger's argument holds clearly for understanding the sense of continuity the selfie has with the pre-digital past. But well into the early 1960s, with regard to both painting and photography, this interest in the pictorial capture of the self and its significant others was by and large an elite practice, which did not extend to ordinary people.

As the camera became more widely available, and after photographic studios expanded and became ordinary places, the possibility of creating images of one's self when needed became increasingly feasible and could transgress class and social boundaries due to the more expanded access to capital and the wider circulation of once class-restricted tastes and social practices. Social events such as weddings tended to offer opportunities to create images of the self, but not through the personal intervention of the individual himself. There had to be an intermediary to operate the camera in creating these images, whether they were professional photographers or kin with cameras, until systems of delayed aperture control became commonly available in the 1960s. These historical developments have created an extensive corpus of images of known and unknown individuals in portraits and self-created portraits. Seen in this sense, selfies as we know them today did not merely emerge out of a vacuum in the recent past, facilitated only by the availability of conducive technology and equipment, most clearly with the advent of camera-equipped mobile phones in the twenty-first century. Instead, the urge for selfies and the contemporary practice of creating them have to be partly located in this general history of interest in creating likenesses of individuals, through personal intervention or through the facilitation of others. In this sense, taking into account these multiple histories and intersections of technologies, Warfield suggests that selfies can be seen 'as a multimodal convergence of older and newer technologies', within which the selfie becomes 'a mirror, and a camera, and a stage or billboard all at once' (Warfield 2014: 1).

Selfies in the Digital Age

How can we understand the nature of the self and the practices of selfie-making in the digital age? To what extent does the present interest differ—if at all—from the pre-history sketched above? The words 'selfie' and 'selfies', considered generally as internet slang, are typical twenty-first century words made possible by twenty-first century technology and attitudes, but fed by a much longer obsession with the self and the formulation of self-portraits. But, as noted by Jones, what is important to remember with regard to photographic self-portraits is that 'technology not only *mediates* but *produces* subjectivities in the contemporary world' (Jones 2002: 950). As a word, 'selfie' was used for the first time in the present sense of its meaning by an Australian man named Nathan Hope, who shared an image of himself sporting an injured lip in a forum post in 2002.[5] But it gained international recognition a decade later when the *Oxford Dictionary* declared 'selfie' its word of the year in 2013.[6] But according to Italie, the term 'selfy' (and not selfie) first appeared in the *Urban Dictionary* in 2005, while photographs tagged as 'selfie' appeared on Flickr and MySpace in 2004 (Italie 2013). But by the time the word appeared in the *Oxford Dictionary*, what was meant by selfie in the contemporary sense and the practice itself was well-entrenched in global popular discourses, which is precisely what led to *Oxford Dictionary*'s public pronouncement. There is a very clear standardisation of what is meant by selfie, insofar as well-known and publically accessible authorities on lexicography are concerned. *Merriam-Webster Dictionary* suggests that a selfie is 'an image of oneself taken by oneself using a digital camera especially for posting on social networks'.[7] According to the similarly clinical and precise definition provided by the *Oxford Dictionary*, a selfie constitutes of 'a photograph that one has taken of oneself, typically one taken with a smartphone or webcam and shared via social media'.[8] For the *Cambridge Dictionary*, 'a photograph that you take of yourself, usually with a mobile phone' can be understood as a selfie, while 'selfies are often published using social media'.[9] In a more extensive and more culturally nuanced and somewhat sarcastic explanation, which captures some of the moods and attitudes of typical selfies, the *Urban Dictionary* says that a selfie is,

> a picture taken of yourself that is planned to be uploaded to Facebook, Myspace or any other sort of social networking website. You can usually see the person's arm holding out the camera in which case you can clearly tell that this person does not have any friends to take pictures of them so they resort to Myspace to find internet friends and post pictures of themselves, taken by themselves. A selfie is usually accompanied by a kissy face or the individual looking in a direction that is not towards the camera.[10]

Obviously, the only reason why people take selfies is not because they do not have 'friends' to take them, as suggested by *Urban Dictionary*. More importantly, this is done because it has been made so easily possible for the person to do so by himself. In other words, today, constructing a self-portrait with a mobile phone camera does not need intermediaries as photographers, and the technology itself is easy and fast. But perceptions of alienation and the urge to transgress feelings of loneliness are not devoid of merit when attempting to understand why some people take selfies. The idea of sharing these images online and the issues of 'friends' and recognition of the self by others are important factors in understanding the phenomenon of selfies, which I will address later in this chapter. One thing that is clear in all these formal meanings is that selfies as seen today are typically captured by late twentieth-century or early twenty-first century equipment, and more importantly, they are captured for the specific purpose of sharing widely on the internet. Referring to selfies, Rawlings (2013) also notes that the practice is 'dependent on advances in digital photography and mobile phone technology, as well as the rise of Twitter, Facebook, and Instagram, among other sites, which supply an outlet and audience for the photos'.

In terms of these understandings, selfies are by definition for wide public consumption and have very little to do with private enjoyment of the self per se. That is, the only way in which the self manifests in this context is not by keeping these images for oneself, but by releasing them to the public. 'Public' here mostly means the internet. As such, the self becomes a public icon open to relentless modes of consumption, perception, as well as mutation. Also, these definitions locate the act of selfie-taking in a thoroughly contemporary situation, and delink it from the broader engagement individuals have historically had with the self and its pictorial re-creation. That is, although a link with a pre-existing tradition can be made intellectually, people who engage in the contemporary practice do not do so on the basis of any consciousness of this historical continuity. Instead, they do so because of very contemporary compulsions and the availability of technology. On the other hand, despite the focus on the self in these definitions, selfies are not merely captured by an individual by herself of only herself. At times, selfies are also of individuals capturing themselves with a group, in the context of which the individual merges with the group, but becomes the focus of attention as s/he displays the agency that made the image possible. These group photos are often known as 'we-fies', about which I will comment later in this chapter. I feel that it is a mistake to delink the practice of selfie-making from the older and longer tradition and interests that have informed the pictorial capture of the self. The selfie needs to be seen as a contemporary manifestation of a much longer obsession with the self.

Globally, there are a number of selfie trends, which researchers have identified across regions. For instance, the SelfieCity Project explored 656,000 photos from five cities, taken between 5–11 December 2013 and posted on Instagram: New York City (207,000 photos), Bangkok (162,000), Moscow (140,000), Sao Paolo (123,000), and Berlin (24,000) (Tifentale and Manocich 2014: 2–3). From this sample, the researchers randomly picked 120,000 photos at the rate of approximately 20,000 to 30,000 for each city, specifically looking for selfies, out of which 640 selfies were selected for each city for further analysis (ibid.: 2). The study notes that people take far fewer selfies than is generally assumed. Although this varied from city to city, only about 3–5 per cent of the images analysed were actually selfies (ibid.). In this sense, the practice of selfies is more 'visible' as an action than the direct productions (selfies) of that action themselves. Significantly, more women than men seem to take selfies, which turned out to be 1.3 times as many in Bangkok as opposed to Berlin, while in Moscow 4.6 times more women took their selfies than men (ibid.). The study also found that most selfies were captured by youth, the average age across all cities being 23.7 years, although in Bangkok, most selfie-takers happened to be in the age cohort of twenty-one years while in New York City, this happened to be 25.3 (ibid.). Interestingly, it also became evident that more older men (thirty onwards) posted selfies on Instagram than women (ibid.). Computer-facilitated facial analysis, which was part of the study, also indicated that more smiling faces were evident in selfies taken in Bangkok and Sao Paulo, while the selfie-takers in Moscow smiled the least (ibid.).

As interesting as these patterns might be in identifying some general trends in the selfie phenomenon across selected cities, by themselves they do not explain the reasons for these variations or individual explanations of why people would be interested in taking selfies and sharing them online. SelfieCity researchers note that their 'project wanted to show that no single interpretation of the selfie phenomenon is correct by itself', and that it was hoping to 'reveal the inherent complexities in understanding the selfie—both as a product of the advancement of the digital image-making and online sharing and a social phenomenon that can serve many functions' (Tifentale and Manocich 2014: 2). What studies like this, based on computer technologies and data mining, indicate is that despite the unravelling of general patterns, they are unable to bring us any closer to individual motivations. This is only possible with a micro-focus on individuals.

It is in such a context that Tiidenberg has noted that selfies should not be seen

> only as photos we take of ourselves with an extended hand, or in a mirroring surface, and share on social media, but as, expressive acts; photographic objects; cultural practices; gestures; means for communicating and understanding ourselves; tools for reclaiming our sexuality, experiencing our bodies or performing particular versions of ourselves; addictive practices that lead to, or amplify psychopathology; tools for gaining visibility; and much more. (Tiidenberg 2018: 7).

Clearly, what Tiidenberg is suggesting is a more nuanced and engaged understanding of selfies by looking closely at the motivations of people who engage in this practice.

What do Selfies Mean? An Incomplete Ethnography of Personal Perceptions

Locating selfies in a specific historical context and within a discourse of formal understanding of what the practice means, as has been done above, is one thing. But what it actually means to people who regularly practice it, or see it routinely but do not practice it, is quite another. In mid-November 2016, when I was visiting the Kirti Monastery in Macleod Ganj, Himachal Pradesh, where the Dalai Lama sometimes resides, I could see people equipped with camera phones and, at times, with selfie-sticks diligently practising their vocation of leisure. I was particularly intrigued by one young man who had come to the temple by himself. He was not too interested in the temple, for religious or other reasons. He hardly photographed the monks engaged in rituals, the murals in the main chamber, the statues of the Buddha, or anything else while I watched. But on one of the balconies, he leaned against the railing, with his back to a range of mountains in the distance, an elevated car park, a cluster of architecturally uninteresting buildings that typify the structures on either side of Temple Road below,

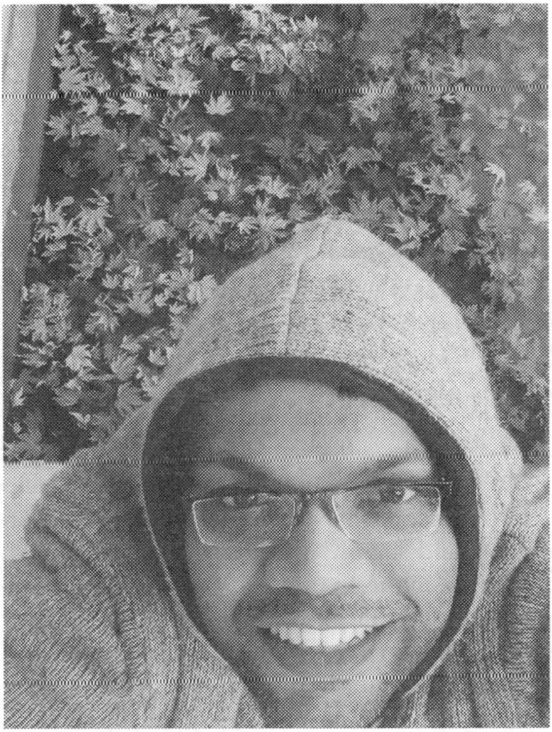

IMAGE 4.2 Typical selfie by Chintan Girish Modi, Shalimar Gardens, Srinagar, November 2016.

Photograph courtesy of: Chintan Girish Modi.

smiled to himself and clicked a few selfies, ensuring that he captured himself from more than one angle from above with the aid of the selfie-stick to which his smartphone was attached. I could not fathom what on earth was aesthetically or otherwise interesting enough in the background for him to pose for a selfie, even as he was not interested in the somewhat more appealing and culturally significant backdrops within the temple itself (although it was certainly nowhere close to the beautiful Buddhist monasteries one could see in Sikkim or Dharamshala). What was his motivation or interest? What was his trigger? What was intriguing about that place and about that backdrop over which he spent considerable time? It appeared that the unimpressive buildings below were not captured in his selfies, while the distant mountains and clouds were, making it seem as though he was leaning against the mountains and hugging the clouds. In other words, he seemed to be creating a photographic illusion or fantasy of himself. But he is simply one among millions of people who do behaviourally similar things. They take selfies, not just because it is a necessity, but simply because it is possible and easy. They also take selfies seemingly so randomly and often because backdrops for selfies that capture the interests of many are scattered across the planet, produced by nature as well as history and the ordinary circumstances of contemporary living.

To get a sense of why people actually take selfies in this manner and what they might do with them, I thought it best to pose an open question on one of the most common forums where selfies are often posted for the purpose of sharing and generating a discourse through 'likes', 'comments', and 'shares,' which is what is anticipated in the very act of posting them online. In this case, I opted for Facebook, to which I have regular access. And also because I have always considered Facebook a forum to explore fads, fashion, news, and politics, which is why I opened an account in the first place in 2008. For me, social networking sites such as Facebook, Instagram, and Twitter are open discursive spaces where written and pictorial texts float across relatively freely, turning them into veritable and constantly mutating ethnographic sites that remain relatively unchartered and un-policed, but at the same time profusely commented upon and taken note of by many. My post on Facebook, which combined a simple explanation of what I had in mind and a request to educate me on why individuals were interested in selfies, was formulated as follows:

> Let me understand 'selfies': While slowly writing my fantasy book on photography, anthropology and method, I realized that I am a bit lost in my attempts to understand selfies as a non-selfie-taker in the era of good cameras in mobile phones. There are plenty of things to read on this though. And India records the highest selfie-related deaths in the world. Mumbai police has just launched a 'safe selfie' campaign to try and minimize

> selfie-related deaths and injuries! Towards understanding why people click images of themselves and what they do with them, I thought I should simply ask the 'experts', the doers via FB: So if anyone has the time, please send a brief note to my inbox responding to the following two questions: 1) Why do you take selfies? 2) What do you do with the images?[11]

The responses I received came from people based in India, Nepal, Sri Lanka, and Ethiopia. I knew all the respondents personally or professionally, and they came from different age groups. But age, national origins, or professional affiliation did not seem to have an effect on the content and direction of their responses. However, for the sake of keeping my somewhat quirky sample minimally 'sociological', I thought of providing a few minor details on the authors of the responses in a series of simple footnotes. To begin with, let me present the views of people who admitted to capturing selfies regularly or irregularly.

According to Sandhya, AS,[12]

> people take selfies because it is a relatively independent endeavor. If you are in a group of friends and wish to capture the moment, you don't have to rely on a passerby or another friend (who will be left out of the picture if he clicks it for your group) to get clicked. Selfies help that way.

What she refers to is the instantaneous nature of the selfie, which requires no external agency as the construction of self-portraits once did. In other words, selfies today are an almost thoughtless effort that anyone can engage in almost anywhere without mediation. She further suggests, 'selfies are actually a pro-naturalness [*sic*]. [They], I think, [have] come to challenge the otherwise "perfect" images, which are often photo-shopped and look unreal. On the other hand, selfies come across as more humble and less mediated counterparts.'[13] Sarah Gervais, while sympathetic towards selfies, agrees with this position when she notes,

> Instagram (and other social media) has allowed the public to reclaim photography as a source of empowerment ... [it] offers a quiet resistance to the barrage of perfect images that we face each day. Rather than being bombarded with those creations ...

> we can look through our Instagram feed and see images of real people—with beautiful diversity. (quoted in Day 2013)

Today, internet-enabled smartphones offer the possibility of self-images to be directly released to the internet quickly, once the lens has captured the photo and saved it in the phone's memory, and without the intervention of other people or editorial mediations.

However, such sharing of self-images in a relatively unmediated state is a matter of personal choice, and not necessarily the defining feature of the technology at one's disposal or a taken-for-granted feature of selfie-practice in general. Widely available technology offered via built-in mobile phone applications allow for quick editing prior to a photo being released online. In 2013, Huawei announced that its smartphone, 'Ascend P6', comes equipped with 'instant facial beauty support' software, which 'reduces wrinkles and blends skin tone' (Garside 2013). This specific use of language was clearly reminiscent of advertisements for 'skin creams rather than computer technology' (ibid.). Very clearly, the company was making use of the 'growing popularity of the self portrait or "selfie"' as a marketing tool for its phones (ibid.). Beyond this, numerous specifically designed software allow people to fine-tune their selfies (or any other image) prior to sharing them online. In general, these are known as 'selfie editors' and 'skinny apps', which 'help us look like we've photographed ourselves in the best lighting every time, blurs our imperfections and can even slim our face the morning after a late night of partying' (Samotin 2017). Among these photo-editing apps which allow people to perfect their selfies prior to their journeys online are: Photowonder, Facetune, Visage Lab, CreamCam, SkinnyCamera, Picmonkey, Perfect 365 (ibid.). While most of these are free, others charge a nominal fee for their use. So clearly, being 'natural' and unmediated is no longer the final word in selfie-creation. Instead, they promote exactly the opposite, the ability to transform the self beyond nature into an icon of acceptance, and create online the kind of self one wants to be rather than the self that is.

Sandhya, in her explanation of selfies, also notes, 'there isn't much scope for creativity in terms of posing' and 'selfies are ironically not for the self. It obviously doesn't have value if it is not shared, or so I believe'.[14] Shared selfies in this sense oscillate between what is allowed to be seen in public, and what is not. Shah refers to this as 'the inherent tension in the world of the social web', 'between hiding and revealing' (Shah 2014). He further notes, 'our private data is a commodity that can buy us conveniences and perks to make life more interesting if not easier', which is where the open sharing of selfies can be located (ibid.). 'Interesting', in this understanding, can mean anything from a pronounced and fashionable online presence to the repetitive posting of selfies for added attention. It is in the space marked by these two variables of hiding and revealing that individuals who share their selfies take decisions on 'what identities to create, what faces to show, what data to offer for public consumption, and how we cope with the double bind of visible invisibility' (ibid.).

Chani Imbulgoda[15] views selfies from a more personal lens. She says,

> I'm also analyzing why people take selfies ... including myself. It's an addiction ... like to see nice [through] pics [of] ourselves ... maybe because we are more self-centered and lonely .... I normally post good ones on fb ... and interested [in] seeing comments and likes ... has become a hobby ... to spare [that is, spend] time ... it's more or less like getting addicted to smoking.

Her reading brings out notions such as 'addiction' and a remedy for 'loneliness' as possible explanations of people's preoccupation with selfies, which are also among some of the better-known popular explanations of the phenomenon. It is within the understanding of selfie-capture as an addiction that some have referred to it as 'a symptom of social media-driven narcissism' (Pearlman 2013). Within the same general idea of narcissism, Marche describes the urge for selfies as 'a disengagement from the self as much as it is a promotion of the self. It is seeing and being seen at once, in the same act' (Marche 2013). John Paul Titlow suggests that selfie-sharing is 'a high school popularity contest on digital steroids' (quoted in Day 2013). For him, selfie-takers who share them online 'are seeking some kind of approval from their peers and the larger community, which thanks to the Internet is now effectively infinite' (ibid.).

Sujata Chandra,[16] another respondent to my inquiry, agrees with the idea of narcissism more clearly:

> [W]e take selfies to feed our narcissism a wee bit more. Life is such, often we want a pretty moment captured, and we have no one around. Selfies are an answer to loneliness mixed with narcissism, along with looking for approval on social networking sites. As dismal as it sounds, that's how I look at selfies ....

The same sentiment is echoed by Marche when he notes, 'the selfie is the masturbation of self-image' because 'it gives control. It gives release. When you feel the urge to become an image, you can, with little effort and almost no consequences. You can call this selfie narcissism if you like' (Marche 2013). For Marche, this 'new narcissism is a natural reaction to the changing technology of image-making and image-distribution' (ibid.). Similarly, Day notes that for many, 'the selfie has become the ultimate symbol of the narcissistic age', because 'its instantaneous nature encourages superficiality' (Day 2013). In this sense, it is possible that selfie-takers 'care more than ever before about how we appear and, as a consequence, social acceptance comes only when the outside world accepts the way we look, rather than endorsing the work we do or the way we behave off-camera' (ibid.). This argument places considerable weightage on selfies and their online sharing in the actual public personality development of people. That is, selfies, comments, and the 'likes' one gets after they are posted online might actually create the guidelines on which a person formulates her/his public behaviour and public engagements. This also shows the core role that photo-editing apps can play in making the digitised self more appealing and accepted on the worldwide web.

Susan Visvanathan[17] looks at the selfie more positively: '[the] selfie records a moment of enjoyment, solitude, boredom, gregariousness. It is like looking in the mirror. It's not necessarily narcissistic, just an asset to living in a digital world. One can delete them if one looks awful.' This understanding, devoid of any negativity in the practice, is similar to what Levin notes when he says, 'taking selfies is simply a harmless past time. As with Polaroid, it is considered little more than a method for capturing a moment in one's life and sharing it with others' (Levin 2014). Tiidenberg also attempts to similarly absolve the relentless negativity that many critics have harshly imposed on selfies when she notes,

> selfies are not something that are good or bad as such. They are a way for us to express ourselves. This can be creative and help us understand ourselves better, or it can be vain, vapid and a source of abuse. What selfies mean depends on the context surrounding them—whose selfies, what's on them, where shared? (Tiidenberg 2018: 7)

She further notes that what a selfie actually means and what it eventually does depends on context (ibid.). What this means is that the emotional negativity often attached to the practice of selfies at the popular level must be looked at cautiously when the practice is read intellectually.

With particular reference to selfies shared on Instagram, Gervais notes in agreement with observers such as Levin and Tiidenberg, 'Instagram also allows us the opportunity to see below the surface. We capture a glimpse into the makings of people's daily lives. We get a sense of those things that make the everyday extraordinary' (quoted in Day 2013). In a sense, given the relative ease in capturing a selfie today, the practice allows for the construction of an incomplete digital diary of a person's travels and moments—both mundane and special. It is in this context that one can understand the enormous popularity of taking selfies in the most ordinary of places an individual might visit—including one's own kitchen—as well as the relatively memorable and iconic places. Why a person might want to take a selfie with a memorable backdrop is easier to comprehend as it has a longer history in photography. In the colonial period as well as in the history of early anthropology, colonial travellers and anthropologists in the field sometimes embedded themselves within the photos that were captured of the places they visited. This was a matter of marking their presence in 'exotic' places. As the camera evolved, one could also see ordinary travellers being photographed in many recognisable tourist locations, from Disneyland in Anaheim to notable monuments across the world. But for this, someone else's intervention as a photographer was necessary. What the mobile phone cameras have done is make this practice much easier and almost thoughtless and effortless. As a result, the emotional difference between a selfie in front of a memorable monument such as the Taj Mahal and one in your own kitchen sitting next to your favourite dish and utensils has somewhat diminished.

Let me now cross over to a slightly different perspective, offered by people who admit that they do not take selfies, but nevertheless have an opinion on the practice. P. K. Balachandran does not spend time on selfies. But in his mind, taking selfies is

> the product of an urge to be noticed. If nobody else cares to take your picture, what do you do? Take one yourself and put it on social media so people can see! These days, everyone wants to be noticed and commented upon. No one likes to be ignored. There is no room for a shy and retiring person. He is seen as a misfit and unsocial.[18]

The idea of attention and of being noticed, also evident in the other explanations, can be seen in this articulation as well. Similarly, Sanjee Goonatilake,[19] who identifies herself as someone who has 'not attempted to take a selfie', offers the following explanation for why her Facebook 'friends' frequently produce selfies:

> they actually have a need for attention and praise. For one reason or another they feel that they are not recognized. There are those who make 'wefies' [selfie of a group of people; see Image 4.3] and there are those who feel like putting a selfie of himself or herself in various poses. I generally oblige myself to put a like for anyone putting a selfie as it will make that person feel good and it does not cost anything to put a LIKE.

What she explains is how networks of obligation and goodwill are created online. Unnathi Samaraweera,[20] following in general terms the same line of thought as the two earlier commentators, notes that she too is 'not a fan on taking selfies'. Nevertheless, as an observer of the process, she notes,

> what I observe from my friends and relatives [is that] it may be a way of developing their social image as they themselves have feelings of [being] neglected or not paid attention [to] by others. To drag others' attention, [the] best way [is] to make a selfie and put [it] on FB (apparently most people think in that way).[21]

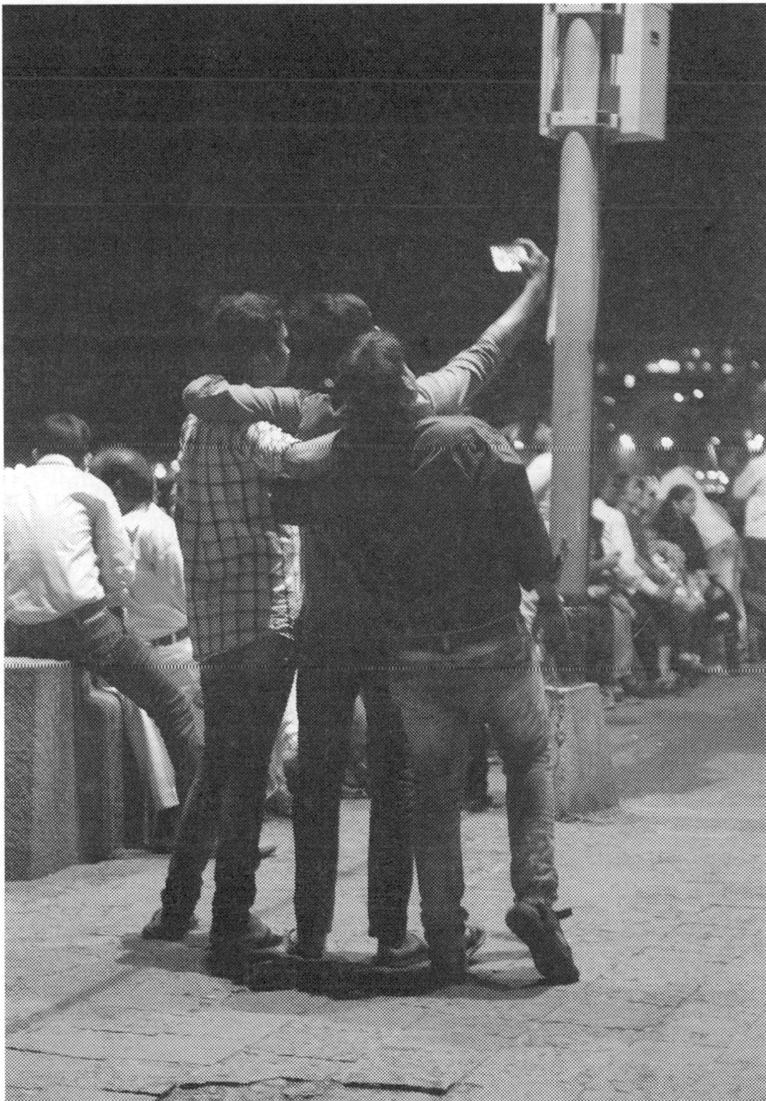

IMAGE 4.3 'Wefie' capture by three young men, Gateway of India, Mumbai, January 2016.

Photograph courtesy of: Author's research collection.

She further notes that if the practice is based on a person's self-perception as being neglected by others, placing selfies online might work as a means of relieving feelings of loneliness.[22] For her, 'it is linked with expressing [a sense of] "happiness"[23] as well'. More generally, according to Samaraweera, 'wherever [people] visit, whatever they do, people have started taking selfies and putting on FB, just to show they live a happy life which may not be [the actual situation] in their real lives'.[24] Mark Leary agrees with the general position articulated above, that is, that selfies have to do with attention:

> From a social psychological standpoint, the selfie phenomenon seems to stem from basic human motives. The first is to attract attention from other people. Because people's positive social outcomes in life require that others know them, people are motivated to get and maintain social attention.[25]

What this brief survey of individual motivations for engaging in the selfie phenomenon—or not engaging in it—shows is that individuals opt for it for different reasons. But even so, there are general themes that seem to recur, which include notions of narcissism and the need to be noticed and accepted, dealing with loneliness, documenting day-to-day life, and so on. But it seems to me that general selfie trends need not be seen as a societal malaise, as some of the more popular anti-selfie opinions seem to suggest. There is an element of addiction, in the sense that many young people in particular seem to opt for it because others do so as well. In this sense, the practice has an element of peer pressure. But on the other hand, selfies are not forced upon anyone, and it is a voluntary practice. The fact that some individuals might spend considerable time on capturing selfies and posting them online is another matter. It is up to individuals' sense of agency to ensure that a fad does not lead to dystopian lifestyles. But that by itself cannot be seen as a symptom of a narcissistic society.

Selfies and the Shadow of Death

Most proponents of selfies view it within a discourse of leisure and life. However, since recent times, it has become apparent that selfies can also be located within the realm of death. It seems to me that the association of selfies with death manifests itself in two ways. One has to do with the death of selfie-takers as a direct consequence of selfie-capture. The second is related to treating forms and places of death as objects of curiosity, which would make backdrops or locations for selfies. It is in this latter context that Levin notes that selfies are 'symbols of the deteriorating moral fabric of civilization; harbingers of a future digital media dystopia in which disassociated individuals callously pose before human atrocities to snap and share the pic[ture]' (Levin 2014). I would like to briefly explore both of these manifestations.

In January 2016, when I was in Mumbai for a brief period, I heard the story of a young woman, Tarnnaum Ansari, who died after she and her friends fell into the sea while attempting to take a selfie with a group of friends at the city's Bandra Fort. A local man managed to save the friends of the young woman, but died himself in the rescue attempt (Shinde 2016). This was not the first time that I had heard of selfie-related deaths; but this was the first time that I noted that law enforcement authorities, at least in Mumbai, were actively beginning to consider the practice of selfie-capture as something dangerous under specific conditions. They had initiated a 'Safe Selfie' campaign, identifying fifteen potentially dangerous places across the city for selfie-practitioners (ibid.). While this specific tragedy seemed to be well-known in the city, I did not see any relenting in the urge for selfies in its public manifestation during my brief sojourn, in either Bandra Fort where the two lives were lost or in many other selfie zones in the city's vicinity which offered the kind of backdrops that people preferred, such as the Gateway of India (see Image 4.4). These backdrops added more meaning in an adventurous sense and to the narrative potential of selfies, which explains their popularity as sites for selfies despite the possible risks.

In a comparable situation in Sri Lanka, the country's railway authorities have taken a tougher stand on people taking selfies on railway tracks with approaching trains as a backdrop, given the increase in selfie-related accidents and deaths on rail tracks in recent times. In mid-June 2017, an official of Sri Lanka Railways noted that

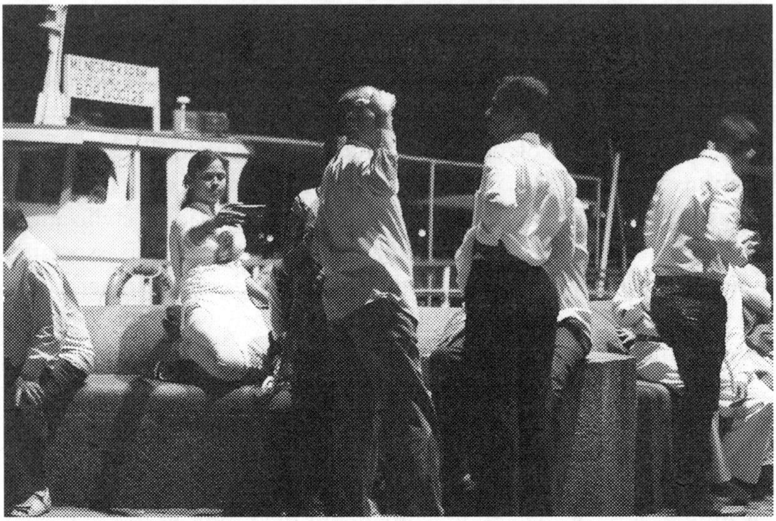

Image 4.4 Selfie-capture near the sea at the Gateway of India, with a passing tug-boat in the background. Mumbai, January 2016.
Photograph courtesy of: Author's research collection.

in the previous six months alone, at least twenty people had died trying to use mobile phones on rail roads, while in the second week of June 2017 alone, four people died trying to take selfies on rail roads (Nafeel 2017). In all cases, they were run over by approaching trains, which were supposed to be their moving backdrops. In this context, the country's railway authorities had 'announced that they will start arresting people who are found taking selfies on the railway tracks or in front of moving trains' (Srivastava 2017). But this phenomenon is a global one. Incomplete statistics from 2014–16 paint the picture provided in Table 4.1.

These figures have been compiled by Zachary Crocket, based on a three-year analysis of Google news archives and Wikipedia, which collected all reported incidents of selfie-related deaths since 2014: 'that is, a death that was *precipitated* by taking a selfie'.[26] The three main causes of death happen to be falling from a high place (sixteen deaths), drowning (fourteen deaths), and run over by a train (eight deaths).

TABLE 4.1 Selfie-related deaths by country, 2014–16.

	India	Russia	USA	Spain	Philippines	Portugal	Indonesia	South Africa	Romania	Pakistan	Mexico	Italy	China
Number of deaths	19	07	05	04	04	02	02	01	01	01	01	01	01

Source: Priceonomics, https://priceonomics.com/the-tragic-data-behind-selfie-fatalities/, (accessed 3 July 2017).

The figures show that forty-nine people had died while attempting to take a selfie and that the average age of the victims was twenty-one years, while 75 per cent of them happened to be male.[27] One has to assume that these figures are incomplete, given the nature of the methodology adopted for compilation. As has been acknowledged by others, under-reporting can skew the actual situation.[28] In addition, one has to assume that such incidents are also reported in languages the analysts could not read, they may not be deposited in the two main sources used for the study, and that many newspaper or government reports on such incidents in many parts of the world might not even be online. Even so, it is obvious that the urge for selfies has taken lives, although this is by no means an 'epidemic'. But when situated in the context of other accidental deaths, selfie-deaths present more morbid interpretive possibilities. Take, for example, the figures of accidental deaths (including selfie-deaths) based on 2015 estimates in Table 4.2.

Again, despite the fact that the figures can be much more comprehensive, they show a number of trends. While there are causes for a much higher number of accidental deaths, selfie-deaths are not the lowest. Also, most accidental deaths have occurred as a result of sporting activities or while going about day-to-day work. Selfies, on the other hand (like erotic asphyxiation), is a non-essential activity. In that sense, a selfie death comes somewhat closer to suicide, given its self-inflicted nature. But suicides result from difficult social and emotional circumstances, when an individual takes her/his own life as a means of permanent escape. But selfie-deaths are not precipitated with an idea of death as its point of departure. Instead, the risk involved

Table 4.2 Accidental Deaths in 2015.

Cause of death	Deaths per year
Erotic asphyxiation	625
Airplane crash	513
Bee/wasp attacks	58
Skateboarding	28
Selfies	28
Accident on Mount Everest	17
American football	12
Shark attacks	8
Vending machines	2

Source: Priceonomics, https://priceonomics.com/the-tragic-data-behind-selfie-fatalities/ (accessed 3 July 2017).

in taking a selfie in life-threatening conditions is something that a person takes for her/his own personal pleasure, within which death is not seen as an end. The contradiction here is that the intention to mark the presence of the self in a place marked by danger or sense of adventure, and to ensure that that moment is captured in perpetuity directly results in the corporeal annihilation of the self itself—although at times, the selfie might survive these dire circumstances. Given this real propensity for selfies to take lives and create pain, just as much as it creates joy for followers most of the time, it also has to be seen as a practice in which the kind of self-restraint and discipline that is routinely necessary to ensure one's own sanctity of life is at times relaxed to become something seemingly addictive and deadly. As the figures in Table 4.1 show, nineteen individuals, or 40 per cent of the total selfie-related deaths took place in India. Selfies that lead to death in this manner are known as 'killfies'[29] in internet slang. In this context, it is hardly surprising that the Minister of Road Transport and Highways in India, Nitin Gadkari, opted to feature himself in a public interest television advert sponsored by his own Ministry and Samsung India, reiterating this discomforting statistic.[30] The video advised viewers in a no-nonsense written text, 'the moments you hold so dear can disappear with one silly selfie'.[31]

The second association of selfies with death occurs when places of death are treated as objects of curiosity and suitable sites or backdrops for selfies. Here, what is at stake is not the life of the self, but the sanctity of death as provided for by most cultures under routine circumstances, and so this is therefore a matter of suspending routine ethics in the capture of selfies. *The New York Post* reported in 2013 the case of a young woman who captured a selfie, framing as her background New York's iconic Brooklyn Bridge upon which a man was trying to commit suicide (Martinka 2013). While the impending tragedy and the rescue effort was in progress, the woman 'turned her back to the scene, angled her phone toward the bridge and snapped a shot', ensuring to present herself with a 'thin smile', making the framing of the selfie 'perfect' (ibid.). This was not an accidental shot in which an attempted suicide was captured while taking a selfie, but a situation where the Brooklyn Bridge became the background for the selfie only because a suicide was in progress. So effectively, someone's pain and impending end of life was suitable enough for a selfie backdrop because these features would add to the narrative potential of the image and the attention it might generate once shared online.

Even more questionable have been the cases of Bahsid McLean from The Bronx, who in May 2013 killed his mother and then 'posed with a picture of her severed head', and the example of Malik Whiter from Florida, who in October 2013 created a selfie in a 'classroom while his teacher was seen going through labor in the background' (Martinka 2013). While these may be seen as extreme instances, they have nevertheless become a part of selfie folklore, offering newer possibilities of looking at the phenomenon as a situation of extreme narcissism, with the misery and pain of others used as a backdrop. While one of the examples above includes the matter of murder, which facilitated the selfie, the other two were situations where the selfie-takers could have helped to stop a possible death in one case or reduce someone's pain in the other. Minimally, they could have offered a degree of sympathy to the aggrieved, as any society would have expected. But instead, they decided that the pain of others in those instances was far more valuable as selfie-backdrops and as a generator of online discourse.

If these cases are considered extreme, there are many other, seemingly less extreme examples of selfies which nevertheless take death or symbols of death as backdrops and sites of selfies. It was in 2016 that I first noticed on Facebook someone I knew posting images of a family funeral, which also included a selfie of herself with the open coffin of her deceased relative in the background. The images were posted with a brief narrative of pain and loss. None of the comments made any negative observations but were standard remarks like 'rest in peace'. But I found the phenomenon somewhat strange and unusual at the time, particularly because of the selfie and the sombre context. But today, one can see that these kinds of selfies related to funerals have become a sub-genre of self-portraits, known in internet slang as 'funeral selfies'.[32] The Tumblr account, 'Selfies at Funerals', offers a cross-section of selfies related to funerals, sourced from social media feeds along with the text that accompanied the photos.[33] But these are from limited cultural settings, mostly within the US, and do not offer a global picture. But one can see in these images and the comments that accompany them a number of features which make specific patterns: (*i*) The images are taken during, on the way to, or after attending a funeral; (*ii*) While the accompanying messages sometimes offer a statement on loss or condolences over the death of an individual, the photos themselves—particularly the facial expressions—do not indicate any semblance of sorrow or sombreness. What can be seen in some images are people posing for selfies with the urns containing the dead individuals' remains. If funeral selfies are to be taken as a genre of recent popular photography, what they seem to do is bring death right back into the chaos of continuing life and leisure. In other words, the self—even after its corporeal demise—is not offered an exit from the mundane world in the short term. In some senses, the departed selves are offered a somewhat marginal reincarnation within the frames of funeral selfies.

In this scheme of things, death, as well as symbols of death, simply become commodities for life and the living, and the sanctity of death that funeral events traditionally offered in many cultures has been removed from that context.

Conclusion: Selfies and the Self

The idea of the self has come up more than once during the preceding exploration. Where is the self situated as an analytical category in the context of the discourse and the dynamics of selfie-capture, which range from the perpetuation of the self in pictorial form online to its forced and ultimate demise in corporeal form? The self, in the modernist sense, was often understood within a universalist idiom as a subject that bore universal experience and had universal applicability. It is this universalist idea of the modernist self that became the target of much postmodern critiques (Haraway 2006). In general, postmodern and post-structural theorists argued for the death of the self. In this sense, for writers like Derrida, Laclau, Baudrillard, and Foucault, it was impossible to conceive that individuals possessed a core, unitary, and rational self comprising an essential nature and independent consciousness (Callero 2003: 117). For them, the self, understood in this fashion, simply signified the political residue of European Enlightenment (ibid.). In this scheme of thought, juxtaposed between modernist and postmodernist understandings of the self, where does the self captured in selfies reside? Do selfies take us closer to the modernist understanding of an overarching and more universal appreciation of the self, given the very universal appeal of this practice? Or, despite the relentless reproduction of their selves pictorially by countless individuals across the world, does it somehow indicate the death of the self, as suggested by postmodernists? Such a death could perhaps result from the seeming trivialisation of the act of selfie capture itself. After all, literally and metaphorically, selfies are produced, reproduced, shared, deleted, reinvented, forgotten, and revisited in an inherently linked life-cycle enacted on the internet. But in such a system, what dies is more the selfie rather than the self itself.

For Foucault, the only way in which the self could be understood was by perceiving it as a direct consequence of power and the result of historically specific discursive systems (Callero 2003: 117). The main limitation of the Focauldian tradition in particular and the postmodern/post-structuralist traditions more generally is their elimination of the assumption of the existence of an agentic and knowledgeable actor within the self (ibid.: 118). In general, such an assumption can only come from the kind of universalist understandings of the self as espoused by modernists. But if we are to look at this situation from the point of view of selfies as a universal practice, what might the practice itself say about the self? Are the human beings not taking and sharing their selfies as agentic and knowledgeable actors, in the sense that they do what they do self-consciously, as people who are both producers and products of social systems? It seems to me that the practice of selfies takes our understanding of the self closer to the modernist notion of the self. This is not to say that the self is universal in all aspects of its possibilities. But there are crucial aspects of what is meant by the self and what the self means to people that have universal applicability if one looks at how people understand what selfies mean to them—as reproductions of the self. These notions, irrespective of place, ethnicity, class, and so on, seem to be part of a system of patterns, which transgresses these borders, making selfies a universal pictorial language with its own massive discursive potential based on a cross-cultural grammar. Selfies take the personal self away from the person and pushes her/his private domain into the public, and allows for the manifestation of the public self and for its social construction as its presence continues in the public domain. But this public self can, and often does, have a life quite independent of the private self.

Seen from this specific perspective, rather than its death in the postmodern sense, at least the practice of selfies has provided multiple forums of rebirth to the self, both as an idea and as a practice of photography closely enmeshed with people's self-identity.

Notes

1. I would like to thank Preetha Hussain of the National Institute of Fashion Technology, Delhi, and Ph.D. candidate at the Department of

Sociology, South Asian University, for providing me her archives on selfie-related material, which immensely helped in writing this chapter.

2. http://www.oppo.com/en/smartphones (accessed 13 August 2017).

3. For more information, please visit the Selfie Researchers Network at http://www.selfieresearchers.com/our-selfies-and-links/ (accessed 29 November 2016).

4. http://www.leonardodavinci.net/self-portrait.jsp#prettyPhoto (accessed 10 July 2016).

5. http://www.dailymail.co.uk/news/article-3061118/Australia-revealed-invented-word-selfie-2000-Aussie-phrases-words-added-Oxford-Dictionaries.html#ixzz4E08Lk2zo (accessed 11 July 2016).

6. Ibid.

7. http://www.merriam-webster.com/dictionary/selfie (accessed 11 July 2016).

8. http://www.oxforddictionaries.com/definition/english/selfie (accessed 11 July 2016).

9. http://dictionary.cambridge.org/dictionary/english/selfie (accessed 11 July 2016).

10. http://www.urbandictionary.com/define.php?term=Selfie (accessed 11 July 2016).

11. Facebook post by Sasanka Perera on 23 January 2016.

12. Sandhya, AS, graduate student of sociology at South Asian University, New Delhi, via Facebook, 23 January 2016.

13. Ibid.

14. Ibid.

15. Chani Vasana Impbulgoda, senior university administrator, University of the Visual and Performing Arts, Colombo, via Facebook, 23 January 2016.

16. Sujata Chandra, sociologist, New Delhi, via Facebook, 23 January 2016.

17. Susan Visvanathan, Professor of Sociology, Jawharlal Nehru University, New Delhi, via Facebook, 23 January 2016.

18. P. K. Balachandran, journalist from India based in Colombo, via Facebook, 23 January 2016.

19. Sanjee Goonetilake, Sri Lankan national based in Ethiopia, via Facebook, 24 January 2016.

20. Unnathi Samaraweera, Lecturer in Sociology, University of Colombo, Colombo, via Facebook, 24 January 2016.

21. Ibid.

22. Ibid.

23. Ibid.

24. Ibid.

25. http://baybaybleis.blogspot.in/ (accessed 2 July 2017).

26. https://priceonomics.com/the-tragic-data-behind-selfie-fatalities/ (accessed 3 July 2017).

27. Ibid.

28. Ibid.

29. http://www.daynews.com/world/world-news/2017/06/sri-lanka-arrest-following-death-selfies-26712 (accessed 1 July 2017).

30. https://www.youtube.com/watch?v=QZdP-G-F0a8 (accessed 1 July 2017).

31. Ibid.

32. http://selfiesatfunerals.tumblr.com/ (accessed 4 July 2017).

33. To get a sense of the variety of 'funeral selfies', please see http://selfiesatfunerals.tumblr.com/ (accessed 4 July 2017).

five

Framing and Performing Intimacy

An Incomplete Social History of Wedding Photographs

From the 1960s well into the 1990s, my parents' home was not a haven for the 'public' display of wedding photographs, or for that matter, family photographs of any kind. And neither is my own home today. In fact, in living areas that we considered 'public', there were no photographs at all. But at the same time, the walls were decorated with other visual artefacts, ranging from three 1950s Parisian prints of well-known paintings by Picasso and Degas in my parents' home, and original paintings by Sri Lankan artists who represented the country's 1990s trend in visual art in my own home. So it was not a radical familial appreciation of minimalist interiors in our homes as some kind of puritanical socio-cultural objective that had led to this situation. Also, this does not mean that we did not, or do not, have wedding photographs in our private collections. In retrospect, it seems to me that this absence is indicative of the fact that we have shied away from the 'public' display of emotion in what we do on a quotidian basis, as well as in the display of cultural objects such as wedding photographs, which also carry such emotions. But the display of such photographs is a routine cultural practice among people across class and ethno-cultural lines, in Sri Lanka and elsewhere in the region and beyond. But there were wedding photographs and photos of other private events that were safely tucked away in the three albums owned by my mother and father, and later in the single album dedicated to my own wedding. Despite this seemingly clinical attitude towards photographs of this kind, my father always had an old but fairly clear black-and-white photograph taken on his parents' wedding day, which I think was taken in Colombo in the mid-1920s (see Image 5.1).

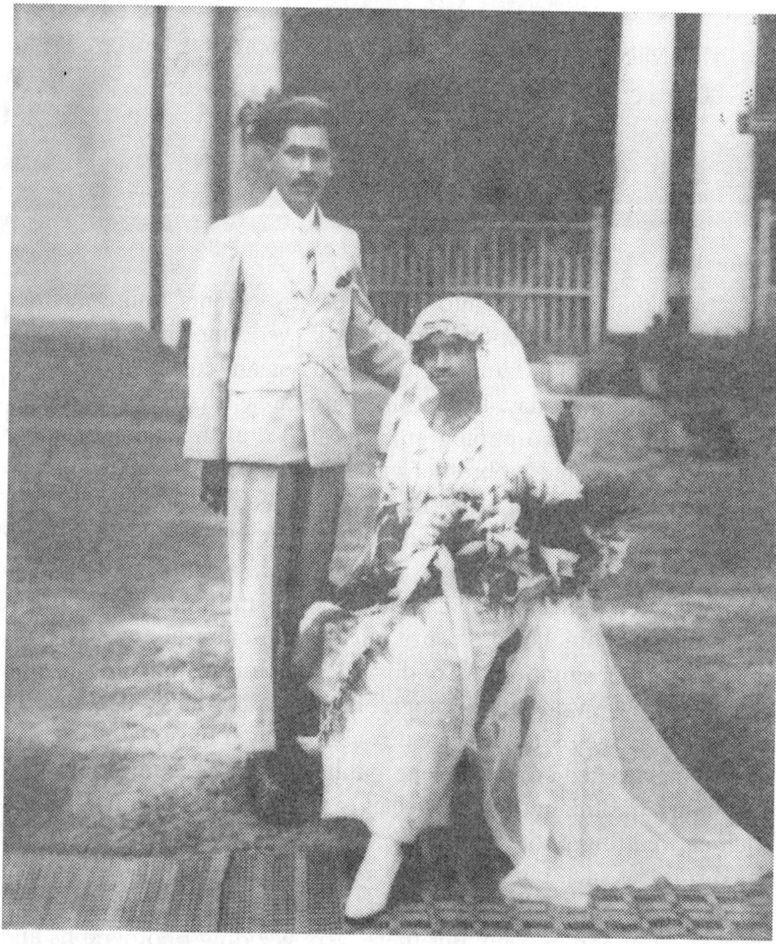

IMAGE 5.1 Wedding photograph of my paternal grandparents, mid-1920s, Colombo.

Photograph courtesy of: Karnika Jayatilake.

It was a simple photo, taken in front of a house with an open veranda, picket fence-like railings, and circular pillars, very common architectural features in many houses built in the late nineteenth and early twentieth centuries, particularly in the 'low country' areas of Sri Lanka. Perhaps this is where the wedding took place, which most probably was the house of a close family member. But the specificities of that information are now lost. My grandfather is dressed in 'Western' attire and my grandmother in a sari but with a head veil, which did not cover her face. She also wears socks with her shoes. Despite the hybridity of her dress, the overall meta-language narrated through the sartorial significations in the photograph made unmistakable references to their time and their social location in that time and place. At the very least, someone with a basic understanding of local cultural history would have deduced that this was an urban, middle-class, and quite possibly Sinhala couple in the 1920s. Occasionally, my father would take this photo from the file in which he kept it in his office and narrate some stories about the two people in the photo. It is as a result of such conversations that I came to know the Anglicised names of my paternal grandparents, that my grandfather was an officer in the colonial Agriculture Department, and that my grandmother was a housewife and that she came from a well-known family of Sinhala Buddhists in the western coastal zone of Sri Lanka. It was only because the photograph allowed these conversations to begin by being a primordial pictorial reference to these personal histories and the general social circumstances of my ancestral kin that I got to know about these people who had died long before I was born. In other words, it was due to this photograph that I grew up with some personal references and anchors to a time I was not familiar with, which had to be understood both in the context of national socio-cultural prerogatives and that of my own family's insignificant location within it.

However, this photograph was never displayed in our house, despite the fact that such displays were commonplace in general. My sense is that it came from two other absences in this scheme of things, which my father must have felt as he thought about this practice of institutionalised pictorial display. Whenever possible, such photographs were not isolated exhibits even within the confines of one's home. They were expected to narrate family histories with reference to their social and cultural status across generations. They were regular features, which were taken for granted and often forgotten by the family members. But equally as often, they also became points of departure for specific conversations, particularly when visitors were involved. In my wife's parental home, a formal portrait of her grandparents in lieu of their wedding photo (which does not exist) was followed by the wedding photograph of her parents, her two brothers, and finally, her own wedding photograph in a single cluster. Similarly, the photo that I have referred to above (Image 5.1) was a long-term fixture in my paternal aunt's home, followed by her own and the photos of her two daughters taken on their wedding days. But my father could not complete this sequence. He and my mother had decided for some reason—clearly defying a very regular practice of their class—not to have a wedding photo. My maternal grandparents also had no such pictorial record, perhaps because their marriage might have been more informal. In such a situation, a solitary wedding photograph from a bygone era posed more anxiety-ridden questions than the kind of comfortable and linear conversations they might have otherwise generated, had it been displayed as part of a cluster narrating family social history.

I have begun this chapter with recollections of my early encounters with wedding photographs and later interpretations of my memories because I think they place in context a number of core aspects of this genre of photography anywhere in the world. Wedding photographs, from the time they initially emerged in the 1840s up to the present, despite the radical changes in technology over time, have never been casual exercises. Although the mood in these images would change in tune with national or ethno-cultural locations as well as temporal moments and global trends within which they are captured, they have always been conscious and planned efforts, which need both time and a considerable degree of patience. On the other hand, wedding photographs have created a historical cartography of how issues of emotion, desire, and interpretations of love and romance might be enacted and displayed for both private and public consumption, depending on how and where these photographs are displayed. In the context of a brief social history of wedding photography, the main theme that I want to explore in this chapter has to do with the absence and the presence of the smile in wedding photographs at different times, and how, in later times, it has helped construct narratives of romance and desire in what might be called a spectacular mode.

Most histories of photography suggest that the first wedding photographs were possibly created in the 1840s, not too long after photography itself was established in Europe, both as a technical effort and a social practice. Given its rarity at the time, it should not be surprising that the initial wedding photographs that have survived in collections are those of social elites, who were quick enough to embrace the practice as worthy of their class tastes and could also afford its costs. One of the first couples to be photographed in this manner was Queen Victoria and Prince Albert of England in 1840.[1] But, as in the case of portrait photography more generally and landscape photography referred to in previous chapters, wedding photography also has to be understood in the context of intertwined histories of related practices. These are the histories of portrait painting and studio-based portrait photography.

For obvious technical reasons, wedding photography began as a studio-based practice (much the same reasons why photography in general and portrait photography in particular began as studio-based practices). This was mainly due to the limitations in technology at the time and the need to control light, as well as the bulky equipment that were not meant to be mobile. In the initial stages in European and later North American urban contexts, couples who were keen to be photographed to memorialise their weddings went to studios before or after the wedding. But when the pioneering brides and grooms who embraced this emergent practice visited studios to have their wedding photographs taken, they were essentially emulating the existing elite social practice of wedding portrait painting. This sequence of practices is not very different from the practice of portrait painting in general, making way for portrait photography when technology provided this possibility, and when trendsetters of the time embraced this kind of photography as an acceptable social practice. In the earlier painterly incarnation of this practice, 'newly wed couples and their family members posed for long periods of time as artists painted them for posterity'.[2] As noted earlier, wedding photography did not begin as a casual practice. It still is not, even though the moods created by these early photographs and the moods in recent wedding photographs the world over have radically changed. In the initial period, taking a wedding photograph meant the investment of considerable time and effort, which required the people being photographed to hold their choreographed poses for a considerable period of time. This was not very different from what was required for portrait painting of the same type. But with photography, the overall time required to pose did come down significantly, although it still required considerable effort. The technological innovations in lighting as well as the invention of lighter and more sophisticated cameras contributed to reducing the mandatory time spent over a single photograph over time, making wedding photography much easier, and eventually pleasurable. But in the initial phase, wedding photography was a singular event. That is, given the time and effort that was needed to make a single photograph, people generally opted for a single photo, which became an artefact displayed in people's homes.

But by the late nineteenth and early twentieth centuries, as technology improved and the posing time for each session was reduced, it became possible for photographers to attempt multiple shots of the same wedding or couple. The reductions in the 'exposure times and general "trickiness"'[3] of the overall procedure also allowed for the photographic capture of the entire wedding party, as opposed to just the couple. A direct outcome of this plurality of photographs was the invention of the 'wedding album'.[4] The wedding album, more than any other cultural practice associated with weddings, revitalised wedding photography from a difficult single exposure to easier, multiple images of different groups in the same wedding, allowing these images to narrate a more complete story of the event. The invention of flash-lighting[5] to be used with cameras in the late 1880s, which became popular and more technologically stable later, allowed for wedding photographs to be captured at the sites of weddings, rather than in the clinically removed, albeit decorated, environs of the studio. The increased mobility of cameras, along with the flashlight, also allowed for better control of light, and enabled photographs of different aspects of wedding rituals to be taken as they took place, both in the interiors of households and churches and in outdoor locations. The invention of these technologies allowed wedding photographs to be fuller, more contextual, and more creative.

In Search of the Absent Smile

From initial times, the posture and mood of most wedding photographs from around the world remained serious and sombre. They were generally devoid of the kind of passion, desire, and notions of romantic love that one may associate with most couples getting married today. Today, even if a particular marriage is not necessarily the result of romantic love and sustained courtship, the photographs meant to capture that occasion are expected to reflect some attributes of romance, desire, fantasy, and so on. Moreover, such emotional attributes are today also closely linked with the fanfare and reverie associated with others who become part of the overall ceremony in a ritual like the wedding, which is after all a noteworthy secular right of passage in the conventional anthropological sense. Compared to contemporary wedding photography, the same genre of photographs from earlier periods indicates a completely different set of preoccupations.

Examples from the very beginning of wedding photography right up to the mid or late 1940s are generally devoid of any kind of lightness in emotional terms. The main feature that was banished from within the frame to achieve this generalised sense of sullenness was the smile. The kinesics frozen on the facial expressions as well as body positions of these period photographs almost exudes a sense of sadness or unhappiness, as if these were the fundamental attributes symbolised by what the wedding represents. The attempt seems to have been to inject a sense of exaggerated seriousness to the wedding photograph, and by extension to how the event was to be remembered in the future. In these circumstances, it is hardly surprising that early wedding photos look the way they do. But interestingly, this structure of emotion seen in wedding photographs from around the world seem quite remarkably consistent across geographic, class, national, and cultural boundaries, as if very different cultural settings somehow took a decisively negative position with regard to the public expression of contentment or happiness, which a smile is often expected to convey. But the smile was not necessarily an indication of happiness in Victorian cultural settings. As Hirsch (1981) notes, if a family wished to appear happy, they were expected to pose in front of their property. The property in the background of their portrait painting or photograph would indicate their success and status in the material world, and hence the ultimate source of happiness. The smile, if it were present in a wedding photograph, would have completely changed its mood, which somehow was kept under control well into the 1940s. As a young man, I often wondered what was making my grandparents look so unhappy in their wedding photograph, taken in the 1920s (see Image 5.1). But even so, compared to other period photographs of the same genre, it appears that my grandmother somehow surreptitiously allowed the vestiges of a reluctant smile to enter the frame—without showing her teeth—while my grandfather adhered to the period norm of being solemn. So how and why was the smile so self-consciously expelled from this scheme of things?

The absence of the smile and the emotions it introduces were not restricted to wedding photography alone. It was something generally seen in photography across genres at the time, which was also adopted by wedding photographs as necessary decorum because it made sense, given the way the marriage itself was understood. Kotchemidova refers to this as the 'invariably serious facial expression of nineteenth-century photos' (Kotchemidova 2005: 2). The smile in this specific context reflected a broader social concern or taboo, and to understand why the smile did not adorn wedding photographs, one must also understand why it was similarly not a part of any other kind of photography that involved a close study of human facial expressions. Fabry notes that it was only by the 1920s and 1930s that the smile came to be considered a 'standard expression' in photographs in general (Fabry 2016). But in practical terms, it was more clearly visible only after the 1940s, after World War II had ended.

Angus Trumble, in his book, *A Brief History of the Smile*, suggests that bad dental conditions partly explain why the smile was not seen in nineteenth-century photographs (quoted in Fabry 2016). He traces the development of dental health as an important criterion that allowed for the later emergence of the smile in photographs (ibid.). As he notes, 'people had lousy teeth, if they had teeth at all, which militated against opening your mouth in social settings' (ibid.). But this does not mean that people did not smile at this time. And it is also likely that if bad teeth were the norm, being seen with such teeth in most social settings would also have been routinised and normalised. As such, this factor alone does not fully explain the nineteenth and early twentieth century's frown upon capturing a smile in a photograph. The inadequacy of technology is also used to explain why the smile is not visible in nineteenth-century photographs. That is, in the initial period of photography, it was necessary to hold a specific pose for a considerable period of time for the camera to capture it, given the longer exposure time in the early cameras (Fabry 2016). It was not easy to hold a smile for too long. As such, it would be natural to adopt easier poses. Even so, by the 1850s and 1860s, in the right conditions, it was quite possible to capture a photograph in a few seconds, and in the decades immediately afterwards, exposure times were made even shorter (ibid.). It is clear that the technology was available much earlier than we generally assume to capture a fleeting expression like a smile—if it was considered worth capturing. Seen in this sense, more than a matter of problematic dental hygiene and lack of the necessary technology, the issue seems to be the smile itself, or the norms governing public smiling and what it means in terms of etiquette.

With reference to Fred Schroeder's 1998 essay, 'Say Cheese! The Revolution in the Aesthetics of Smiles', Kotchemidova offers a cultural explanation that goes beyond the concerns of dental hygiene and technology in explaining the absence of the smile in early photographs (Kotchemidova 2005). She notes that the standard expression in early group photos and portraits emulated the established practices of European portraiture, which generally tended to depict solemn faces, 'occasionally softened by a Mona Lisa curve of the lips' (ibid.: 2). So the smile was not a norm when the self and his significant others were captured for posterity in paintings or early photographs. Instead, it was an occasional or even an accidental occurrence. This is because 'in the fine arts a grin was only characteristic of peasants, drunkards, children, and halfwits, suggesting low class or some other deficiency' (ibid.). Within these conventions, the smile was clearly a sign of low social status or a matter of being uncouth. And such a feature was obviously not worthy of posterity. In the transmission of the conventions of portrait painting to photography, this class-based sense of solemnity in the construction of a person's likeness was blindly simulated. These conventions, meant initially for portrait painting, were considered the ideal form of behaviour when a person faced the camera. Further, general beauty standards in the late nineteenth century privileged a small mouth, which would also be challenged if a smile were to invade this sombre cultural repertoire (ibid.). As such, it was no surprise that the first photographic studio established in London in 1841 adopted the 'locution "say prunes" to help sitters form a small mouth', devoid of a smile (ibid.).

There is another dimension to the absence of the smile, which I suggest is embedded in the Christian understanding of the wedding, and the manner in which this understanding was later codified and generalised as the ideal associated with the secular practice of wedding photography. In terms of general Christian belief, marriage is a gift from God, and had to be taken seriously precisely due to this reason. As a result, the wedding, the ceremony that ritualised the marriage, was expected to be conducted in a church, effectively in the presence of God. More than any other kind of marriage tempered with religion, it is the Christian marriage, through its wedding ceremony, which is directly sanctified by religion in a place of worship. This association of religion with marriage is clearly outlined in most standard Christian marriage wows taken during weddings, as typified by 'as is Christ to His body, the church, so I will be to you a loving and faithful husband' and 'as is the church in her relationship to Christ, so I will be to you'.[6] As the visual history of wedding photography informs us, it is this kind of religiously sanctified wedding that was initially photographed in studios, churches, or other locations.

The central issue here is not the location *per se*, but the bond the ceremony and the couple involved had with religion. This was not a matter of fun, but a solemn moment in the presence of God, or one that was sanctified by God. Seen in this sense, the smile as a reflection of non-seriousness, frivolity, or the kind of negative cultural attributes referred to earlier in terms of the nineteenth-century classist interpretation of social decorum had no place in a respectable wedding. The same could also not be captured in a photograph. After all, it was not a moment of romance, but a solemn moment when a man and a woman had been wedded with the sanction of God. Given the genesis of early photography in general and wedding photography in particular in sites of strong Christian belief, as is the case with Europe and North America, this cluster of belief and context provided crucial codification to wedding photography in its initial phase. Although the practice was quite soon transmitted to very different cultural settings defined by other religious and socio-cultural practices, the codified modes of behaviour and posturing initially constructed in the pioneering settings became part of the overall package that accompanied wedding photography as a practice. In other words, what the rest of the world received was this model of wedding photography, with its inbuilt Christian ethos accepted as a necessary part of decorum. But as the practice was adopted in different cultural and social settings, its initial religious lineage was conveniently forgotten. Only its posturing and the sense of etiquette remained in place.

To some extent, this overall mood and the absence of the smile also comes from the way the marriage as an institution, and the wedding as the societal vehicle that initiates the institutional principles the marriage incorporates, were conventionally understood. Adshade and Kaiser note that, 'the formalization of family structure through marriage creates a key economic and social institution for distributing resources and for the production of consumption goods as well as children' (Adshade and Kaiser 2008: 1). In this scheme of things, the marriage formally brought men and women together 'in genetic reproduction and household production' (ibid.: 2). As suggested by Rose, the 'home', which is created by a socially sanctioned union, 'was to be transformed into a purified, cleansed, moralized domestic space. It was to undertake the moral training of its children' (Rose 1999: 75). In addition, it was expected to 'domesticate and familiarize the dangerous passions of adults, tearing them away from public vice, the gin palace and the gambling hall, imposing a duty of responsibility to each other, to home, and to children, and a wish to better their own condition' (ibid.).

In this context, the fundamental way in which the marriage and its result, the family, was understood was in terms of an avenue for legalised and socially accepted procreation, as a site for disciplining family members, and a place of economic production for the sake of society as well as personal well-being. As such, the immediate benefit that marriage brings to men is that the life chances of the 'children they are helping rear carry their genes improves' if the women are seen by society as 'their' 'wives', further regulated by specific penalties for infidelity (Adshade and Kaiser 2008: 2). This is about the clear and undisputed continuation of a specific genetic line or family name, which ultimately bears upon ownership of property and inheritance. Similarly, as further pointed out by Adshade and Kaiser, marriage as an institutional arrangement is 'preferred by women if they value genetic continuance and if contractual matching increases the consumption levels of both themselves and their offspring' (ibid.). That is, 'both men and women prefer marriage in that they receive benefits to bonding that are independent of consumption and childbearing, what we might call "love"' (ibid.). So marriage was an opening to a very specific set of social and economic responsibilities, none of which included issues such as desire, romance or their public expression as a necessity for its sustenance. This does not mean that these attributes were not associated with marriage or the family life that followed. But they were carefully controlled, regulated, and generally expelled into the darkness and the relative invisibility of 'bedrooms'. They were effectively out of sight and beyond discourse. Lauren Berlant aptly articulates this state of affairs when she notes that within marriage, 'people are schooled to recognize as worthwhile only those desires that take shape within the institutions and narratives that bolster convention and traditions of propriety' (Berlant 2012: 44).

It seems reasonable to accept that the absence of the smile in early portrait photographs in general and wedding photographs in particular was part of the cultural heritage of Victorian upper-class social decorum, tempered by religion and class, which was packaged into the structure of normative period behaviour when facing the camera. Although not invented specifically for wedding photography, this practice was nevertheless adopted by wedding photography as well, because its semantics coincided comfortably with dominant understandings of marriage as an institution. More importantly, what spread to the rest of the world from Europe with the invention of the camera and photography was not merely the technology, equipment, and the taste for different kinds of photography. With these obvious features, one could also see the diffusion of idealised and standardised patterns of behaviour in specific situations, such as in the case of portrait and wedding photography, even as sartorial codes associated with weddings showed much more resistance to this kind of cultural homogenisation and the ability to innovate and hybridise when compared to postures and normative behaviours. The globally banished smile in wedding photographs was simply one of these diffused and readily adopted cultural traits. But with the smile, what was also banished from these photographs was a sense of love, romance or desire, which we now associate with such photographs. This is an issue I will explore later in this chapter.

The Emergence of the Smile

Seen in the sense outlined above, the smile in wedding photographs that we take for granted today, as well as in photography more generally, is a norm rooted in our time rather than in the first ninety years of photography's history. That is why in contemporary times, most people naturally presume the smile to be a generic ingredient in such photographs, without reference to time. Just as much as its absence marked a specific norm in an earlier time, its presence marks a similarly generalised value in our own time. But how did a non-existent and frowned upon practice find expression in what is now a taken for granted and an anticipated practice? We have already seen how pre-existing traditions in landscape and portrait painting had an impact on photography by influencing the emergence of new photographic conventions through the simulation of painterly conventions. Although photography and painting remained, and continue to remain, separate practices with their own, very distinct ways of dealing with the visual, regular interactions between the two also continued at different levels, and at different moments. At times, these interactions meant that practices adopted by one tended to influence the other. According to Trumble, as the Edwardian period in British social history commenced and continued, people began to 'smile in effervescent ways' in painted portraits, clearly evident from about 1895–1914 (quoted in Fabry 2016). Consequent to this change, the smile was gradually accepted in photography as well (Fabry 2016). That is, it received acceptance as a legitimate social practice within the same social classes which had shunned it in the previous era. This transformation in attitude in painterly conventions made it possible for the smile to be transmitted onto photographs as well. But it had a more dramatic impact on wedding photography as the entire mood in these images was transformed into something much more festive and celebratory from the decidedly sullen and solemn portraits of the previous era. Nevertheless, the emergence of the smile, which can be understood as the empowerment of an 'aesthetic of the teeth' (Kotchemidova 2005: 3), was a gradual process. It was also a transformation that impacted photography in general, and not merely wedding photography.

As Kotchemidova explains, 'open smiles' typify twentieth-century snapshot photography, which includes family pictures, yearbook portraits, as well as wedding photos (ibid.). With specific reference to wedding photographs, King notes, 'one cannot but be struck by the sameness of expression on the faces, from the bride and groom all the way to the flower girls. It is, what's more, a standard look, with all the participants mouthing cheese to summon up smiles' (quoted in ibid.). If sullen, unsmiling faces were the generic feature of wedding photographs in the nineteenth and early twentieth centuries, standardised smiling faces, in the manner described by King, had become the norm of the twentieth century. And this was more visible after the 1940s, and since the end of World War II. At least to some extent, it seems that the returning soldiers from World War II came to their homes with a sense of relief that the War was over, and that they had survived it. The smiles many of them carried on to their own wedding photos, which was adopted by others, was a symbol of this relief as much as it was an emergent norm in photography at the time. As Image 5.2 indicates, my mother-in-law, Kamala Rajapaksa, sports

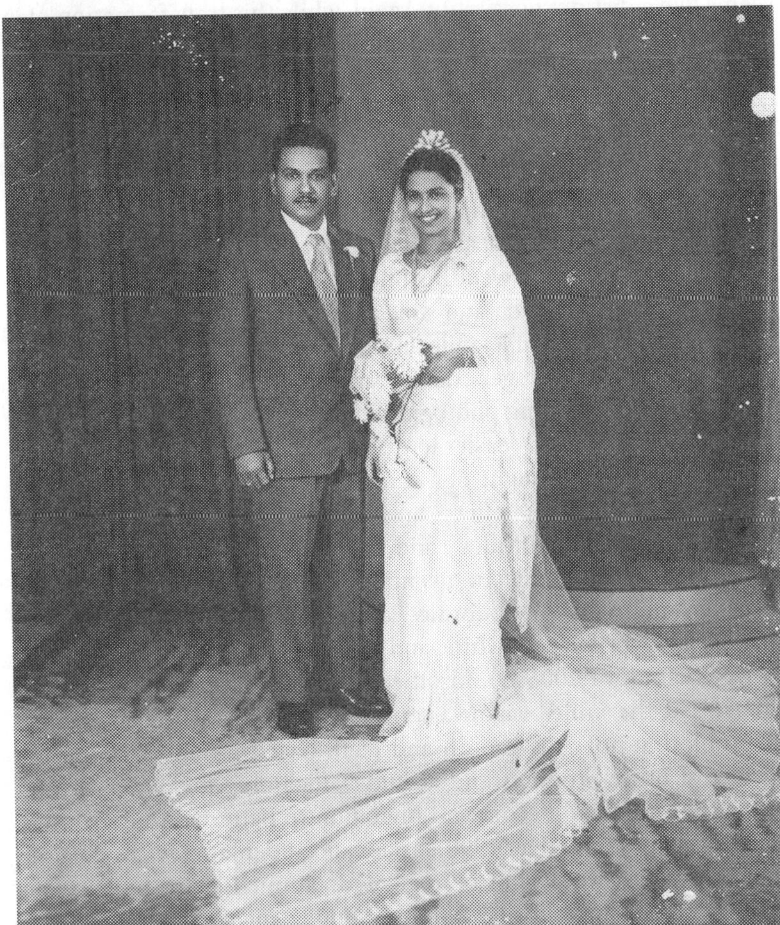

IMAGE 5.2 Wedding photograph of Simpson Wijertane and Kamala Rajapaksa, 1956, Broadway Studio, Matara, Sri Lanka.

Photograph courtesy of: Anoli Perera.

a broad smile in her wedding photograph taken in 1956 in Matara in southern Sri Lanka, even though my father-in-law still does not have a smile. But even in his case, the transformation in attitude is clear enough. He is not sullen and is seemingly more relaxed than his photographic ancestors. And his facial expressions suggest that a smile seems like a distinct possibility. Again, while this transformation may have had its roots in the broader Euro-American popular cultural contexts, its appeal has been global.

However, this combination of a clear smile adorning the lips of the bride and the groom's relative reluctance to be so obvious with a smile has become almost an acceptable norm since the arrival of the smile in wedding photography. When I say that the smile 'arrived' in wedding photography, that arrival is clearer with brides. While grooms also often smile in their wedding photos, equally as often, they do not. But they are not as sullen and stoic as in early wedding photographs. If there is an absence of a smile among grooms, it is compensated for with a far more relaxed general demeanour. Image 5.3 would indicate that in my own wedding photograph, my wife's smile is very obvious, while mine is not much easier to distinguish as a smile as opposed to my father-in-law's 'thought' of a smile.

Schroeder (1998) offers an argument located squarely in twentieth-century attitudes and commerce that explains the emergence of the smile in twentieth-century photographs, which directly implicates orthodontics and mouth product advertising that visually privileged white and perfectly aligned teeth (quoted in Kotchemidova 2005: 3). In other words, as the twentieth century progressed, the smile became a commercial vehicle as well as an asset in promoting not only mouth and teeth-based products, but also a variety of other products and attitudes, including the 'looks' of film stars. The smile had become an invitation to better and finer things. According to Schroeder (1998), as advanced dental services ensured that the mouth would not be regulated as much as in the previous century, its constant closure in formal public engagements, including in photographs, was no longer necessary (quoted in Kotchemidova 2005: 3). In the context of these newly emergent social circumstances, the smile became a new virtue and social reality that was constantly

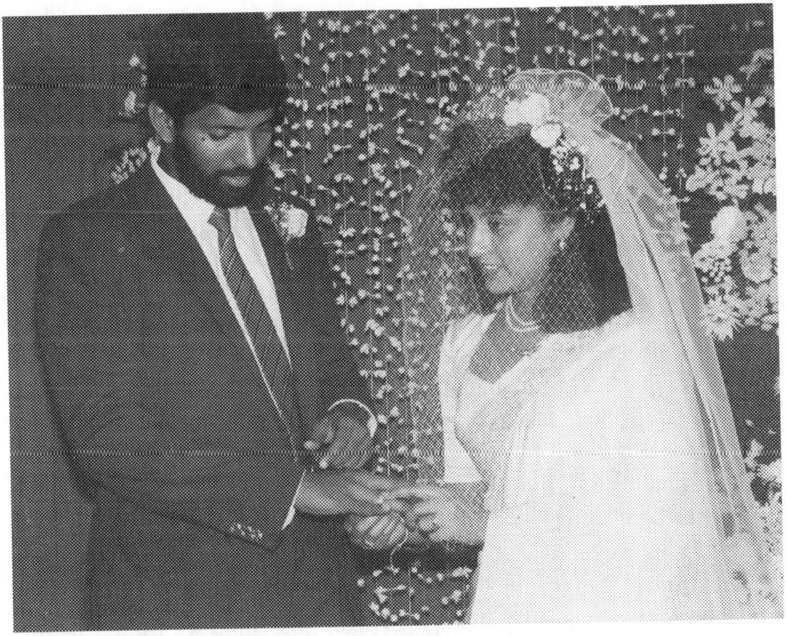

IMAGE 5.3 Wedding photograph of Sasanka Perera and Anoli Wijeratne, 1988, Hotel Ramada Renaissance, Colombo.
Photograph courtesy of: Author's family album.

reproduced on a mass scale in photos (Kotchemidova 2005: 3). While commerce certainly played a crucial role in ushering in the smile to the midst of twentieth-century photography, the dental argument—as in the case of explaining the absence of the smile in the previous time—can only be seen more as a contributory and supporting factor. It is in this context that Kotchemidova suggests that rather than considering the emergence of the smile as a matter of 'mouth liberalization', it might be more reasonable to perceive it as a cultural construct rooted in twentieth-century conditions and attitudes (ibid.). As she notes, 'aesthetic criteria change over time and, in any case, the toothy smile was adopted as a standard in a certain time, place, and media culture, namely, twentieth-century American snapshot photography' (ibid.). Given the wide cross-border reach that American popular culture has had since the beginning of the twentieth century as a result of the global influence of American political, commercial, and cultural power, its role in marketing the photographic smile makes contextual sense. The toothy smile, often captured and typified by the locution 'cheese', is also an American cultural invention that emerged in the twentieth century. The smile that adorned photographs in this fashion was given a significant public boost through its broad public adaptation by the US film industry, as evidenced in the smiling faces of Hollywood characters that have floated around the world in the form of posters and other similar cultural artefacts since the 1930s. One of its more obvious promoters in the 1950s was Marilyn Monroe with her seductive, and what appeared to be a permanent public smile, who is also supposed to have proclaimed, 'keep smiling, because life is a beautiful thing and there's so much to smile about'.[7] Once it arrived in the global visual domain, what Kotchemidova calls the 'say cheese' smile (ibid.) dominated snapshot photography as well as wedding photography globally.

Eastman Kodak, the American camera, film products and services company, also played a crucial role in the popularisation of the smile in the public domain in the US and beyond. From the late 1800s, Kodak produced or partially funded the production of numerous manuals, which were aimed at promoting their own products as well as popularising photography by offering tips on how to use a camera (Kotchemidova 2005: 4). These tips were not only technical ones, but also included what might be considered artistic advice on framing, using light, and even posing. In terms of posing, the smile was presented as a necessary feature in standard portraits. As a pioneering company which focussed on harnessing the profits of touting consumption as a form of pleasure, in 1893 Eastman Kodak introduced the 'Kodak Girl' as its major commercial icon, which lasted for nearly eighty years (ibid.: 5). In terms of visual language, she was constructed as a young, stylishly dressed woman, 'shooting pictures of children, vacations, outings, and picnics with a portable camera', who was enjoying 'herself fabulously' (ibid.). More importantly, 'the message of consumer happiness radiated from her ever-present smile' (ibid.). Given Eastman Kodak's global power as a very successful company in general, and a camera and photo equipment company in particular, its role in globally popularising the smile as a quintessential twentieth-century public expression of happiness cannot be underemphasised. That is, happiness or seeming happiness as exemplified by the smile was already a commodity. In this context, numerous companies had opted to use the smile as an important sign quite widely in their advertisements by the 1920s. This was symbolic of the recognition of the expressive value of the smile as a conveyor of a universal meaning of human happiness (Schroeder 1998, quoted in Kotchemidova 2005: 10). It is in this context that a textbook published in 1920 suggested that the way to indicate that someone was enjoying the product he had acquired was to show him using it with a smile, such as 'a man smiling as he puffs at his cigar' (Tipper 1920, quoted in Kotchemidova 2005: 10).

As I have outlined above, the adoption of the smile as an ideal in general photography in the twentieth century allowed it to travel to wedding photography as well. More than anything else, the smile transformed the expressive semantics of wedding photography. It gave wedding photography of the twentieth century a generic collective global personality imbued with expressions of happiness, which we are now familiar with as a sign. And this generic global understanding has travelled well into the twenty-first century as well. But this is not a simple matter of adopting the smile in wedding photography. This innovation in attitude became possible because the institutional understanding of marriage, based on ideals of economic production, procreation, and societal and individual responsibilities, was self-consciously invested with additional attributes. Particularly after World War II, marriage and the wedding ceremony also came to be seen as sites of desire, romantic love, and passion, which were discursive elements made invisible in the previous era. Therefore, the ways in which formal weddings were organised, and particularly how they were photographed, also tended to capture these newly empowered attributes. As such, weddings had to become performances, which narrated the notions of glamour, desire, romantic love, and passion in ways that cultural norms in different locations allowed. It is precisely this broader transformation that made it possible for the smile to be embraced as the central feature of wedding photography. That is, it did not come to wedding photography simply because it was already established as a core element in twentieth-century snapshot photography more generally. The adoption of the smile in twentieth-century photography in general, accompanied by the transformed understanding of the marriage and the wedding, which was symbolised by the smile, made the smile's entry into the semantics of twentieth-century wedding photography understandable and inevitable. In other words, the smile became the anchor for the newer field of significations that twentieth and twenty-first century weddings provided for.

Wedding in the Realm of Fantasy

The ideals of glamour, romantic love, and passion, which came to define weddings and wedding photography more clearly in the second half of the twentieth century, came into being as a gradual process. And the specifics of their interpretations changed according to local cultural conditions, the affluence of the individuals getting married, the structures of taste that people contributed to, and so on. But these significations were more visible after the 1990s and had to do, at least partially, with the global evolution of a strong consumerist ethos, which cuts across national as well as socio-cultural borders. In addition to the global changes in sexual mores, which have been ongoing since the end of World War II, much of the symbols of glamour and passion were also borrowed from the signs created by Hollywood through its films. In South Asia, the Mumbai-centred Bollywood film industry's fantasy-like films offered more proximate models for simulation.

If the smile had been the defining feature of global wedding photography since the middle of the twentieth century, by the twenty-first century, the general focus of wedding photography had moved more squarely into the realms of romance, love, fantasy, make-believe and spectacle, while the smile remained a central anchor to the overall mood. But in what manner has wedding photography moved into the realm of fantasy and the spectacular; how does it function; and what does this shift mean in cultural and epistemological terms?

It seems to me that very specific interpretations of what is understood as 'love' places in context some of these transformations, in both epistemological and cultural terms. Niklas Luhmann explains that love, and more specifically, passionate love, needs to be understood as a code which is the central authority that can help to make sense of situations generally related to love (Luhmann 1986). He explains how expressions of love have radically changed from the idealised notions of love in the medieval period to its more romantic interpretations in the modern period (ibid.). Notwithstanding the vastly different cultural and social mores in different parts of the world, which govern expressions of love, such a general transformation can be fathomed partly as a result of the globalisation of ideas and tastes. One classic example is the globalisation of the recognition of Valentine's Day as the day of lovers, and the routine adoption of the heart and red roses as global significations of love across cultures. Of course, commerce played a more crucial role in the spread of these ideas, rather than their self-conscious adaptation as symbols of love across the world. Although Luhmann's reading is inspired by an understanding of the historical evolution of love in Western Europe, from the medieval period to the present, much of what he says is applicable today to its more global manifestations as well when it comes to symbols and modes of signification with regard to ideas of love. The circulation of these symbols, significations, and attitudes is not that dissimilar to the circulation and resultant adoption of the smile in wedding photography across different cultural and ethno-national borders in the world. To be more precise, in order to participate in the expression of love in the modern period, this transformation was needed at the level of semantics. In this context, wedding photography as well as the recently emergent pre-wedding photography have to be seen as fields of meaning where these semantics are given visual and performative expression. It is through this kind of photography that codes of love, or their articulations in the Luhmannian sense, move to the realm of commonsense and performance, beyond what is ritually needed in weddings. This happens when an array of cultural expressions of love is embraced in specific cultural domains.

Understood in this manner, passionate love can be more specifically comprehended as the 'semantics' of communication (Luhmann 1986). That is, what is expressed is not necessarily only for the consumption of lovers, but also for significant others in the social and cultural worlds in which they live. But today, these images have a mutating life well beyond the circles of lovers and their significant others. This is why at present, these images often percolate far beyond the personal worlds of the people concerned into a much broader realm of discourse through forums such as social media. It is here that the kind of wedding and pre-wedding photography that we see at present can be more clearly understood in terms of their broader performative and discursive intentions. They are not merely pictorial records of the moment in which two people have entered into matrimony. If at all, such recording is the most basic anticipation attributed to these photos. The official and legal sanctity of a marriage would be attested by secular documentation in terms of law and the regulations of the State, or in religious codification, where personal laws decide on the status of marriage. Photographs of these events attempt to transform a routine rite of passage into something memorable, extraordinary, and spectacular. In other words, these photos are supposed to signify the passion of love and romance, so that these states of feeling can be made tangible and be constructed pictorially for the expressed purpose of simulated memory and broader communication. Once these images enter the internet via the personal accounts of innumerable brides, grooms, their kin and friends, they also effectively become objects of public consumption. That is, wedding photographs are no longer merely private cultural artefacts. Instead, they are also public displays of private passions, desires, and romance.

For Luhmann, love plays a core role in what he suggests are the abstract and individualised means of social relations in the modern world (Luhman 1986). For him, the entire society is in any case a social system comprising of communications. That is, the system of intimacy that love offers links individuals (ibid.). Through wedding photographs, this linking is not only with regard to the couple, but through them, as noted above, to the discourses and worlds beyond them as well. And more importantly, they are linked in a way that makes the nature of the relationship clearly decipherable, and allows it to be de-coded and turned into a consumable part of quotidian collective discourse. From that point onwards, the love of individuals travels formally from private domains into the broader and publicly accessible discourses on intimacy, which by the very nature of this entry is accepted in the public domain as socially legitimate. And the core significations in this field of symbols embedded in wedding photographs are linked to commonly understood notions of tradition, royalty, glamour, fairy-tale understandings of romance, specific colour schemes, and so on. Although there is a general standardisation of these themes, there is considerable variation in the way they manifest, depending on local cultural contexts and the structures of taste the individuals are a part of. In discourses on weddings today, including in the formal sales pitches of wedding organisers, these and many other such possibilities are known as 'themes'. For instance, the website The Knot offers a large variety of wedding themes for American couples within three basic thematic types, which include rustic weddings, beach weddings, and vintage weddings, in addition to advice on the selection of colours and related matters.[8] All of these themes are in turn expected to help in pictorially articulating the passion in love, even in situations where a marriage may be taking place devoid of passion or even love. In that sense, wedding photographs become an autonomous text symbolising an idealised and hyped sense of love and passion, which does not necessarily have to reflect the lives of the people concerned. Instead, they are supposed to refer to a popularly accepted ideal of love.

Thanuja Perera-Childs, writing with reference to her 2016 wedding in Hertfordshire, UK, notes that she and her husband, Kevin Childs, preferred a wedding that related to nature and the outdoors,[9] and this theme is clearly reflected in the iconic images of both pre-wedding and wedding photographs (see Images 5.4 and 5.5).

While the couple selected the theme for their wedding photographs, the actual structuring and choreographing of poses and the planning of individual photographs was the prerogative of the photographer.[10] In other words, he brought in his expertise to

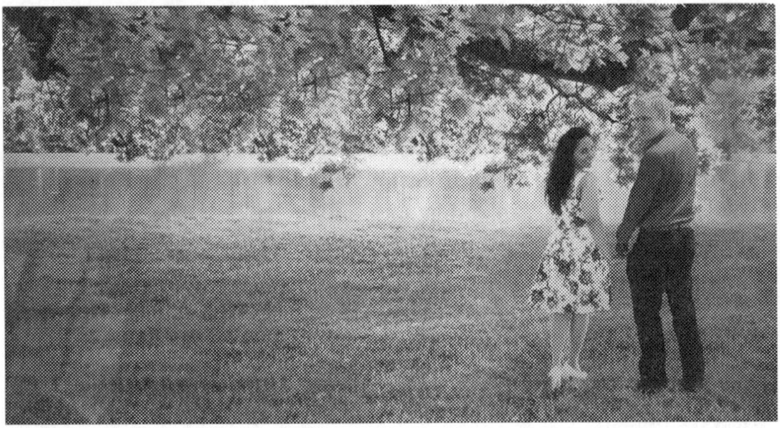

IMAGE 5.4 Pre-wedding photo of Thanuja Perera-Childs and Kevin Childs.
Photograph courtesy of: Thanuja Perera-Childs' personal album.

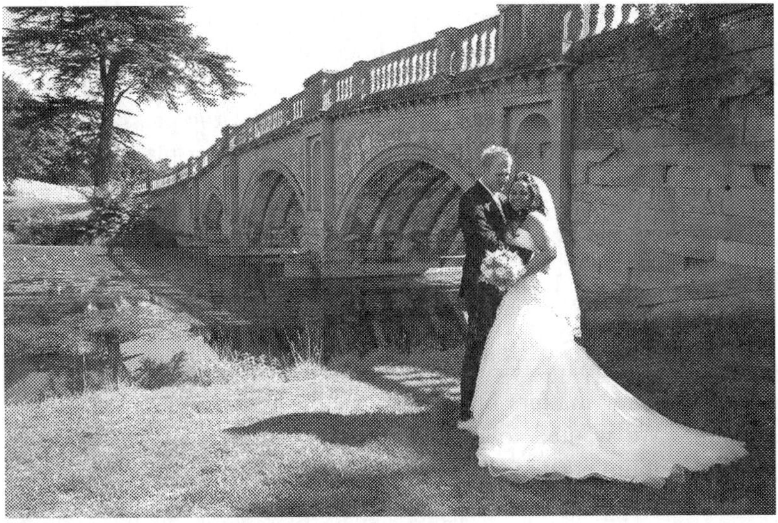

IMAGE 5.5 Wedding photograph of Thanuja Perera-Childs and Kevin Childs.
Photograph courtesy of: Thanuja Perera-Childs' personal album.

ensure that the theme or the significations the couple had decided upon were performed well enough to make photographic sense. This structured organisation has also ensured two specific moods in the photographs of the two occasions. That is, the pre-wedding images elicit a clear sense of informality and relaxation, while the wedding photos construct a much more conscious sense of formality. However, compared to the first generation of wedding photos referred to earlier in this chapter, these look much more relaxed and happier, ensuring that the contemporary idealised prerequisites of marriage, which oscillate between love to passion and desire, have the space to express themselves in the photos.

On the other hand, in this particular case, the intention to have pre-wedding photographs, which are now an important part of the couple's wedding album, did not come from the couple, but from the photographer. As Perera-Childs explains,

> It wasn't our idea, but was suggested by the photographer. He said he wanted to familiarise us with the camera and to find out our 'beauty angles and chemistry'. So we agreed to let him take a few photos in a nearby park. He also wanted us to wear something nice and matching. The photographer ended taking 100 of photos and later sent us edited versions. Even though, we didn't want to do [a] pre-shoot, after seeing the photos we thought we might buy them in an album.[11]

Although the photographer's reason for suggesting pre-wedding photos was technical and professional, it ensured two things—the creation of a need that did not pre-exist, and the building of an emotional linkage to this newly created need, which had now become an album. Beyond the carefully structured performativity of the photos, the primary reason why the couple wanted to have these images was for matters of memory in the future. As Perera-Childs explains, 'We wanted to remember our wedding. So we wanted a wedding album created.'[12]

Raihana Sayeeda Kamal, referring to her 2016 wedding and the associated *haldi* ceremony in Dhaka, Bangladesh, notes how various issues linked to these two events, which were photographed, were decided upon. The *haldi* ceremony, also known in Bengali as 'Gaye

Holud', is an important ceremony mostly observed in the wider Bengal region, including West Bengal in India, and Bangladesh. It usually takes place one or two days before the legal and religious sanctification of the wedding. While separate ceremonies are held for the bride and the groom, from a photographic point of view, what appears to be more important in contemporary times is the ceremony involving the bride. As she is made to sit on a low dais-like chair, natural hair colour known locally as *henna* is used to decorate her hands and feet with complex designs conventionally associated with these occasions. In addition, turmeric (*haldi*) is applied by those assembled on her face and hands. All of these cultural practices involving design and colour have made photographing the event an integral part of the overall wedding where it is practised. The ceremony, which takes time, has now moved to a more stable and standardised cultural plain from what used to be a religiously-oriented ceremony informed by ideals of Hinduism. That religious preoccupation no longer plays an important part in the ceremony as it has effectively crossed religious, community, and ethnic boundaries. What is important in this discussion is that this ceremony offers as many photographic opportunities as a pre-wedding shoot would in other places.

Kamal decided on the main colour of her wedding, which relates to the dress, interior decorations of the venue, as well as floral arrangements.[13] She was also the author of the overall themes of the two different events. But even here, she was closely advised by designers as well as the photographer on how to make these decisions.[14] The importance of this close relationship is self-evident. That is, it is the photographs that will remain in a physical sense to remind one of these moments (other than memory itself); and these photographs should be able to present as complete a narrative as it was possible of what was attempted. As a result, it was necessary to ensure that what was decided—in terms of aesthetics and themes—was clear enough in the images. In her *haldi* ceremony, the field of signification was inspired by the imagery of 'flower gardens' and ideas of 'fairy tales', while at her wedding, the main theme was 'royalty and glamor' (see Images 5.6 and 5.7).[15]

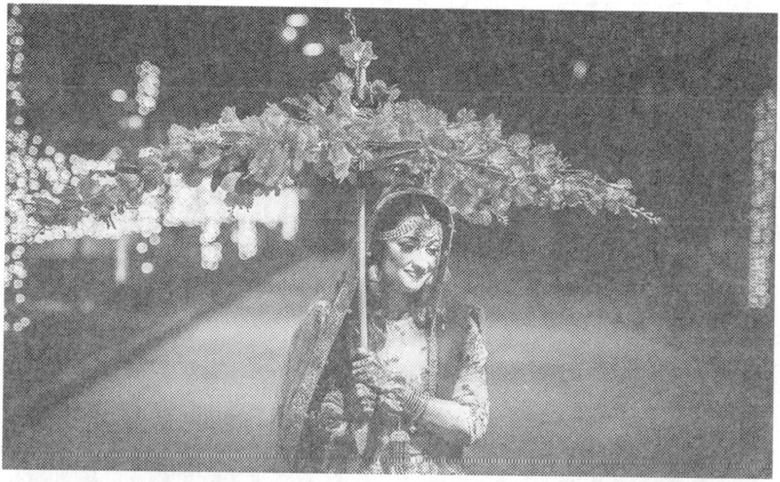

IMAGE 5.6 Themes of gardens, fairy tales, and royalty. *Haldi* and wedding photos of Raihana Sayeeda Kamal. Photography by Jobayer Hossain Shuvo. *Photograph courtesy of*: Raihana Sayeeda Kamal's personal album.

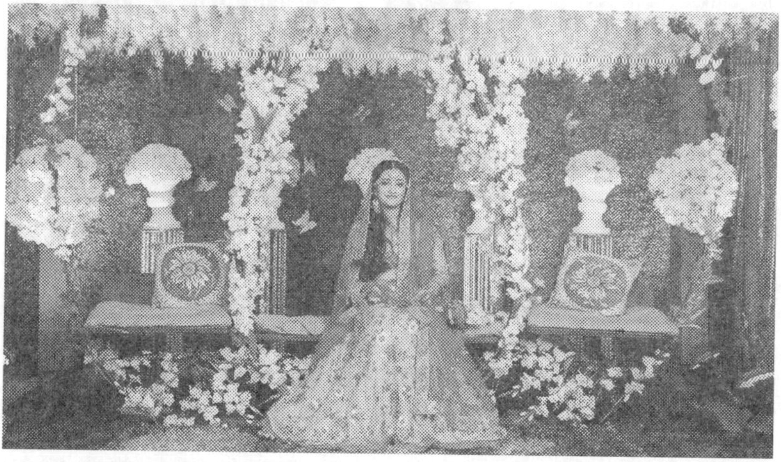

IMAGE 5.7 Themes of gardens, fairy tales, and royalty. *Haldi* and wedding photos of Raihana Sayeeda Kamal. Photography by Jobayer Hossain Shuvo. *Photograph courtesy of*: Raihana Sayeeda Kamal's personal album.

Lakruwan and Nadee Kariyawasam's 2017 wedding took place in Kalutara, Sri Lanka, a coastal town on the western seaboard with considerable access to a number of internal water bodies and 'green' settings, which are popular backdrops for portrait photography, particularly with regard to weddings and pre-wedding photography. The wedding itself was preceded by a pre-wedding shoot, which used themes of nature and the outdoors. This thematic preoccupation is evident in all the images in the couple's collection, which have been shot near streams, on the beach, among flora and fauna, and so on (see Image 5.8).

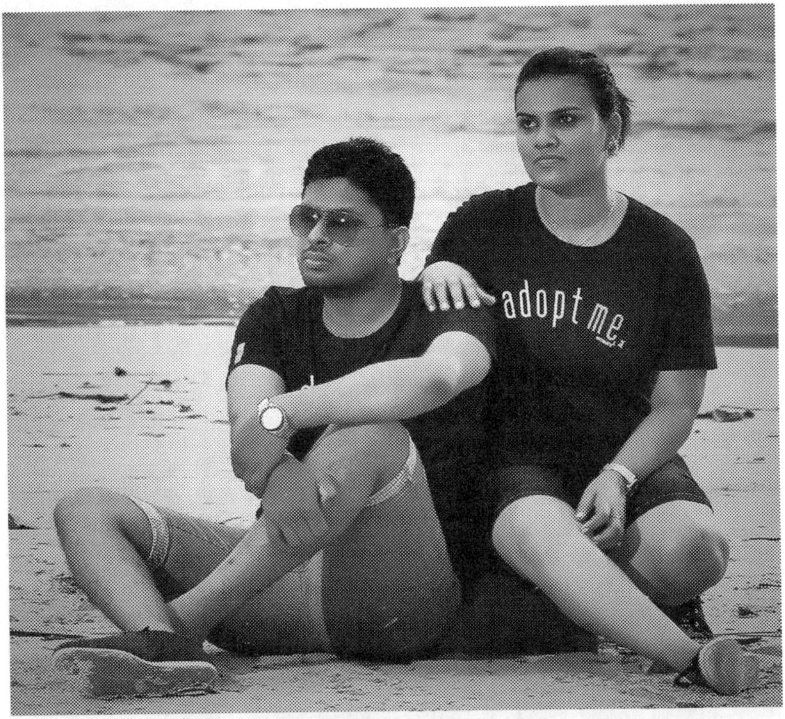

IMAGE 5.8 Themes of nature and the outdoors. Pre-wedding photos from Lakruwan and Nadee Kariyawasam.

Photograph courtesy of: Lakruwan and Nadee Kariyawasam's personal album.

Also, as in many other pre-wedding shoots, the secondary theme is that of relative informality, in terms of both attitudes and moods as well as clothing (see Images 5.8 and 5.9).

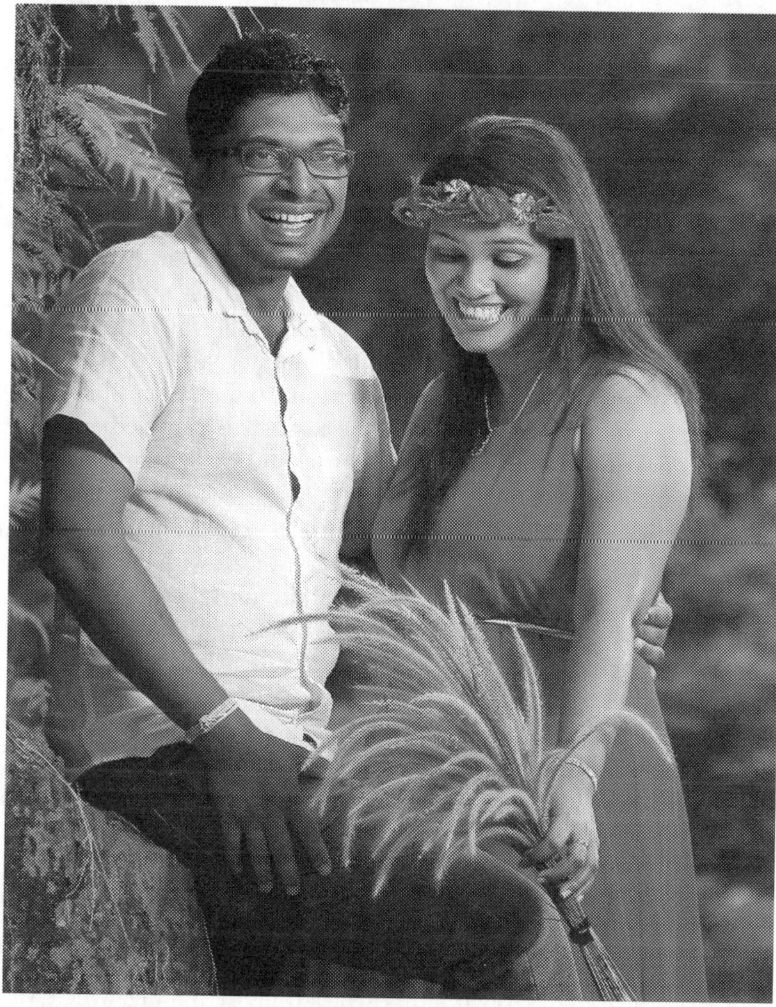

IMAGE 5.9 Themes of nature and the outdoors. Pre-wedding photos from Lakruwan and Nadee Kariyawasam.

Photograph courtesy of: Lakruwan and Nadee Kariyawasam's personal album.

Comparatively, the theme as well as the mood of their wedding photographs are more controlled and sedate, dictated by a sense of 'tradition' which both the bride and the groom had agreed upon, and had worked on over a period of one year leading up to the wedding itself.[16] 'Tradition' in Sinhala Buddhist weddings is a major preoccupation, particularly in times of enhanced photographic possibilities. The Sinhala Buddhist wedding, as it is understood today, does not have a very long history. In the Buddhist scheme of things, the marriage and the wedding were seen as the means to enhance the suffering in *samsara* or the cycle of life and death due to the attachments they encourage. As a result, except for the weddings of royalty and the elites, in the pre-colonial era, the Buddhist wedding was an insignificant social affair in terms of ritual. But Sinhala Buddhist middle classes wanted a more 'respectable' wedding ritual with which they could compete for status with their Christian counterparts, whose social power was enhanced in the colonial period. So the present Buddhist wedding as a model was based upon the basic structural elements and practices borrowed from the nineteenth-century Christian wedding, as it was practised in colonial Ceylon.[17]

Particularly after Independence in 1948, there were many attempts to indigenise the rituals and ceremonies associated with the marriage, depending on the tastes and socio-political circumstances of the people concerned. One vehicle through which this was attempted was by introducing elements into wedding practices, which were understood within an idiom of 'tradition'. Often, the main modes of expression used to induce this sense of tradition were invented traditions infused with a sense of historical depth, introducing elements of music through instruments inherited from the pre-colonial past and recreated sartorial attire, which were expected to usher in a sense of tradition or a continuation from the distant Sinhala and Buddhist past. It is in this last sense that notions of tradition have to be understood in the context of the Kariyawasams' wedding. The bride opted for what is known today as the Kandyan sari.[18] It is a Sri Lankan version of the Indian sari with minor variations in draping, which was initially the attire of women of elite families in the central hill regions of Sri Lanka. The groom opted for what is commonly known as the 'nilame dress',[19] or what is now thought of as men's attire from the Kandyan period. It is essentially a highly standardised version of pre-colonial official attire of the Kandy court. Officials wore very specific costumes, depending on their rank. These included specific headgear, ways of wearing the cloth, the jacket (or there would be no jacket at all), specific shoes (or, if it was required, going barefoot), the kind of weaponry or other paraphernalia carried, and so on. As a result, these attires had very specific caste, social, regional, as well as hierarchical meanings. Image 5.10 indicates a Kandyan family comprising both men and women in 1900, wearing some of these costumes long before they were subjected to the kind of generalisation and standardisation that has happened today, particularly within a discourse on wedding photography. This photograph was taken eighty-five years after the Kandyan court and kingdom had fallen to the British and the political meaning of this costume had died. However, it still retained some local cultural significance. But soon after Independence, many cultural artefacts, practices, and symbols of the Kandy period of Sri Lankan Kingship—including its dance forms—were popularly adopted as the most authentic references to tradition and the pre-colonial past. This choice was also encouraged by the State itself by adopting the same symbols for State functions.

In this reincarnated and reinvented persona, these costumes, widely used in weddings, no longer have their original caste, region-specific, professional or hierarchical meanings. As a field of significations, these costumes and places where they are used—such as weddings—have been standardised and simplified to refer in a linear fashion only to simple and uncomplicated understandings of tradition. But in this sense, in contemporary usage, the ideas of tradition visually—albeit superficially—and a sense of historicity embedded into these costumes are popularly accepted without confusion. It is in this broader context that the Kariyawasams' wedding theme needs to be understood. And it is within this thematic consideration that the photographs of this event have been framed (see Image 5.11).

The examples of these weddings and their implications for photography make one point very clear. That is, they are no longer private social practices meant to be carried out in the presence

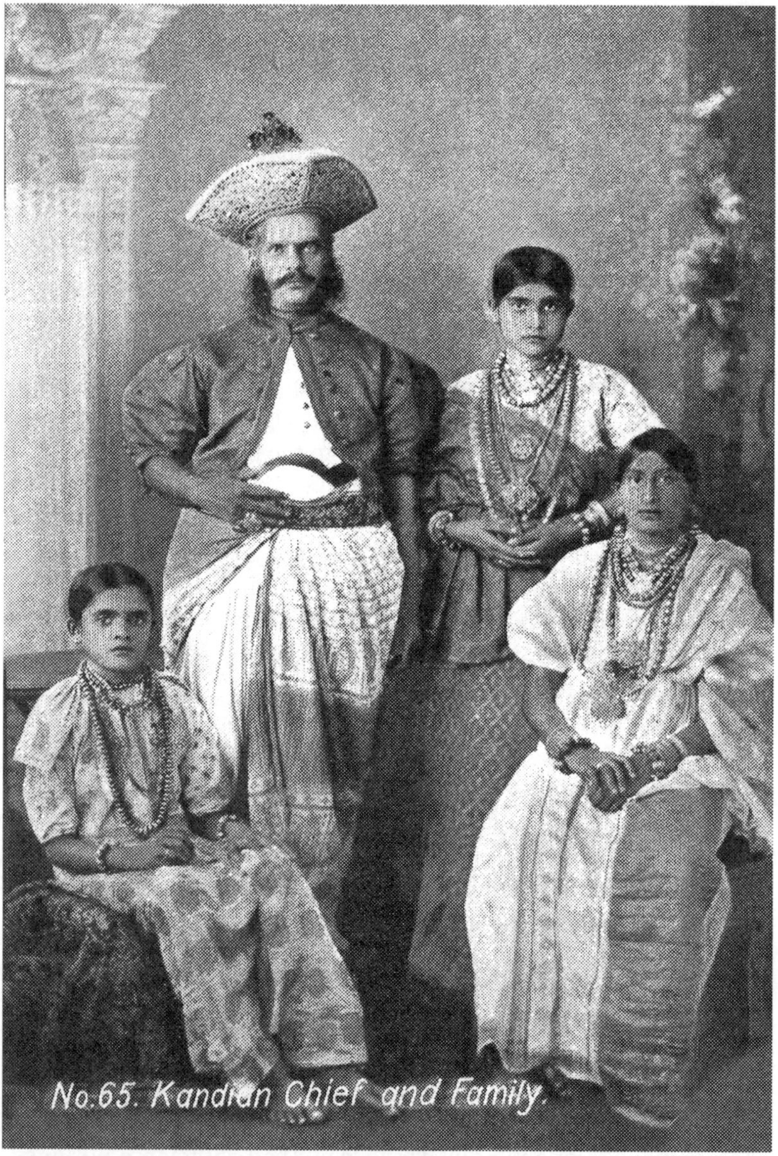

Image 5.10 Kandyan family, Ceylon, 1890.

Photograph courtesy of: Plâté Limited, Colombo 3, Sri Lanka.

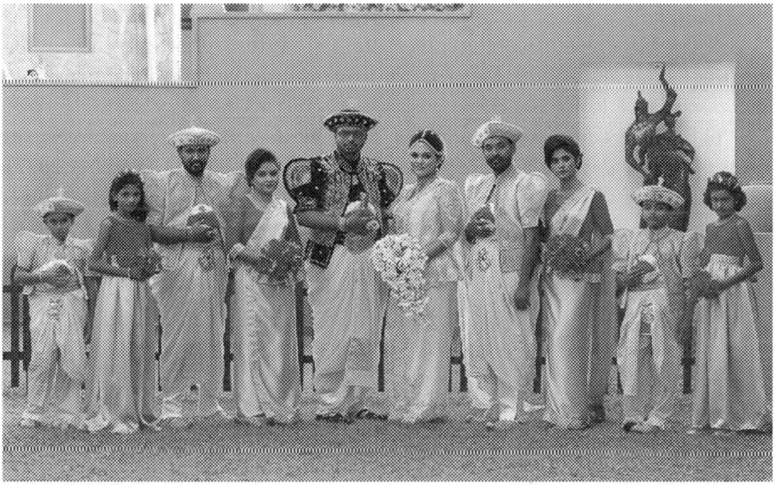

IMAGE 5.11 A theme of tradition. Wedding photos from Lakruwan and Nadee Kariyawasam.
Photograph courtesy of: Lakruwan and Nadee Kariyawasam's personal album.

of close kin and friends. Particularly due to the possibilities of photography combined with the wide reach of the internet, they have become theme-based performances enacted not only for the purpose of marriage, but also for the purpose of expanding the 'news' of the event considerably beyond the realm of the private, and well into the public. But the overall symbolic references to these performances remain ideas of love, desire, and passion, which cut across cultural and geographic domains.

NOTES

1. https://www.theweddingsecret.co.uk/magazine/history-of-wedding-photography/ (accessed 31 October 2017).
2. http://www.brighthub.com/multimedia/photography/articles/102414.aspx (accessed 31 October 2017).
3. https://www.theweddingsecret.co.uk/magazine/history-of-wedding-photography/ (accessed 31 October 2017).

4. Ibid.

5. For a brief history of the camera flash, see https://photography.tutsplus.com/articles/a-brief-history-of-photographic-flashglobalphoto-4249 (accessed 31 October 2017).

6. For the complete versions of these vows and other examples, see https://bible.org/article/sample-wedding-vows (accessed 19 December 2017).

7. https://www.goodreads.com/quotes/289384-keep-smiling-because-life-is-a-beautiful-thing-and-there-s (accessed 3 December 2017).

8. For more information, see https://www.theknot.com/wedding-themes (accessed 26 June 2018).

9. Email communication from Thanuja Perera-Childs, 3 January 2018.

10. Ibid.

11. Ibid.

12. Ibid.

13. Email communication from Raihana Sayeeda Kamal, 27 February 2018.

14. Ibid.

15. Ibid.

16. Email communication from Lakruwan Kariyawasam, 16 May 2017.

17. For a detailed analysis of inventions and innovations in the Buddhist wedding since the British colonial period, see Gombrich Obeyesekere (1988).

18. Email communication from Lakruwan Kariyawasam, 16 May 2017.

19. Nilame was an official in the pre-colonial Kandyan royal court.

six

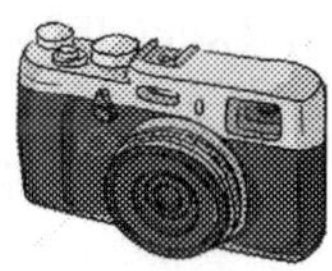

Why Visual Anthropology and Visual Sociology?

A*s I started* teaching my course, 'Photography and Method in Sociology and Social Anthropology', in 2013, it was not meant to be a course taught from a position of authority of knowledge, which university courses are generally expected to be. I was not speaking from my perceived status as a teacher with advanced knowledge to students who were yet to acquire such knowledge. Instead, my position was that this was an exploration based on a question and a relative lack of knowledge. The question was: Why was it necessary for visual anthropology and visual sociology to emerge as separate sub-disciplines beyond the mainstream when in my mind, both sociology and social anthropology were capable in intellectual terms to deal with the visual within the methodological and theoretical approaches available to them? As a result, we hardly referred to visual sociology or anthropology in the class. The histories we read explained how the sub-disciplines began, but not necessarily why. My interest at the time was in any case not to trace the history of these two sub-disciplines. Rather, I was keen to see how a serious interest in the visual might be maintained at the centre of anthropological or sociological practice in the mainstream, since in my own institutional circumstances it seemed more than possible. As a result, neither I nor the students in my class were thinking of what we were reading, doing, and thinking as a set of practices in visual sociology or visual anthropology. There was no confusion; we were in the mainstream of the disciplines, but we were trying to deal with a category which most of our academic counterparts were not keen to deal with.

Today, anyone within the social sciences and humanities, or even beyond these broader systems of knowledge, would have at least heard of the subfields of visual anthropology and visual sociology, which work exclusively on the visual in both social anthropology and sociology. But what is not as self-evident is what necessitated the emergence of these subfields in the first place. One can begin such an exploratory journey by attempting to answer the following three questions:

1. Is it because mainstream sociology and anthropology somehow could not successfully address the visual within the theoretical and methodological apparatuses available within the disciplines? That is, were there inadequate analytical apparatuses built into these disciplines to deal with the visual, either as a research object or as a cluster of methods for information collection? If so, was there an inherent intellectual lack in these two disciplines?
2. Or was it a matter of intellectual disinterest and arrogance, coupled with the methodological and theoretical conservatism of most colleagues in the mainstream of these disciplines, and the resultant unwillingness to engage with possibilities that were situated beyond the conventional limits set by the written word? That is, was it because dealing with the visual was considered too 'soft' or 'non-scientific' to maintain the 'scientific' provenance of the discipline?
3. Or was the desire of those colleagues with a pronounced interest in the visual to carve out a safe intellectual comfort zone for themselves with an obsessive focus on the visual an overriding factor?

As I proceed with this exploration, trying to answer these questions, my focus will mostly be on photography's implication in these two broader disciplines, rather than on the visual more generally. That is, I will mostly attempt to answer these preliminary questions by looking at the place of photography in sociology and anthropology over time. What I have outlined above are the general questions I hope to explore in this chapter. And I pose them here this starkly because as I read through the available histories of the visual in sociology and social anthropology, it is not always clear how things have transpired the way they have, and why. But when posing these questions here, I see no valid intellectual reason to maintain a distinct differentiation between the recent histories of sociology and social anthropology and the emergence of their visual counterparts. It seems to me that the visual subfields of both have emerged for very similar reasons. As such, I will look at the emergence of interests in the visual via visual sociology and anthropology as a single discourse, even though I am quite mindful of the fact that the formal histories of visual sociology and anthropology are written as if they are airtight disciplinary histories. Due to this reason, my brief survey of these two histories will focus on them individually.

My own position can be attributed to two basic reasons. One, with regard to contemporary practice, it is very difficult to maintain any sensible or useful distinction between mainstream sociology and social anthropology as matters of discourse if we do not self-consciously take into account institutional histories and the different disciplinary histories associated with these two disciplines in the first sixty or so years of their existence. That is, much of the seeming separation of identities in sociology and social anthropology has been maintained by the sustenance of separate departments of sociology and social anthropology in most universities where these disciplines are taught. This has been further entrenched—mostly within university systems—by vehemently protecting the accidental and historically contingent erection of borders between the two. This was made further possible by the differentiated theoretical development in the two disciplines in their early historical moments, when it was easier to categorise E.B. Tylor or Malinowski's ideas as strictly anthropological theory and Robert Merton or C. Wright Mills' ideas as part of the body of sociological theory. This was possible when social theory as a general body of ideas had not yet evolved into an encompassing body of knowledge that could cut across all systems of knowledge in the social sciences and humanities, as was evident later in the twentieth century. Similarly, this separation made sense at a time when the object of inquiries in these two fields were understood somewhat artificially on the basis of historical accidents, rather than on the basis of intellectual necessity. After all, both fields took human society and culture as their major emphases. It is in this context that Bourdieu (1995) notes that the boundary between sociology and social anthropology, which he refers to as ethnology, is an example of a spurious border. As such, in contemporary practice, despite the continuation of some of the earlier borders, it is possible to perceive these disciplines as closely interconnected fields of inquiry.

Second, if one were to explore the institutional and theoretical evolution of the mainstream in both disciplines to the extent possible, it would be quite evident that in contemporary times, neither has shown a pronounced and sustained interest in the visual. This is so despite the fact that at different moments in their intellectual histories, both have engaged with the visual in some ways, only to leave that interest behind as time progressed. This association with the visual once upon a time is of course much more obvious with regard to anthropology, as partially referred to in Chapter 2 and elaborated in Chapter 3.

Why Visual Anthropology?

Away from the experts, in the commonsense of social anthropology and, to some extent, in the social sciences more generally, there appears to be a rather strange assumption of what constitutes the disciplinary terrain of 'visual anthropology'. That is, it is assumed that visual anthropology must somehow engage in its intellectual discourse purely by privileging the visual alone. In a number of casual conversations with some of my students in Delhi since 2011, this assumption has often emerged as a matter of routine. Christof Thurnherr's contention is that 'traditionalists seem to lay more stress on the verbal', while 'supporters of technologically more inclusive ways of doing anthropology tend to disproportionally favor the visual' (Thurnherr 2012: 31). Although it does not seem reasonable for me to make such a broad and simple generalisation without falling into problems of over-simplification, this also appears to be one of the components of the popular commonsense in the understanding of visual anthropology or sociology. Thurnherr also notes that neither the visual nor the verbal in anthropology can 'sensibly be of use without the other' because, as he proceeds to stress further, 'even in visually based research the pencil remains an indispensable tool' (ibid.). The very need to belabour this obvious methodological commonsense points to the widely held belief that the visual somehow has to make its case by itself for it to be thought of as a legitimate discursive and intellectual practice.

I consider this erroneous assumption an intellectual poltergeist that has often hovered in the background, creating a strange fear of the visual within mainstream social anthropology. It is strange, not because the visual in this context is feared because it is scary as such, but because it is thought to be intellectually too soft, difficult to objectify, embedded in what is seen as layers of subjectivities, and finally, almost impossible to quantify. The preoccupation with these considerations offers at least a partial explanation for the emergence of visual anthropology as a formal sub-discipline, which has self-consciously located itself away from the gaze of the mainstream. In this sense, visual anthropology has made its presence felt since the mid-1970s and the early 1980s, as has visual sociology.

I take it as a matter of obvious fact that contemporary mainstream anthropology's interest in the visual more generally, and in photography more specifically, is unfocussed and inconsistent at best. This has happened in spite of the very close relationship that photography had with early anthropology, as outlined in Chapter 3. Today, the crucial issue is not that visual anthropology and sociology have not globally evolved their own recognisable intellectual personalities, but what these manifestations represent for mainstream anthropology and sociology vis-à-vis visuality's location within these disciplines in terms of research. It is important to work out what the inherent intellectual limitations, if any, were in mainstream sociology and anthropology that made them shun a concentrated engagement with the visual, which necessitated the exiling of those interested in the visual to the academic hinterland of the two disciplines, from where the two sub-disciplines emerged later.

The establishment of visual anthropology marks two other important developments, which are generally not emphasised in most discussions on the history of these developments. In terms of the first of these, as interests in the visual migrated to visual anthropology and were mostly restricted within its sub-disciplinary borders, most concerns with the visual were effectively banished from mainstream anthropology. Naturally, this means that most studies that had anything to do with photography since the 1990s have taken place within visual anthropology in particular and not within mainstream social anthropology. That absence is quite evident today. In a sense, one of the most inherent intellectual biases of both sociology and anthropology over time has been their preference for the written and the spoken word—in that order. One can see this as a kind of methodological reductionism, which has evolved historically. As noted by Ruby, 'anthropology is a word-driven discipline', and in that scheme of things, 'it has tended to ignore the visual-pictorial world perhaps because of distrust of the ability of images to convey abstract ideas' (Ruby 1996: 1350). In this unenviable situation, the idealised 'promise of visual anthropology is that it might provide an alternative way of perceiving culture-perception constructed through the lens' (ibid.). More precisely, visual anthropology is based upon the assumption 'that culture is manifested through visible symbols embedded in gestures, ceremonies, rituals, and artifacts situated in constructed and natural environments' (ibid.: 1345). These general interests are also reflected in the American Anthropological Association's Society for Visual Anthropology, one of the first professional bodies set up (in 1984) specifically with a focus on visual anthropology. Among the activities it promotes are:

- Promoting the study of visual representation and media, taking into account both research methods and teaching strategies.
- Its members are interested in 'works in film, video, photography, and computer-based multimedia [that] explore signification, perception, and communication-in-context, as well as a multitude of other anthropological and ethnographic themes'.
- These interests encompass 'all visual aspects of culture, including art, architecture and material artifacts, as well as kinesics, proxemics and related forms of body motion communication (e.g. gesture, emotion, dance, sign language)'.

- It 'encourages the use of media, including still photography, film, video and non-camera generated images, in the recording of ethnographic, archaeological and other anthropological genres'. In the process, Society members are expected to 'examine how aspects of culture can be pictorially/visually interpreted and expressed, and how images can be understood as artifacts of culture. Historical photographs, in particular, are seen as a source of ethnographic data, expanding our horizons beyond the reach of memory culture.'[1]

Given this rather obvious sense of visuality in both the production of culture and action, it is further assumed that if it is possible to see culture, then, as pointed out by Ruby, 'researchers should be able to employ audiovisual technologies to record it as data amenable to analysis and presentation' (Ruby 1996: 1350). This is a sensible point of departure. But the more crucial question is this: Is it not possible to explore all this within mainstream sociology or anthropology in the first place? What is the need to evolve a separate sub-discipline to explore these questions? But when a 'divorce' is imminent and convenient, and is also ready to be accommodated without contestation, such questions will not arise.

The second development is closely linked to the first. That is, scholars interested in the visual in general and photography in particular welcomed and promoted the construction of visual anthropology as a sub-discipline. This is because it enabled them to create an active domain of intellectual inquiry into the visual that had some linkages to anthropology, while interest in the visual remained central within the sub-discipline and was not occulted or marginalised, as had been the case within the mainstream. But what this effectively led to is the institutionalised distanced position that photography and the visual have occupied since then on the margins of mainstream anthropology.

Despite the wide thematic possibilities offered by a focus on the visual, once this became a core interest within the contours of a sub-discipline, visual anthropology, in practical terms, came to be 'dominated primarily by an interest in pictorial media as a means of communicating anthropological knowledge' (Ruby 1996: 1345). This essentially means ethnographic films, photographs and, at a different level of focus, exploring pictorial manifestations of culture (ibid.).

Why Visual Sociology?

Writing in 1998, Douglas Harper sought to identify two main areas of visual sociology in general. The first of these is the making of photographs by researchers or the people they are studying. This was expected to be done in the course of fieldwork, and particularly in the midst of interviews or regular processes of observation (Harper 1988: 55). The second is the study of photographs created by people in day-to-day social interactions (ibid.).

Compared to social anthropology, however, sociology did not so clearly 'develop an intimate relationship with photography' (Schnettler 2013: 42). Its relationship with visuality more generally is also less pronounced compared to social anthropology. With particular reference to American sociology, Jurgen Raab (2008) has suggested that the initial use of visual documents in sociology, including photographs, was from the years 1903 to 1915 (quoted in Schnettler 2013: 42). In this particular context, a number of essays were published in the *American Journal of Sociology*, which used photographs for two specific purposes: first, to generally illustrate the written text, or second, in an attempt to provide photographs as visual evidence of what was being argued (ibid.). Among these essays were Anne MacLean's 'The Sweat-Shop in Summer' (1903), Sophonisba Breckindrige and Edith Aboth's 'Chicago's Housing Problems: Families in Furnished Rooms' (1910), Howard Woodhead's 'The First German Municipal Exposition' (1904), and Natalie Walker's 'Chicago Housing Conditions: Greeks and Italians in the Neighbourhood of Hull House' (1915), among others (Schnettler 2013: 42). With particular reference to the Chicago School of Sociology, Harper notes that despite its heavy emphasis on surveys, secondary research, and statistical analysis from the 1930s onwards, which helped to create an important component of its intellectual identity, the school nevertheless briefly experimented with photography in the 1920s (Harper 2016: 238–39). This, however, never took off as a serious methodological intervention.

Just as anthropology's somewhat longer romance with photography came to a sudden end in the first decades of the twentieth century, sociology's brief association with photography ended more abruptly post-1916 (Schnettler 2013: 42). Schnettler's explanation for this rupture makes sense to me. That is, tables, formulae, and graphs replaced visual texts such as photographs as a direct result of the influence and impact of statistical methods in sociology (ibid.). We know that American sociology embraced such allegedly 'more scientific' techniques rigorously and quite early, compared to other sociologies of the world. And this romance began much before techniques like photography had the chance to take root within American sociology. This was also the time when American sociology had the power to show the paths that other sociologies might want to follow. As described in Chapter 3, if photography in the initial stages of social anthropology offered the discipline a veneer of being 'scientific' and evidence-based, after the first decade of the twentieth century, statistics and statistics-based illustrations came to be considered the 'only legitimate forms of scientific illustrations' (Stasz 1979, quoted in Schnettler 2013: 42). As we know, this specific intellectual personality, which was initially embraced by American sociology, became one of the key identity markers of sociology more generally as the twentieth century evolved.

There is a clearer history of visual sociology's emergence in the United States. Writing with particular reference to this context, Douglas Harper notes that the late 1960s and 1970s were the initial period 'when visual sociology was germinating' (Harper 2016: 238). He notes that this was also the time in the context of the US when 'the methodological god of quantitative methods had been coincidentally challenged by emerging qualitative methods and visual sociology became a small part of that movement' (ibid.). These general circumstances allowed for the kind of thinking that was necessary for professional associations interested in the practice of visual sociology to come to the fore, as well as visual sociology as a sub-discipline to emerge within sociology. Harper notes that the 'brazen attitude' towards these possibilities was also a product of the times (ibid.). According to him, Howard Becker's now well-known 1974 essay,

'Photography and Sociology', added to this atmosphere of confidence amongst supporters of visual sociology and helped in the creation of formal institutional possibilities for visual sociology in times to come (ibid.).

Harper contends that many early American sociologists who formally thought of themselves as visual sociologists, or who were keen to work within sociology by employing a significant engagement with photography, were influenced by the possibilities offered by documentary photography of the time (ibid.: 239). It is easy to see how this interest might have been viewed as hopeful when looking at the approach and possibilities of 'the New Journalism' movement (ibid.). Within its practice, photographers were keen on capturing much more than merely good images. They looked upon their willingness to involve themselves to some extent in the lives of the people whom they photographed as their method, as well as their strength (ibid.). It is in this context that one can understand Danny Lyon's long-term project that evolved over a number of years and focussed on the American Civil Rights Movement, and John Kerry's edited book that documented the anti-war movement amongst US service personnel (ibid.). Harper suggests that a number of other photographic interventions in the 1970s can be considered 'phenomenological studies of the photographer's own communities and circumstances', which include Peter Simon's photographs of the hippie movement (1975), Bill Owens' exploration of his own suburban experience, Larry Clark's study of drug addicts in suburban contexts (1971), among others (Harper 2016: 239). What resulted from these projects were not simply photographs as a means of documentation. They were effectively photographic narratives, which came about as the result of the photographers' long-term immersion within the situations that interested them. In other words, these images were not captured as a matter of fleeting moments, but were the result of a process that was close to what we consider today as 'fieldwork'. And that too, from the perspective of a veritable 'insider'. The scholars who opted for visual sociology in the initial period were not only inspired by these examples, but were also already using photography seriously in their work at the time. They were looking for ways to solidify and institutionalise their intellectual practice, which needed a more supportive home than what existing US mainstream sociology was willing to offer.

It was Howard Becker's essay, 'Photography and Sociology' (1974), that effectively offered the initial guidelines for the practice of visual sociology. As an individual located well within the emerging movement of visual sociology in the US, Becker promoted a practice that combined an intellectual intensity with a commitment to and skill in photography, typified by documentary photographers on the one hand and an adherence to sociological concerns, objects, and methods on the other (Becker 1974). Clearly, Becker's intention was to ensure that the emergent field did not stray too far from its sociological roots and lose its scientific provenance in a maze of subjective images.

The Visual in Sociology and Social Anthropology in Contemporary Times

The engagement with the visual in sociology and social anthropology has come about as outlined briefly in the two histories presented above. But these two histories of separation and emergence, I suggest, has come to a single point of convergence—that is, the clear exile of the visual from the mainstreams of both sociology and social anthropology and its relocation in the sub-disciplinary domains of visual sociology and anthropology. My earlier suggestion—that there is no particular use, intellectually, in making these two histories distinct—had been made from this vantage point. They have led to the same place.

But where and how does this new disciplinary domain manifest now? By the late 1990s, a number of influential books dealing with the subject had already emerged, clearly indicating that visual anthropology and sociology were in the process of establishing themselves, with their own formal corpus of knowledge that was quite separate from the mainstream knowledge production in both sociology and social anthropology. These include *Principles of Visual Anthropology*, edited by Paul Hockings (1974); *Anthropology and*

Photography, edited by Elizabeth Edwards (1992); *Fields of Vision: Essays on Film Studies, Visual Anthropology and Photography*, edited by Leslie Devereaux and Roger Hillman (1995); and *Rethinking Visual Anthropology*, edited by Marcus Banks and Howard Morphy (1997). This, of course, is in addition to numerous essays published in journals such as *Visual Studies*, *Visual Sociology*, *Visual Anthropology*, etc., which includes the following, published in the 1990s (among many others): Wyne Mellinger, 'Representing Blackness in the White Imagination: Images of Happy Darkies in Popular Culture, 1893–1917' (1992); Ellen Ramsey, 'Picturing the Picturesque: Lucius O Brien's "Sunrise on the Saguenay"' (1992); Janet Davis, 'Spectacles of South Asia at the American Circus, 1890–1940' (1993); and Dominic Alessio, 'Capitalist Realist Art: Industrial Images of Hamilton, Ontario, 1884–1910' (1992). This textual production collectively indicates an increased interest in the place of the visual in general, and photography or visual media's place in visual anthropology and visual sociology in particular.

However, the clear emergence of these sub-disciplines and their own textual production also indicated in no uncertain terms the mainstream's consistent and continuing lack of interest in engaging with the visual, and the robust institutionalisation of this disinterest and its formalisation. It is in this context that Taylor's argument, that visual anthropology was at once both highly visible and quite marginal within mainstream anthropology, makes sense (Taylor 1998: 534). It was highly visible due to its self-conscious exit from the mainstream and its decision to encamp by itself in the disciplinary landscape beyond the mainstream. It was effectively the metaphorical 'poor cousin' of anthropology, who had left 'home'. But at the same time, that exit itself ensured its invisibility within the quotidian intellectual deliberations in the mainstream. But despite its clear evolution outside the mainstream as a sub-discipline with a very specific focus, even by the mid-1990s the domain of visual anthropology was not clearly understood or, at the very least, was not defined in a manner that had broader acceptance. This lack of clarity was evident in the kind of fundamental questions about the nature of visual anthropology that were posed in debates at the time:

(a) Is it a kind of anthropology that was primarily articulated through 'visual media, as distinct from anthropology articulated through the expository prose' (Taylor 1998: 534)?

(b) Or 'is it anthropology that attends to visual aspects of material culture, or even to the visual dimensions of sensory experience as a whole' (ibid.)?

These observations, raised with regard to visual anthropology, can also be applied to visual sociology at the same time. The first query emanated from a confusion that emerged when considering visual anthropology's perceived mode of expression, that is: Was this kind of anthropology to be seen or read? Partly, it seems to me that this confusion stemmed from confusing visual anthropology in general with aspects of anthropological practice that could be more easily located in visual anthropology than within the mainstream—such as ethnographic film. However, ethnographic film as a practice had emerged long before visual anthropology formally entered the intellectual landscape and became a reasonably accepted part of mainstream anthropology. But obviously, it was not something that every anthropologist opted to practice. It was seen as something that one could engage in while undertaking more serious field research. The second concerned its focus of attention in terms of research and intellectual interest. To be more precise, this query was about where certain kinds of anthropological inquiry should be located. For instance, the issue here was whether human practices such as art and craft, where visuality is centrally implicated, or end-products such as ethnographic films should ideally be located in mainstream anthropology's regular discourse or within the specialised discourse of visual anthropology. In today's academic and intellectual circumstances, where visual anthropology and sociology have found wide and credible expression, defining their borders and methods is not my concern. In any event, by now there is sufficient agreement on such matters, as the emergence of crucial works such as the ones above and many more since then would indicate. What these confusions highlight, however, is that until relatively recent times, what visual anthropology and sociology were all about and what to do with them were constantly raised questions.

Writing in the late 1990s, Caulfield attempted to answer the question of what constitutes areas of interest when it comes to visuality, with particular reference to sociology. He noted that visual imagery (not merely photographs) can be of sociological interest due to the following three reasons:

1. Photographs or artworks might reflect the 'life worlds and social relations of their makers and users' (Caulfield 1996: 57). For example, with reference to Mary Stokrocki's essay, 'Through Navajo children's eyes: Cultural influences on representational abilities' (1994), he points out that the cultural and social significance of themes such as land and animals evident among Native Americans is clearly seen in the artworks created by Navajo children (ibid.). Similarly, with reference to T.J. Clark's *The Painting of Modern Life: Paris in the Art of Manet and his Followers* (1984), Caulfield suggests that the social aspects of modern urbanism are clearly embedded in Edouard Manet's painting depicting a Parisian barmaid (ibid.).
2. Images can often be understood as 'formative elements of social life' (ibid.). Caulfield suggests that the display of cultural artefacts such as family photographs might work as a forum for children to internalise important moments in family histories, understood within idioms such as 'achievements' or 'happiness' (ibid.). That is, such photographs could be seen as mechanisms of family and societal training in ethics, goals, and so on. If so, such images would constitute a legitimate domain of sociological inquiry.
3. In a more straightforward manner, imagery such as photographs or painted portraits may carry embedded documentary information on the people they depict (Caulfield 1996: 57). Caulfield points out that John Thompson's photographs of London in Victorian times actually also offer an evidence-based sense of the city of the time, as clearly seen in Adolphe Smith's 1877 book, *Street Life in London* (ibid.). In a similar fashion, as Christina Cameron and Jean Trudel point out in their 1976 book, *The Drawings of James Cockburn*, the

> water-colour paintings of colonial Quebec by Cockburn can be understood as a faithful pictorial record of town scapes and everyday life (ibid.).

What Caulfield explains for sociology makes equal sense for social anthropology. But what is more important is the manner in which he explains how such images might be used intellectually. His attempt offers a clear early answer to those uninformed commentators who assumed that images in the social sciences must speak for themselves. However, as Caulfield explains, 'because they are immanently social objects, pictures tend to do none of these things transparently' (Caulfield 1996: 57). As a result, 'deriving sociological information from them requires critical sociological reading' (ibid.). What Caulfield has attempted is essentially a methodological justification for the practice of visual sociology.

To make a case for the wider acceptance of visual methods as the twenty-first century began, Pink refers to four important texts. These are Marcus Banks' *Visual Methods in Social Research* (2001), Pink's own *Doing Visual Ethnography* (2001), Gillian Rose's *Visual Methodologies* (2000), and Theo van Leeuwen and Carey Jewitt's edited book, *The Handbook of Visual Analysis* (2001) (Pink 2012: 2). As noted earlier, the production of texts (among other practices) within a specific methodological orientation, as in visual sociology or anthropology, is a marker of that method's perseverance and longevity. For Pink, the publication of these books 'marked a moment in the social sciences and humanities where for a number of reasons the visual was becoming more acceptable, more viable and more central to qualitative research practice' (ibid.: 3).

Teaching Visual Sociology and Visual Anthropology

By the beginning of the twenty-first century, visual anthropology and sociology, while trying to maintain their artificially separated twin sub-disciplinary status on much the same lines as mainstream sociology and social anthropology, had clearly emerged as independent academic sub-disciplines. Much of these disciplines' visibility and academic credibility have come from their ability to introduce and maintain academic teaching programmes in a number of universities. These, along with the increasing corpus of writing, are the main markers of their independent presence, vitality, and visibility. Writing in 2013, it was in this context that Schnettler notes that in the preceding years, it was possible to see a 'vibrant intensification in the field of visual sociology and in visual research methods' (Schnettler 2013: 41). Referring to visual anthropology in particular, Bank notes that demands for courses among students has grown, as a result of which MA-level courses in visual anthropology have been formulated in the UK and elsewhere (Banks 2001: 2). In addition, other options for courses focussed on visual aspects have become increasingly available in undergraduate-level teaching programmes. In his assessment, this development is led by visual anthropology, while 'visual sociology is also a relatively well-established sub-discipline, and visual approaches can be found in other research areas such as social psychology, educational studies and the like' (ibid.). As a result of this establishment, today a number of university-level courses in visual sociology and anthropology are offered in many countries, while this interest is also represented by dynamic professional organisations (Pink 2003: 179). These professional organisations aid in research as well as the regular dissemination of ideas. This is a taken for granted reality in the contemporary academic landscape in Europe and North America.

However, such an expansion has not taken place to any serious degree in South Asia. For instance, no formal and fully-fledged academic programmes offering courses in visual sociology or anthropology can be seen anywhere in South Asia. In Bangladesh, visual anthropology as a single course (among many other regular anthropology courses) was initially introduced at the Department of Anthropology at Jahangir Nagar University.[2] Similarly, the Department of Anthropology, University of Dhaka offers a Visual and Media Anthropology Programme for its postgraduate candidates.[3] This programme aims to:

A. Develop curriculum and module for visual and media anthropology teaching, learning and research.
B. Enhance the capacity of the young faculties [that is, teachers] and the post graduate students through development of conceptual and theoretical understanding about visual and media anthropology.
C. The lab facilities and training on the use of the computer based digital visual technologies will help to enhance the understanding of post graduate students about the role of the new visualizing technologies increasingly used in our technology-driven world.
D. Improve capacity to the innovative use of images and interactive technology to explore, communicate and interact with data.[4]

As is evident, however, this programme emphasises the development of technical skills and making available technical facilities to practice visual imaging, as opposed to intellectual or theoretical advancement, or sustained research. In other words, this is a course that has been predefined by market requirements and not intellectual curiosity. In the same sense, Shahjalal University of Science & Technology in Sylhet also offers an optional course in visual anthropology in the final semester of its Bachelors degree programme.[5] In general, these programmes are geared towards offering BA, MA, and sometimes M.Phil and Ph.D.-level optional courses rather than any kind of comprehensive training in visual research in either sociology or anthropology. The only notable comparable example in India is the course 'Visual Culture', offered as an optional course in the sociology programme in the undergraduate colleges of Delhi University. It expects to introduce students to 'the construction of seeing as a social process' (University of Delhi 2015: 67). 'Through case studies covering various visual environments', the course's aim is to 'contextualise everyday visual culture within larger social debates around power, politics, identity and resistance' (ibid.). Here, there is more emphasis on considering the visual and the process of seeing in theoretical and conceptual terms, linked to recent debates on these issues. In universities in other parts of the region, however, visual sociology or anthropology does not seem to have made any impact. As such, it has not been part of any serious debate on the methods of research or its theoretical impactions.

Despite this rather abysmal situation with regard to the study of the visual in sociology and social anthropology in South Asia, beyond the region numerous other fields of inquiry such as cultural studies, queer studies, cultural geography, and consumer research make wide use of visual methods of research and formulate approaches that are 'discipline specific' on the one hand, and 'borrow from existing examples in visual anthropology' on the other (Pink 2003: 179). It is this interaction that has also allowed visual sociology and anthropology to develop on their own terms as well as acquire a legitimate presence in the academic landscapes where they have emerged. In a sense, this means that visual anthropology and sociology are now established well enough for them to exert their influence, particularly in terms of method and approach, on other areas of study with an interest in the visual. In this sense, one can perhaps argue that visual sociology and anthropology have gone beyond the immediate circumstances of their genesis to create a much broader composite area of work, which Pink describes as 'a new stage in the development of visual methodology as a field of interdisciplinary and post-disciplinary practice that spans scholarly and applied concerns' (Pink 2012: 4).

Notes

1. http://societyforvisualanthropology.org/ (accessed 11 March 2018).

2. I am thankful to Ratan Kumar Roy in the Ph.D. Programme at the Department of Sociology, South Asian University for providing me some of the information on the status of visual anthropology in Bangladesh.

3. For more information, see the URL of the programme: http://anthropology.du.ac.bd/pages/content_details/background-and-overview (accessed 10 March 2018).

4. http://anthropology.du.ac.bd/pages/content_details/background-and-overview (accessed 10 March 2018).

5. For course details, see http://www.sust.edu/d/anp/curriculam#about-school1 (accessed 10 March 2018).

seven

Photography, Research, and the Liminality of Ethics in Contemporary Times[1]

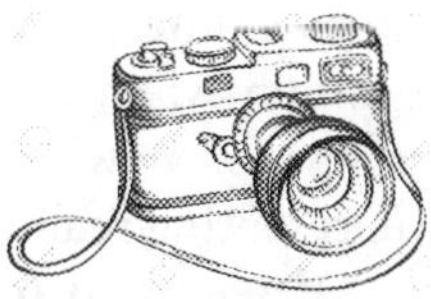

Because images surround us, it is easy to overlook the work that goes into making and producing them—work that is always based on particular viewpoints. As responsible social scientists, however, it is vital to take into account the full range of ethical considerations and implications involved in making, using, and disseminating images.

Marion and Crowder (2013: 3)

In the past, and to a certain extent even today, I tend to spend considerable time with a camera whenever I travel. Much of my effort in such situations has not been to capture reality, as it might exist in totality within a single frame. This is because I know this is not possible, given the fact that a single frame that can be effectively captured by the camera at any time will leave much beyond the frame as well. But as Prosser has noted, 'the still camera and movie camera ... replicate accurately what is set before them. However, more significantly, they do so at our bidding' (Prosser 2000: 124). To emphasise a commonsense position that is often forgotten in popular debates on the 'truthfulness' of photography, any frame captured with the camera is merely a fragment of the overall complex of temporal moments within which society, culture, and life evolve. As such, while the accuracy of what the lens captures in this sense can be accepted, this is clearly done at our 'bidding', as we want it, and at our convenience. So the accuracy of what has been captured on film has to be assessed on the basis of many factors, which vary from the simple framing conceived by photographers to the politics of a specific time, place, and intention. In this context, a taken-for-granted position when dealing with images is that they 'always represent a particular view', and as a result, 'images cannot accurately be seen as representing reality or truth' (Marion and Crowder 2013: 3).

It seems to me that the overall sense of a photograph is best understood when taken in the context of Prosser as well as Marion and Crowder's commonsense above. Taking into account what has been said so far, my interest generally when I use the camera in situations of leisure is not to capture images 'accurately' in an evidential sense, but often out of context—knowing quite well that much of the narrative of what is evident within the frame continues beyond it, and is lost to viewers and even to me as time passes by. In this sense, whatever fragments of realities are captured become at best blurred and incomplete. In a discursive domain, such images do not exist without interpretation. It is the act of interpretation, often by photographers and also by scholars, which offers these photos their context and a more complete sense of 'life'. So any photograph, if it is to make sense in a research or social situation, must necessarily be placed in context and interpreted. Photographs cannot be autonomous texts with their own independent voice.

In this scheme of things, some time ago a friend of mine pointed out that my photographs almost never included people as their main focus. If at all, they were in the background or at the edges of the frames, or with their backs to the camera, almost devoid of consequence and seemingly the result of accidents of time, space, and movement. And she was right. The placement of people in my photos in this manner has often reminded me of the way Adolf Hitler had located individuals in the context of the massive buildings with gothic pillars and other imposing structural features that he had painted as a failed art student in Austria early in his life. Hitler's interest lay in the large buildings and their details, and not in the caricature-like small human figures he sometimes painted in the foreground. This was because his grandly destructive and insane dream articulated in *Mein Kampf*, which had not yet become a reality, was more easily encapsulated in the grandiose buildings that he painted. My way of dealing with the human presence in my photos was a conscious decision, but not in the manner conceived by Hitler. For a long time, I had self-consciously avoided photographing people because I could not be sure if I was violating their sense of privacy and personal space every time I took a photograph. It was also too tedious to seek permission to photograph them all the time.[2] It is precisely the kind of concerns that I had encountered that Rose Wiles, et al. refer to when they note, 'when taking images of groups of people in public spaces or at events it is not practical, or indeed necessary, to obtain consent from people present' (2008: 14). But 'informed consent' and 'privacy', as understood in these situations, have clear limits in today's circumstances, where the eyes of roaming cameras are focussed on almost everyone, and almost everywhere. This is more clearly the case when we deal with photography delinked from clearly predefined research processes. I will address this issue later in this chapter.

However, I did not see the kind of discomfort I had experienced when a visiting colleague from Germany at the seminar, *The Anxious Century: Discourses Waiting to be Born*, in 2008[3] presented her photographs taken in Karachi and Peshawar, and went on to narrate how she simply pointed her camera and photographed whatever and whomever she wanted. I was convinced that some of the photos showed men intensely, and seemingly unhappily, gazing directly into her camera. She referred to some of these men as 'this Taliban' and 'that Taliban', and these casual references themselves made no sense to me. Her narrative reminded me of the limitless possibilities of photojournalism in situations where the ethics of photographic exposure might be expelled to the margins of consciousness. I asked her about the ethics of this engagement, and if she had considered that the people in her photographs might not want her to photograph them, but remained mute in the context of the power relations within which she and her actions were more advantageously located. But she could not see what my concern was. It seemed to me at the time that I was concerned about the ethics of photographing people, particularly when there was a possibility that these images might travel well beyond the camera itself or from the photographer's private collection to other discourses such as conferences, publications, and so on, over which the photographer may not have much control. In such contexts, the privacy of the people captured in the images could not be guaranteed.

But in both these examples involving my own anxiety and my colleague's lack of anxiety over what to photograph and what not to, I am referring to photographs taken in public spaces, which had no connection to research as such. The distinctly different concerns over the ethics of photography between my German colleague, a full-time professional photographer, and myself as a field anthropologist seemed to come from our respective realms of professional training and practice. At the time, I was mostly looking at photography as a matter of leisure and not so much as a matter of research, and my colleague was looking at it as a matter of work and a source of income. We were also looking at photography from two very different ethical perspectives. In 2008, when this interaction took place, and before that as well, I had thought that my own, more stringent sense of photographic practice, informed by considerations of field research ethics generally associated with mainstream social anthropological research, was the more reasonable approach.

But today, twelve years later, I am no longer sure if my own position regarding photographic ethics is applicable, or even practical any longer, given the radical changes in the general circumstances of our lives as well as in the ways we practice photography today. We live in a time where we are consciously and unconsciously photographed all the time as a result of the surveillance systems set up by governments, private companies, home owners, as well as the constantly roaming and gazing eyes of ordinary people's private cameras, embedded in mobile phones. Similarly, we are not the only ones inadvertently or consciously photographed in this sense. We do the same to others as well. This is very much an integral part of our collective social life today. These possibilities of over-photography are a result of the democratisation of technology and the affordability of its access, along with the familiarisation of photography as a practice. And this practice goes beyond a focus on individuals and objects and encompasses groups, landscapes, and so on.

In these circumstances, photography has moved away from recording events, people or things that may have been considered within the purview of monumentality or memorability to photographing quotidian ordinariness where everything and everyone has the potential to be photographed by friends and kin as well as by unknown others, and vice versa. I am constantly surprised by the number of people who know that I am in a particular place at a particular time, even though I may not have consciously informed anyone of my presence. That information becomes available due to the freely circulating images on social media, taken by people both known and unknown to me. In these pictures of ordinary events, my presence is embedded, consciously or otherwise. The ordinary has become memorable, simply because memorialising something in the form of a photo has become effortless, to the extent of being almost thoughtless. In the same sense, the ordinary has also become discursive as long as images circulate on relatively unrestricted forums such as social media. But what is photographed in this manner could equally, and as easily, be unnoticed, forgotten or routinely deleted, giving a very short span of life to the act of photographed memory. Alternatively, such photographs, after being released online, could acquire an afterlife of their own over which the photographer or the subjects in the photographs might not have any control, or even any knowledge of.

In these constantly photographed global circumstances, how does one fathom what ethics in photography in research and intellectual contexts might be? Is posing such a question even possible in contemporary circumstances, where cameras have become ubiquitous? My sense of anthropological field ethics, which initially emanated from the pre-1980s ethics recommended to members of the American Anthropological Association, no longer seem to provide the answers that it had, in somewhat circular ways, since the 1980s to the middle of the first decade of the present millennium. My exploration of these issues will take place mostly via a consideration of photographs taken in non-research contexts, which is where much of my own photographic interests lie. This is also because I strongly believe that such photographs offer considerable research possibilities, and might work as posers for significant intellectual quests beyond photographs generated in specific research projects.

Parameters of Contemporary Debates of Visual Ethics

With reference to recent debates on ethics in the context of using visual materials, Andrew Clark suggests that in general, these concerns can be summarised into three basic categories of anxieties. The first of these comes from the assumption that visual research methods and the data they generate give rise to very specific ethical concerns (Clark 2012: 17). The main reason for this assumed specificity is the perception that the 'the visual is somehow different in form or method to word and number-based data' (ibid.). That is, what is seen and can be easily recognisable, such as photos or film, poses much more obvious concerns for ethics, given the immediacy with which people might react to such data, compared to things that people might read as written text. Obviously, at a simple level, the way in which someone reacts to a published image of someone known to him or her is going to be very different from the way the same person might react to a sociologist's interpretation of a specific incident in which s/he might have taken part. The second set of ethical concerns emanates from the perception that the present review procedures generally followed by research institutions, universities, and the like, as well as currently operational ethical frameworks and codes of practice 'are unsatisfactory for visual material' (ibid.). This anxiety stems from the fact that many ethical codes may have been designed with data other than visual material in mind, and therefore might be difficult to apply to visual methods. The third cluster of anxieties relates to the uncertainty on 'how to proceed when ethical conventions applied to other methods and data seem inappropriate for visual material' (ibid.).

This final concern is obviously an extension of the second. It questions the reasonability of ethics evolved in situations to specifically deal with non-visual data and research contexts, if they are to be applied to visual contexts as well. These concerns emerge from a background where, even now, there appears to be no wide-ranging visual ethics in social research in the same way that more general social science or sociology/anthropology research ethics have been circulating for a considerable period of time. And that too, in the midst of numerous debates, and processes of institutional soul-searching and fine-tuning. This, however, does not mean that there is no idea about what ethics in such situations might mean. Hence the existence of the debates that Clark refers to. The issue is the absence of a general codification of a certain basic consensus when it comes to dealing with visuals in social science research.

Marion and Crowder outline what they call 'seven key issues in visual ethics' (Marion and Crowder 2013: 5) as a set of initial ethical parameters for dealing with visuals:

> 1. Negotiating representational authority, including the triadic relationship between researchers, subjects, and audiences.
> 2. The decontextualization/circulation of images (and the problem of lack of control).
> 3. Presumed versus actual outcome of image display.
> 4. Relations with and responsibilities toward research subjects/communities.
> 5. Balancing privacy versus publicity (depending on subjects' wishes).
> 6. The importance of communication with and consent of subjects/communities at every stage of the research process.
> 7. The collection and dissemination of visual materials within the context of globally expanding media savvy and presence. (ibid.: 11, 5–7)

Even though these are presented as 'key ethical considerations in visual research', by their own admission, Marion and Crowder do not argue that these seven issues can be seen as 'an ingredient list for ethical research' involving images (ibid.: 6). And, more importantly, they do not suggest that their list is a 'recipe' that could simply be followed, but suggest instead that each of the issues is to be pondered over vis-à-vis the way they might relate to one's own research (ibid.). In other words, what they have suggested is a general commonsense, which they have attempted to codify as a non-binding reference-cum-ethical list to be thought through when working with images, and particularly when dealing with photography.

It is obvious that their ideas have been culled from pre-existing general ethics on social research. Also, many of these are more obviously applicable to photographs taken in clearly defined research contexts, as suggested by the consideration on 'negotiating representational authority' (ibid.: 11). Every time I accompanied students to the 'field' for training in field research techniques at different times from the 1990s to about 2009, I drilled into them the need to clearly seek permission from everyone before taking any photographs (see Image 7.1). This was necessary because photography had already become something ordinary and easily doable, initially in print form, and later digitally. Although research ethics in general was a mandatory part of pre-field training instructions for these groups, photographic ethics had no formal reference in the structured instructions that were given. My intervention was merely due to my own interest in photography and the reflection on ethics that had gone into it. In any event, in southern Sri Lankan villages and small towns where these forays

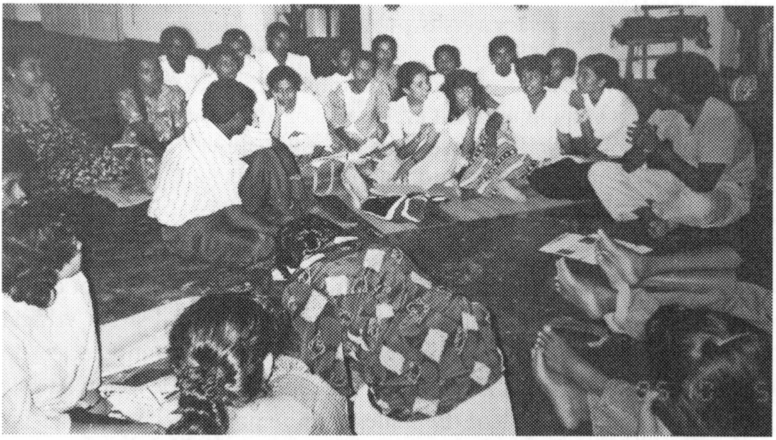

IMAGE 7.1 In-field discussions with students from University of Colombo on research ethics, photo ethics, and dynamics of training in progress, Koggala, Sri Lanka, 1995.

Photograph courtesy of: Dr Anula Ratnayake.

mostly took place, no one said no to requests to capture images. This is partly because what was being done was well understood by the communities concerned, to whom it had been explained prior to field visits as well as while the process was ongoing. It is also the result of the fact that universities still enjoyed a certain degree of social and political esteem, within which all of our activities were perceived.

In the initial period, these images did not proceed beyond the limited reports of the process produced at the end of each programme. The students sometimes made copies for themselves. But in most cases, they remained in the library of the Department of Sociology at University of Colombo—largely unread or under-read. Much later, I recall informing the people who were willing to be photographed while we were in their villages and streets that some of these images would also end up online. That was when I had briefly set up a blog dedicated to these programmes for wider discussion. Again, there was no resistance, due to the same reasons given above. But in the latter case, the images had a much wider reach and discursive potential than the first example, and clearly none of the people involved (the people in the photos as well as the student and faculty photographers) had any control over where these images might end up. Today, I assume that such images would go even further, given the reach opened up by forums such as Twitter, Facebook, Instagram, and so on, to which the present generations are so naturally linked. But at the time, we reminded ourselves of two facts as a matter of self-conscious explanation to ourselves: first, we had formally asked for permission with regard to all acts of photography, and had also explained that they might end up on the internet. Second, these were not images of exceptional circumstances, or exceptional moments or places. Instead, they were very ordinary moments in the day-to-day lives of ordinary people in their routine contexts of living and working.

Image 7.2 comes from a similar research situation in Dambana in southern Sri Lanka, where I was part of a team attempting to make a documentary film on the indigenous community, the Veddas. In addition to the film itself, the project also involved a heavy emphasis on photography,[4] which included photographs taken by young people from the community itself, as well as myself and other members of the

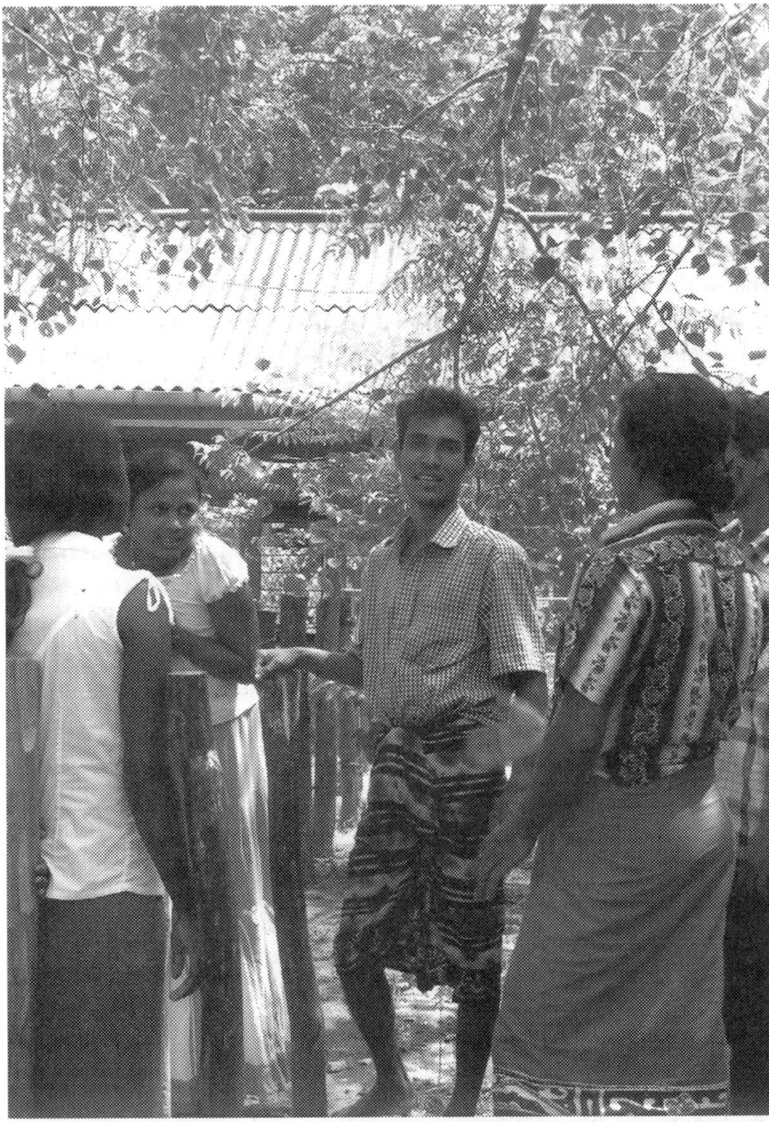

IMAGE 7.2 Research and film project participants in conversation, Dambana, Sri Lanka, 2009.

Photograph courtesy of: Author's research collection.

research and film teams. All photos generated by this project, including Image 7.2, were captured with the consent of the participants via somewhat elaborate negotiations with the community leader. And, as noted above, many of the local youth were among the photographers. Similarly, Image 7.3, which shows a conversation between the community chieftain and my team members, was taken by me with his permission. Consent for making the film, taking photographs, and getting the community involved in both the film and photography was part of a very formal and lengthy process, involving many days of negotiations that culminated in written approvals. This was possible because, with regard to photography as well as filming, our presence and what we were doing were largely controlled, almost to the extent of being choreographed. This permission was taken from the chieftain, who also took part in the film. The conversational moment captured in Image 7.3 was necessitated to show the chieftain the photos that we as outsiders as well as the members of his own community had

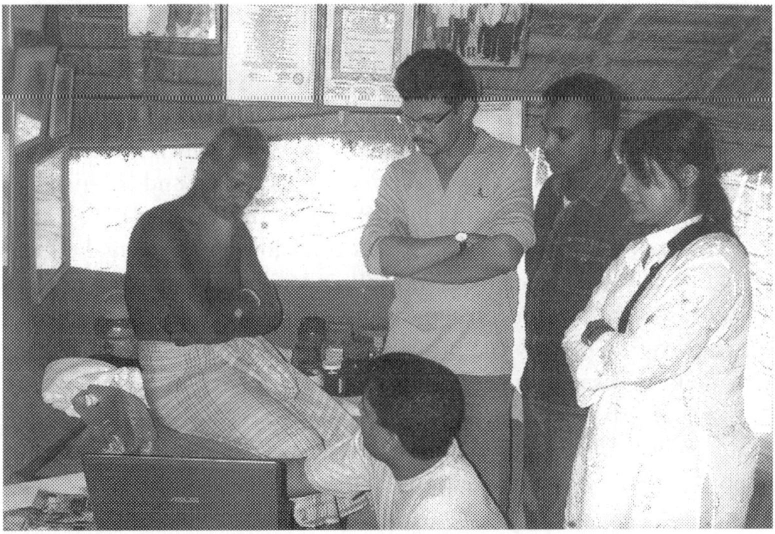

IMAGE 7.3 A conversation about photos, Dambana, Sri Lanka, 2009.
Photograph courtesy of: Author's research collection.

taken prior to the making of the film. The laptop was the repository for these images. The photograph stands as testimony to our attempt to deal with some of the issues referred to in the seven points outlined by Marion and Crowder. Interestingly, the photograph also partially captures the impact of photography in the life of the chieftain himself. On the walls right around the space where he usually meets visitors, a large collection of photographs featuring his father as well as himself on different occasions with national and regional political and social leaders helped to create his public personality. In that sense, he understood the work and politics of photography quite well.

The point I wish to make here is this: When it comes to photographs taken in the context of a research project where photography has been formally factored into the overall research process, thinking ethically in the conventional sense becomes much easier and simpler. In such contexts, the kind of issues raised by Marion and Crowder become less challenging to address and negotiate with. This is because ideally, general research ethics should also govern how one captures images and uses them in predefined research situations. But the problem is, images do not merely come from such research contexts. What about images produced in other situations, marked by leisure and everyday interactions? What about photos from the colonial archives, personal archives of people from the past whose provenance might be lost, images that come to us from online sources, and so on? How are research ethics implicated in these situations where photographs pre-exist any notions of research or a consciousness of visual ethics? It is in such a context that Tarr observes that 'visual methods in social research have become more mainstream over the last twenty years, driven in part by the profusion of digital devices with cameras that make access and production of images far easier...' (Tarr 2015). However, as she also notes, even though images have become more commonly available, 'ethical guidelines have sometimes struggled to adapt' to these evolving situations (ibid.).

Anxieties over Informed Consent, Anonymity, and Privacy

According to Tarr, the two most important ethical issues which tend to pose complex challenges in visual research in recent times are 'informed consent' and 'anonymity' (Tarr 2015). In keeping with my own anxieties about photographing people due to the difficulties in constantly seeking consent referred to at the very beginning of this chapter, Tarr notes that ensuring informed consent 'is particularly challenging with photographs because it is difficult to ensure that every subject has given their consent to the photo being taken and used for research purposes' (ibid.). In a visual context, getting informed consent refers not only to getting authorisation to produce photographs or a film, as the case may be, but also to reproduce and display the material among different audiences as well as in very different contexts (Clark 2012: 19). It is in this context that Pink has said that the public display, publishing, and wider circulation of visual data without the consent of the people in the images is ethically questionable (Pink 2007). Harper has pointed out the manner in which some practitioners have referred to earlier examples from photojournalism and photo-documentary to argue that no harm can possibly befall individuals in photos if it is a matter of 'showing normal people doing normal things' (2005: 759). This is a matter of relying on earlier precedence on seemingly related practices to deal with, or rather, escape from, a dilemma in a thoroughly contemporary research situation. Then the question is: If the visuals are about such ordinary circumstances, then why are they needed in published works in the first place? What would they add in terms of both information and discursive merit to an argument?

All these debates and ideas have emanated from research situations where visual approaches have been built into the research process. But, as already noted, consent is not a difficult issue to address in controlled research conditions or even in field research sites, which are manageable in terms of scale within which a researcher would spend a considerable period of time. But the difficulty arises when one has to address issues of consent with regard to photographs generally taken outside of a research context, where these issues would not have emerged in the first place. In many non-research contexts, such as in situations of evolving political action or public social fanfare, the consent of a subject is often assumed.

Particularly in today's ubiquitous and camera-heavy environment, if one takes part in a political rally or a wedding, the likelihood of being photographed is considerable. And similar possibilities exist of these photographs being shared in news or social media. If one goes to these kinds of public gatherings, consent to being photographed as well as for the genesis of their afterlife online or in print is a 'given'. In this context, we know quite well that—ideals apart—there will be no photojournalism if informed consent in its most inclusive and radical form is fully put into practice. Hawkey and Jeffrey, writing on the basis of their experience in what they call 'humanitarian photography', argue that informed consent 'offers little to protect the rights or dignity of people we photograph', and also works to 'reduce the photographer's ability to capture spontaneous and compelling images' (Hawkey and Jeffrey 2016). For them, two specific understandings of ethics govern the practice of their genre of photography. In general, this can be subsumed under documentary photography where images ideally should record facts on the ground in an evidential sense. To be more precise, their concern is whether a particular photograph they have taken 'accurately depicts the life of the subjects and the situation in which they live', and whether these images 'depict the subjects with respect and dignity' (ibid.). Their overall argument is that these two ethical considerations would be seriously compromised if 'informed consent', as it is understood today, governs their photographic practice (ibid.). Hawkey and Jeffery note that if a discussion on 'informed consent' were to take place prior to the capture of an image, it can easily lead to a change in the behaviour of the people to be photographed (ibid.). As a result, 'the resulting photograph is no longer accurate' (ibid.). This is a clear example of the difficulties involved in implementing 'informed consent' on the ground, at least with regard to this kind of photography.

Even today, when the gaze of the camera has become ubiquitous and is taken for granted, many people are concerned about street photography or public photography. That is, they are anxious of the possibility of being photographed somewhere, and of those images being shared online or published. This concern emanates from issues of privacy as well as informed consent. It was in such a situation of anxiety that Sophie Wilkinson wrote in protest when she found that an image of her having a meal in an underground train in the UK had been posted without her knowledge on a Facebook page called 'Women Who Eat On Tubes' (Wilkinson 2014). She says that she felt 'hurt and humiliated' by the image as well as by the comments it had generated (ibid.). But Wilkinson's is merely one of many similar examples of people who have been offended at seeing their image in public without their consent. I was one of them too, for a long time. But today, I have begun to realise that there is no possibility of avoiding this if we are keen to be in the public sphere as a routine and necessary part of our lives. In certain ways, this is like the postmodern position on the 'death of the author' when one's text enters the public domain, as the result of which the author's hold on the text comes to an end. When it comes to publicly captured imagery, although we are not the 'authors' of these images, our right to control them comes to an end by virtue of our being in public spaces by our own volition. This is a necessary and largely unavoidable aspect of contemporary living.

With reference to this situation, Friedman has noted that in the context of contemporary life, four words in the English language are in the process of becoming obsolete, and might be dropped from the vocabulary. And these words are 'privacy', 'local', 'average', and 'later' (Friedman 2014). Particularly with regard to privacy, he notes, 'everyone with a cellphone camera is paparazzi, everyone with access to Twitter and a cellphone voice recorder is a reporter and everyone who can upload video on YouTube is a filmmaker, everyone else is a public figure—and fair game' (ibid.). Although perhaps mildly exaggerated, the overall reality that Friedman has painted is a fact of contemporary life. That is, in the kind of context he has outlined, which is global, it has now become a matter of routine for 'anyone to record, film or photograph anyone else anywhere and share it with the world' (ibid.). What Friedman has animated through his words is the nature of the contemporary global public sphere that has been constructed by the combination of two elements: our attitude to public life in general, and our acceptance and practice of the ubiquitous and invasive technologies that we have come to embrace thoughtlessly. The latter, of course, partly refers to day-to-day things like the wide circulation of cameras and the ability to capture images of routine events and people, and the availability of easily accessible technology to share these instantly online. As a result of this state of affairs, we 'cannot assume anything is private anymore' (ibid.).

In this general situation, 'privacy', as we used to understand it even in the twentieth century, no longer applies in the same manner in present times in the twenty-first century. And this is most obvious when it comes to public photography, and our possible implication in it as a photographer or as a subject. In such situations of public photography, consent is generally subsumed under other assumptions such as 'the public's need to know', 'freedom of expression', 'newsworthiness', 'the ubiquitous prevalence of cameras', and so on. But most people who engage in public photography will not think of it in such specific or categorical terms. This is particularly so for leisure photography. Such thinking is an afterthought on the part of reflective scholarship. It is in such generalised contexts that Tarr has suggested that researchers who might want to use images generated in non-research situations can bypass the issue of informed consent by opting for the following approaches:

> 1. By using only photos that are taken in public spaces;
> 2. By avoiding the use of photographs of individuals who are not participating in a clearly defined research project. (Tarr 2013)

But this is hardly a concrete solution to enforce ethics. With regard to the first approach, what exactly constitutes a public space is itself often difficult to fathom. Even if one can recognise a park, a beech, the grounds of a public monument, or a similar space as a legally defined public space, the potential to be photographed in such a space does not naturally emerge from its legal or publicly endowed status as a public space. After all, many people, including myself, would prefer to go to a public space and not be subjected to photography. But as I have noted above, this level of privacy is no longer plausible. It is not a reality in our time. As such, the potential to be photographed in a public space emerges not from its legal or public status, but from the reality that cameras embedded in day-to-day objects such as mobile phones have not been banned from such places in general, and photography or videography in particular might also not be specially prohibited in these places. Also, we as a species who have readily embraced cheap technologies, from mobile phone-based cameras to the internet, have not collectively and convincingly sought to enforce an end to public photography or its online circulation. As such, we have to assume that images taken in a 'public space' are acceptable for other people's leisure, for research, news, and other purposes because everyone stands the same chance of being photographed by the State, private entities or individuals, whether one wishes to or not, due to the taken-for-granted technological, behavioural, and attitudinal conditions of contemporary times.

Steve Schlackman's (2016) musings with regard to street photography also throw some light on this situation. Obviously, street photographs taken by professional or hobby photographers are very close to the kind of photography in public spaces that I have discussed so far. As Schlackman notes, in general, 'if a photographer is shooting from a *public space*, such as a street or a park, he or she will usually have the right to do so without the consent of the subjects' (ibid.). This comes from the assumption that if one can see something from a public space, it is possible to take a photograph of that object or event (ibid.). The point he is trying to make is that considerations of privacy become limited when they intersect with the realities of contemporary public space. As he argues, if privacy is understood as 'the state or condition of being free from being observed or disturbed by other people', 'it would be objectively unreasonable to expect privacy on a city street or on a crowded subway' (ibid.). To put in context Schlackman's ideas more clearly, a person gives up 'any expectation that you cannot be "observed or disturbed by other people" by virtue of entering a public space or being in a position where you can be seen by others in a public space' (ibid.). Effectively, in contemporary times, the moment one steps out of the protected realms of private space into public space, much of one's privacy, particularly with regard to being photographed, comes to an end.

It is to this overall situation that Azoulay refers when she notes, 'the modern citizen has renounced the exclusive right to his or her image in favour of an economy of images' (Azoulay 2008: 124). In that economy of images, each individual has the potential to capture other people's images while at the same time, s/he gives up their own rights of privacy and allows others to capture their image as well. This works as an unavoidable social contract of contemporary times by virtue of living under conditions that have made this possible. As she further argues, correctly, despite the intrusive nature of contemporary photography, 'every participant not only contemplates what can be seen but is also herself, exposed and visible' (ibid.: 96). Her observations are not made in a negative sense, but in a situation where the over-exposed nature of contemporary global realities is adequately taken into account. In this state of affairs, images are constantly captured, routinely stored electronically, and equally as often, released on the internet.

In these general circumstances, let me briefly refer to two images I have captured in public space, which would put some of these issues into further context. These are Images 7.4 and 7.5. Image 7.4 shows a woman taking a photograph with her mobile phone camera in the public grounds surrounding the Taj Mahal in Agra, India. I have called it 'The Lady with the Camera'. Thousands of people like her and myself visit this specific site everyday and capture thousands of images, like both she and I have done. Many of these might end up online as well. These images capture not just the Taj Mahal or other adjacent structures, but people who have come to visit the place as well. My camera initially captured her accidentally as I was gazing around for an interesting angle from which to photograph some of the monumental structures with sprawling lawns in the foreground. She was trying to photograph a distant building, while the photograph she took also captured the people walking towards her along the footpath on which she stood. My accidental encounter led to a conscious decision to take her picture while she was engaged in the same practice. I have no idea how many other people (if any) might have captured my attempt as well.

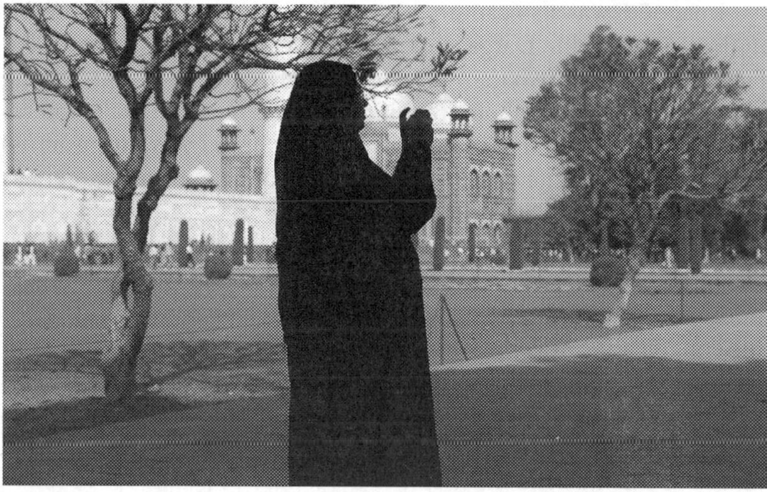

IMAGE 7.4 'The Lady with the Camera', Agra, India, March 2012.
Photograph courtesy of: Author's research collection.

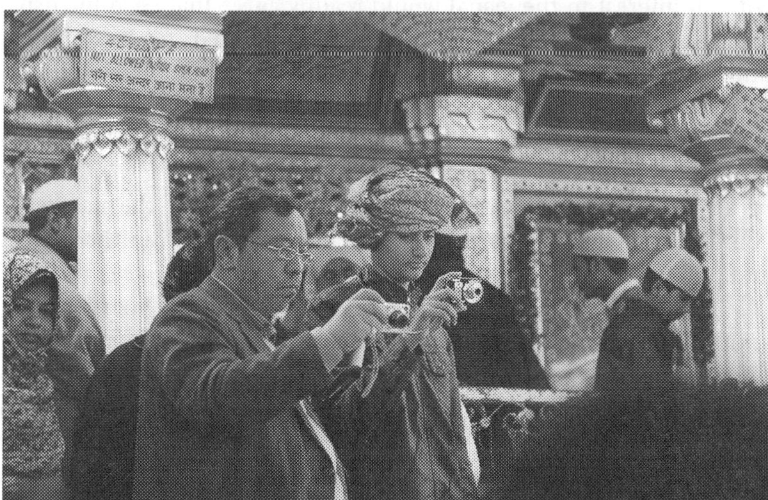

IMAGE 7.5 'Focussed'. Nizamuddin Darga, New Delhi, India, January 2011.
Photograph courtesy of: Author's research collection.

Image 7.5 was also captured in a public space, within the interior of the Nizamuddin Darga complex in Delhi, which I have called 'Focussed'. It shows two men very deliberately, and in both cases using just one single hand, photographing with two small digital cameras the people and the activities in front of them. Since I was sitting across from them, they quite possibly photographed me with my camera as well, the same way that I photographed them.

In both public spaces referred to in these two photographs—one in an open space and the other within a cluster of buildings—thousands of people were congregating, and one precondition of this congregation was the deliberate and self-conscious relaxation of personal space and privacy. My sense is that in today's circumstances such as these, most people are conscious of the fact that cameras are often gazing at them and accidentally or consciously capturing images of them all the time. This is the nature of public space today. But this kind of public photography needs to be distinguished from the covert or clandestine photography utilised by some journalists and researchers in specific contexts. Most reasonable researchers with an interest in the visual would readily agree that such intrusive approaches are clearly unethical. But compared to this, public photography captured in public spaces, such as those I have referred to above, where all individuals (including the photographer) have a reasonably equal chance of being photographed, can be thought of as reasonable objects of research and reflection. Viewing such images in terms of anonymity or privacy in the context of the nature of contemporary public space is difficult to sustain, both in theoretical and practical terms.

These two images also offer me the opportunity to reflect on another related matter with regard to visual ethics. Of the numerous different approaches to research ethics, the most common perhaps are the consequentionalist, non-consequentionalist, principalist, and ethics of care approaches (Wiles, et al. 2008: 6–7). It seems to me that if one's focus is on photographs produced in non-research conditions, any thinking on visual ethics in such contexts might best be served if it is based on a consequentionalist approach. The basic assumption of this approach is that the ethical decisions that researchers make should ultimately relate to the kind of consequences their actions might precipitate. That is, the outcome of an action—such as the publishing of a particular photo—should be clearly thought through prior to undertaking that specific action (ibid.). As Wiles, et al. note, one needs to be certain that a specific 'action is morally right if it will produce the greatest balance of good over evil' (ibid.). But the publishing or the use of a photograph in an intellectual endeavour is not only a matter of good over evil in terms of benefits, but can also be for a much less august consideration. Even this would vary from the simple generation of knowledge on the one hand, to the career enhancement of the researcher her/himself on the other. But if we are using images taken in a non-research context by the researcher or by others, the issue of 'benefits' may never touch the subjects in the images. But what does it mean when images become publicly accessible via scholarship or discourse of some other kind? This is the issue that needs to be most seriously considered when dealing with images from public spaces. Hence, when I considered the merits of using Images 7.4 and 7.5 in this book as photographs taken in public spaces, I could see no potential danger to the people within their frames, whom I do not personally know. These were very ordinary images taken in public spaces, depicting people taking photographs, an act that thousands of other people were also engaged in on those days at the two sites. But I also knew that their publication would not bring them any specific benefits, although it might very well benefit me in making my argument pictorially clearer. My final assumption was that by virtue of being in the contemporary public space from which cameras have not been specifically banned, consent is implicated in these two images, while anonymity is no longer possible in this kind of public space.

The second aspect of Tarr's solution with regard to informed consent suggests the avoidance of photographs of people not specifically participating in a clearly identified research project. This, I suggest, is much less pragmatic. In contemporary circumstances, most photographs are generated by people in non-research everyday conditions. Images 7.4 and 7.5 are merely two out of many such examples in my own collection. For creative researchers, such photographs may offer nuanced reflective possibilities. The mere possibility that a specific photograph may pre-exist the intent of research need not disqualify it from being considered for research as well as writing. If we adopt this precondition based on cautious and radical avoidance, which as an ideal makes sense, entire archives otherwise available for research would be lost. This would include images we have captured in conditions of leisure, family albums, colonial archives, and so on. Given this reality, the first conditionality—that of opting for photos from public spaces—notwithstanding the liminalities of what public space might mean in specific conditions, offer much better leeway for the use of photography in research, and root it more seriously in contemporary conditions.

Ensuring the 'anonymity' of a person or locations in a photograph is the other main ethical challenge that Tarr (2013) refers to. But sites and people are 'difficult to anonymise' in a photograph (ibid.) without causing serious structural damage to the photo itself. On the other hand, 'strategies for making people anonymous, such as pixelating faces or putting black bars over their eyes to make them less recognisable are more frequently associated with criminal activity' (ibid.). This unduly links the use of such images in social research to a popular understanding of criminality, which brings in its own negative baggage. But nowadays, pixelating images with the use of computer software is entirely possible as a means of making images (particularly of people) less recognisable. Although issues of anonymity and confidentiality are central concerns in most conventional social research situations, and are rightly recognised as core aspects of good practices in research, these twin issues become far more challenging in contexts of visual research. As Clark observes, 'it is often impossible, impractical, or even illogical to maintain the anonymity and confidentiality of individuals in artwork, photographs and film' (Clark 2012: 21). And having to disfigure images to maintain anonymity and confidentiality 'may destroy the very purpose of producing data visually' (ibid.).

What is intriguing is the seemingly different ways in which the issue of anonymity applies to different kinds of images. The concern with anonymity has obviously been borrowed from social research ethics in general. But this seems to be a concern for people working with still photographs—or it has been made into a concern for them. Comparatively, however, this does not seem to be an issue in the well-established traditions of ethnographic filmmaking. In almost no major ethnographic film production is it possible to see specific efforts to anonymise participants in the films. And these are not still images, but moving images, where one can argue that there is a better chance of recognisability. Also, ethnographic films are mostly an effort of a conscious and well-designed research and film project. These images, therefore, are not accidental footage captured in public interactions. In such conditions, as with still photography under similar conditions, it can be argued that informed consent as well as anonymity, if necessary, could be guaranteed more easily. But there is no consistent tradition or convention in this direction in ethnographic filmmaking. Perhaps, as some observers have noted, this is because attempting to anonymise either individuals or even places in such films would be contrary to the very act of making such films (Pink 2007).

The options suggested as a way out of this situation include 'waiving anonymity with the explicit consent of the research participants, or avoiding taking or publishing identifiable images' (Tarr 2013). It seems to me that the issue of anonymity of place or people understood in the above sense would be very specific to a certain kind of research undertaken in specific circumstances, where privacy and secrecy are of paramount importance. These assumptions therefore cannot be generalised to research situations more broadly. Specifically, such conditionalities would govern in places and contexts where issues of security and personal safety of research participants might be significant considerations. For instance, when I had interviewed members of Tamil insurgent groups in Sri Lanka as part of my Ph.D. research in the 1990s, and Sri Lankan military officers involved in the wars against Tamil insurgents in northern Sri Lanka and Sinhala insurgents in southern Sri Lanka in the first decade of the present millennium, one condition under which many of them spoke to me was an assurance of their anonymity and privacy. While these conversations allowed me to understand the violence in Sri Lanka considerably better than would otherwise have been possible,

I have never explicitly written about them. They were never recorded at the time nor any notes kept on the details in order to assure the expectations of privacy and anonymity. And certainly no photographs were taken. Some of these people also acknowledged their direct roles in implementing specific incidents of political violence, including targeted killings. In such cases, the use of images should not even be considered within the basket of techniques at the disposal of a researcher. This is because such a choice makes very little contextual sense in ethical, methodological, or commonsensical terms.

When it comes to photos taken in the public space, as discussed above, and for images from private or colonial archives, the issue of anonymity needs to be decided on the basis of both informed research ethics and commonsense implicated by the realities and practices of contemporary times. This is not necessarily something for which one can expect to have 'all weather' rules. For instance, with regard to the colonial-period images in this book, secured from clearly identified formal sources, the issue of consent could not stretch beyond the current copyright holders or 'owners'. This is because the people depicted in the photos as well as the photographers were deceased long ago. And the collections of which these images were a part have changed hands many times over the years, while some also have a public presence online. In my own situation, I decided to deal with entities that had claims over specific images over a long period of time. In such cases, a copyright payment and a formal letter of consent resolved the issue of consent.

On the other hand, when it came to images from my own family collection, the decision to use specific images was my own. I assumed that since they are in my possession and quite possibly nowhere else, I should be able to take what amounts to an 'informed family decision' rather than an ethical decision on consent in the technical sense. When it came to images from the albums and collections of extended family members, I opted to consult the kin who are the present guardians of the collections concerned, and proceeded to take formal written letters of consent from them. A similar approach was used for images from other people who had shared their own personal collections for this book. Many images of this kind have been reproduced in

Chapter 5, dealing with wedding photography. The process adopted was much more formal, and was initiated through a Facebook post on 29 December 2017. It made the following request:

> If anyone is interested in sharing selections of their wedding and pre-wedding photographs with me, let me know. I hope to draw inspiration and cultivate ideas from these for my chapter, 'Framing and Performing Intimacy: An Incomplete Social History of Wedding Photographs' in the forthcoming book, 'A Fragmented History of Seeing: Photography, Anthropology and the Fear of the Visual.'[5] I am keen to see how and where these images are shot and how they are framed. Later, I may want to talk with some of these folks to better understand some of the details. If I plan to use any of these images in my book, I will write to the individuals concerned for permission. But for the moment, I am only interested in seeing some of these photos. Feel free to email me or send a Facebook message.

The post received fifteen comments and sixty-six 'likes', indicating the interest it generated. Some people proceeded to send in their images by Facebook mail (later Messenger), email, as well as physically in portable storage devices. With regard to the images that have finally been reproduced in the book, I sought specific written consent from the 'donors' as well as additional information via email. The same process was adopted for other personal images from individuals, which have been used in other chapters. So the issues of both consent and privacy were resolved in these cases formally through written consent.

But a more commonsensical approach had to be adopted with regard to the images in my research collection of colonial-period family portraits of unknown families and individuals from different parts of India, whose provenance has been completely lost. That is, it was nearly impossible to find out with any degree of accuracy who the people in these faded and forgotten photographs might be. These are effectively images from the past with no foreseeable sense of personal or legal ownership, not very different from the undifferentiated colonial archives freely available in public collections. These were, in effect, abandoned images or images sold to dealers by unknown people because their family linkages had been lost. I made the decision to use these images based on the fact that they had been secured from different informal dealers in Delhi and Mumbai over a period of about six years, dealers who had thousands of such photos in their un-catalogued collections, which are picked up by different people for varied reasons. I was one of those 'customers' who had purchased the images that have been used in this book.

Institutional Responses to Visual Ethics

Let me now briefly focus on how organisations with a core interest in visual research address the issue of ethics. I find it intriguing that the visual research ethics of many such organisations remain generally under defined. One obvious example is the International Visual Sociology Association. Its Code of Research Ethics is formally known as 'The International Visual Sociology Association (IVSA) Code of Research Ethics and Guidelines',[6] and is meant to guide 'visual researchers'. As a document, it is clearly a comprehensive body of social research ethics. However, this body of ethics is not that different from similar bodies of ethics promulgated by other professional research associations. It is in such a context that Wiles, et al. note that such general issues tend to be 'relevant to all research but the ethical issues raised by visual research are, arguably, distinct from those raised by purely textual data' (Wiles, et al. 2008: 8). They also note that the 'general nature of these professional codes and guidelines mean that the ethical issues relating to visual methods are not specifically addressed within most codes' (ibid.). To a large extent, these observations hold true. The International Visual Sociology Association's specific focus on issues such as photography is marginal at best. The only specific reference to photography comes within the subsection 'Use of Recording Technology', which states:

> *Researchers obtain informed consent from research participants, students, employees, clients, or others prior to photographing, videotaping, filming, or recording them in any form, unless these activities involve simply naturalistic observations in public places and it is not anticipated that the recording will be used in a manner that could cause harm.* Efforts to respond ethically to

> unintended circumstances and consequences are necessary in a multi-mediated environment. Reasonable efforts may include the visible use of technology (e.g. the led light on video cameras). Informal as well as subsequent formal permissions to record and make public these recordings may be in addition to formal informed consent procedures for research subjects.[7]

Again, it is clear that what is suggested is applicable mostly to photography in predetermined research settings. The only variation to this norm is selected photography in public spaces, implicated in the reference to 'naturalistic observations'. If such photographs are likely to be used in research, researchers are reminded to ensure that they do not bring any harm to the people in the photographs. That is, this position frees images taken in leisure or news contexts in public spaces for potential research. That decision, however, has to be taken by the researcher informed by the overall ethical considerations of social research, commonsense, as well as a clear understanding of photography's place in quotidian circumstances of contemporary life. In a sense, it is in such a context that I have also taken some of the decisions referred to earlier in this chapter.

In comparison, the code of ethics of the British Sociology Association's Visual Sociology Group offers far more extensive guidelines, which relate directly to the use of visual data in research. Of the sixty-nine clauses in the 'Statement Of Ethical Practice For The British Sociological Association—Visual Sociology Group',[8] twenty-one specifically address aspects of using or dealing with visual data in social research. The first of these, Clause No. 5, subsumed under 'Professional Integrity', notes:

> 5. In terms of research incorporating visual data, researchers should consider the potential risk of the dissemination of their results to themselves, the discipline and the individuals in the setting. For example, using politically sensitive images of right wing groups or youth violence may put the researchers and the individuals depicted in the visual data in danger of retaliation. Risk to personal safety should be taken seriously in the strategy and design of any given research project.[9]

This deals with issues of anonymity and the safety of the individuals involved, from researchers to the people depicted in images. As discussed earlier, these considerations apply to very specific research contexts involving issues of security and personal safety, in which the use of photographs needs to be seriously thought through. Similarly, one section of Clause No. 7 notes:

> 7. ... Of particular pertinence to the researcher(s) using visual methods are duties under UK Copyright Law. When using participants' own photographs, the researcher(s) should make the participant aware that, as creators of images, they (the image-makers(s) are legally the owners. Thus the researcher(s) must have the participants' permission to use the photographs in publication (including publications on websites).[10]

Here, the emphasis is on explaining that images created by researchers, as part of a research process, are owned by the researchers in the UK context. Even so, it suggests that researchers in such situations must still seek the permission of the participants prior to publishing these images. What the generality of such rules indicates is that they deal with a number of basic parameters which involves the following:

1. The safety of participants in research, depicted in visual data;
2. Maintaining the anonymity of such individuals where necessary;
3. Visual data and their implication in law if they depict illegal activities;
4. Legal ownership of visual data;
5. Informed consent prior to publication of visual data when it comes to images produced in research contexts; and
6. Images and issues such as copyright.

In 2001, the American Anthropological Association, in collaboration with the Society for Visual Anthropology, issued a statement titled 'AAA Guidelines for the Evaluation of Ethnographic Visual Media'.[11] This was revised in 2015. While accepting that 'ethnographic visual media (specifically film, video, photography, digital multimedia, and exhibition) play a significant role in the production and application of anthropological knowledge and form an integral part of the discipline's course offerings and research outputs',[12] the statement's sole focus is on how to evaluate such output in scholarly terms.

The statement also acknowledges that 'visual representations offer viewers a means to experience and understand ethnographic complexity, richness and depth, which are the distinguishing features of anthropological knowledge',[13] in the context of which 'visual media convey critical forms of knowledge that written accounts cannot'.[14] Despite this importance given to visual media in the context of the anthropological scholarly world, dominated by the power of the written word, and hence the statement's advice on how to evaluate such material, it is silent on how to produce them. In fact, AAA does not offer any specific guidelines on visual research, despite its recognition of the crucial importance of visual data within forms of anthropological knowledge. Ethical considerations that will necessarily come up in all such research are expected to be covered by the general 'Code of Ethics of the American Anthropological Association', initially approved in 1998.[15]

However, over the past eight years, the Society for Visual Anthropology has been organising ongoing annual forums on ethics coordinated by members of its Ethics Committee, which are presented during the annual sessions of the American Anthropological Association. These interventions are expected to reflect on 'the ethical dimensions of anthropological imaging'.[16] These discussions, presently available online via video, address visual ethics in the context of clearly grounded case studies. These include Miguel Diaz-Barriga and Margaret E. Dorsey's discussion, 'Can the Border Wall be Photographed? Public Anthropology and National Security';[17] Sabra Thorner's discussion, 'Indigenizing Photography: Interfaces and Ethics in Contemporary Australia';[18] Thet Shein Win's presentation, 'Persistence of Vision: The Ethics of Artistic Labor in the Visual Effects Industry';[19] Brent Luvaas' presentation, 'After Anonymity: Visual Ethics and the Culture of Online Self-Promotion';[20] and Barbara Hoffman's discussion, 'Images in the Cloud, Ethics on the Ground';[21] among others. While these discussions have generated some very interesting and reflective thoughts on ethics in very specific situations of visual research (including photography), they do not seem to have led to the emergence of a coherent body of visual ethics within the Society for Visual Anthropology.

However, given its broad applicability, a brief focus on Barbara Hoffman's 'Images in the Cloud, Ethics on the Ground', shows the potential of such deliberations in constructing a coherent body of research ethics that may be applicable both in specific situations and in broader contexts where visual methods might be used. With special reference to students in her classes who belong to the millennial generation, Hoffman asks, '[W]hat is informed consent when the investigator is a member of the first generation to come of age with MySpace, Facebook, Twitter, Instagram, and Tumblr?'[22] Her broader implication is that issues such as informed consent would mean something very different thing to this generation. This is because people of this generation tend to live in a time over-saturated by imagery. In this specific context, she further asks whether 'all possible uses of photos and video taken in the field be covered in the document interlocutors are asked to sign?'[23] Or, alternatively, if any images can be 'taken for granted in this age of ubiquitous visual documentation of everyday life?'[24] Hoffman marks the distinct difference in concern for visual ethics between herself and the present generation of her students in the following observation: 'Uploading project imagery to Instagram, Facebook, Tumblr, and blogs immediately raised issues of accessibility, privacy, permissions, informed consent, and long-term implications to me in ways that seemed quite distinct from those of my students.'[25] But it does not appear that the reflective knowledge base on ethics that scholars such as Hoffman and others have opened up on the basis of very real experiences on the ground when dealing with visual research has led to a larger codified system of ethics at the Society for Visual Anthropology.

What becomes quite clear when exploring the nuances of the codes of conduct adopted by mainstream professional organisations is that most bodies of rules have been evolved by assuming that visual data in general will be generated as an inbuilt part of the research process itself. Or, as in the case of the AAA, there are no references to visual data at all. Or, as with the Society for Visual Anthropology, there is discursive space to discuss visual ethics, without an apparent institutional mechanism—yet—to lead these ideas towards codification as a general body of ethics. As Clark has noted, what is implicit in the development of bodies of ethics by organisations such as the International Visual Sociology Association and others with a clear interest in visual research referred to above is their encouragement of an 'aspirational' spirit, as opposed to a more robust 'prescriptive or exhaustive instruction' on visual research procedures (Clark 2012: 19). It seems to me that Clark's explanation for such seeming flexibility is linked to the kind of ethical issues that visual researchers might face in less straightforward contexts, as opposed to what one might expect when using conventional research methods, and hence the difficulty in resolving these issues in the abstract or prescriptive sense (ibid.).

While many of the ethical positions proposed by organisations such as the International Visual Sociology Association and the Visual Sociology Group of the British Sociological Association may be applicable to photography in pre-defined research situations, or can be modified to suit these contexts, none of them directly or robustly attempt to deal with photographs generated from contemporary social conditions, delinked from research at the time the photos originated. This is mostly because such situations are too liminal and nonlinear, and are difficult to fathom, define, and grasp. It is to such liminal contexts that Prosser referred when speaking of the lacuna in the availability of broadly accepted principles of ethical practices pertaining to visual methods and theoretical positions (Prosser 2000). This lacuna makes it difficult to make informed judgements on visual ethics devoid of contradictions (ibid.).

In such situations, much is left to the commonsense of researchers and to their personal dynamics within which they might interpret the visual ethics that confront them, based upon the general ethical principles of social research and personal decency, which hopefully will be an integral part of their professional training and habitus.

Notes

1. Some of the ideas discussed in this chapter were initially presented in the essay, 'Privacy, Consent and Public Photography in "Over-exposed" Times', published in 2018. This is scheduled to be published in the *Visual Arts Journal*, 2020, India Habitat Centre.

2. Most of the observations above are taken from my lecture, 'Intricacies, Ethics and Anxieties of Fieldwork in Sites of Contestation' delivered at the workshop 'Doing Research; Doing Ethnography: Workshop for Young Sociologists', organised by the Indian Sociological Society and XXXVII All India Sociological Conference at Indian Institute of Technology, Delhi, 9 December 2011.

3. The seminar was co-organised by Nukta Art and Goethe Institut Karachi, 25–26 October 2008,

4. More details on this project is presented in my essay, 'Photography's Methodological Absence in Social Anthropology in South Asia: Some Preliminary Thoughts for Consideration' (Perera 2018).

5. Please note that since 2017, when this Facebook notice was posted, the chapter title referred to and the title of this book have changed.

6. Visit the IVSA's website for the complete text of 'The International Visual Sociology Association (IVSA) Code of Research Ethics and Guidelines', available at http://visualsociology.org/?page_id=405 (accessed 24 December 2017).

7. Emphasis added. See http://visualsociology.org/?page_id=405 (accessed 24 December 2017).

8. For the full text of the Statement Of Ethical Practice For The British Sociological Association—Visual Sociology Group, please see http://www.visualsociology.org.uk/about/ethical_statement.php (accessed 24 December 2017).

9. http://www.visualsociology.org.uk/about/ethical_statement.php (accessed 24 December 2017).

10. Ibid.

11. The complete statement is available at: http://www.americananthro.org/ConnectWithAAA/Content.aspx?ItemNumber=1941 (accessed 30 June 2018).

12. http://www.americananthro.org/ConnectWithAAA/Content.aspx?ItemNumber=1941 (Accessed 30 June 2018).

13. Ibid.

14. Ibid.

15. https://s3.amazonaws.com/rdcms-aaa/files/production/public/FileDownloads/pdfs/issues/policy-advocacy/upload/ethicscode.pdf (accessed 30 June 2018).

16. http://societyforvisualanthropology.org/about/ethics/ (accessed 30 June 2018).

17. http://societyforvisualanthropology.org/about/ethics/diaz-barriga-dorsey/(accessed 29 June 2018).

18. http://societyforvisualanthropology.org/about/ethics/sabra-thorner/ (accessed 29 June 2018).

19. http://societyforvisualanthropology.org/about/ethics/thet-win/ (accessed 29 June 2018).

20. http://societyforvisualanthropology.org/about/ethics/brent-luvaas/ (accessed 29 June 2018).

21. http://societyforvisualanthropology.org/about/ethics/barbara-hoffman/ (accessed 29 June 2018).

22. Ibid.

23. Ibid.

24. Ibid.

25. Ibid.

eight

PHOTOGRAPHY AS A 'FLEETING, CASUAL AND UNTHINKING' PRACTICE

I'm particularly curious about the photo you took of the pain viennois, those long-ridged rolls of bread that drew you in closer and closer. I'm sure your lens was clean enough to eat off, since you held it for so long only centimetres away from the tray of food.

Ode To The Thoughtless Photographer, by Fernando Gros[1]

A *close relative of* mine, who belongs to my generation, spends a considerable amount of time photographing food when she goes out, which is often. Sometimes she does this at home, too, when the food is not ordinary, such as during a party. A sandwich decorated atop with lettuce, a colourful salad, an ordinary curry, a seemingly happily decked lobster, a blue drink in a tall glass with a tiny umbrella precariously perched on its rim, and anything else equally capture her interest. She practices her ubiquitous and all-weather photography with her mobile phone. Some of these photos end up on her Facebook page with minimum written text, merely noting when, where, and sometimes with whom. But many others remain in her upgraded camera memory as a mass of clutter without any clear division into separate folders, until she runs out of space. When that happens, she routinely deletes some images on the basis of a very casual glance over them, making space for the new ones. And this cycle repeats itself. Fleeting culinary memories are almost routinely captured, and equally as routinely released to the internet and quite as casually deleted. With her, photographs have exceptionally short lifespans and equally shorter memories. Passing moments barely become memories before they are discarded, both in their pictorial form and perhaps in terms of remembrance as well. The reason for such casual deletion of photographs is because what was photographed had no significant reference to a memorable moment or an object in the first place. That is, some of these photographs are hardly records of moments with specific references. They are glimpses of a fleeting existence that probably do not conjure up even a fragmentary recollection in most people's lives. And yet, she religiously engages in this practice routinely. It is a part of her life. It is literally a fleeting, thoughtless, casual, and almost a reflexive action without the investment of much time or thought.

However, such photography is a part not only of her life, but also that of many other people. They would photograph, if not fleeting culinary moments, then equally ordinary gatherings in the most ordinary of places with people one meets all the time, or with people one does not know personally, and whom one is not likely to meet again. They would photograph some unknown person singing on stage. When I invited a colleague to a Western classical music concert in New Delhi in 2016, he promptly fell asleep in the middle of the concert, proceeding to snore loudly. I could see the glares being cast in our direction because of the noises emanating from my sleeping colleague. Then he suddenly woke up, and without hesitation fished out his mobile phone and took a number of photographs of the performers on stage with the flash on, while the camera let out computerised clicks to indicate that an act of photography was in progress. More glares were now coming our way. And this action was from a man who had already indicated his disinterest in classical music. As part of our routine life, we will see this kind of photography wherever we go. Someone might simply photograph a young woman in a mall, posing next to an expensive car as part of an advertising routine. Another might be drawn to the Christmas promotion an airport had put up in its public area, with a large and aesthetically questionable representation of Santa Claus. Often, none of the people objectified in these photos are the significant others of the photographers. They might never meet, see or hear of them again. Some of the objects or fields of clutter photographed are so ordinary in the present circumstances that one might never think of them again. Yet, they are diligently photographed. And they are casually deleted when the need arises. What kind of photography would this be?

How does one explain this casualness and thoughtlessness in photography? And what does it do to memory? Or can this even be explained in terms of memory? What does this practice say about a person's taste in the sense articulated by Pierre Bourdieu? And where in the history of photography is this practice located?

As I have explained with regard to the recent manifestation of selfies in Chapter 4, this kind of casual and fleeting photography has to be understood as a quintessential social practice of the twenty-first century, informed directly by the lifestyles and, more importantly, by the technologies widely available in this specific time. This practice could not have originated in any time other than the present, in which a number of technologies have come together to make this possible, and inevitable. These are digital photography, its wide availability through powerful cameras embedded in mobile phones, the internet and easy access to it via mobile phones and other devices that allow such casually captured images to be shared widely, albeit equally as casually, and finally, what appears to be a globally prevalent attitude where many people think of such casual photography as a norm or an acquired 'taste' of the times, which needs to be engaged with in order to be part of this time. This, then, is the backdrop against which such photography must be located and made sense of.

When I refer to these photographs as casual, fleeting or thoughtless, I do not mean, however, that they are devoid of meaning. What I mean instead is that to capture such images, one need not invest much time or thought. It is precisely due to this reason that many such images have a very short lifespan. That is, such photography has no clearly defined references to specific moments or times important in the life of the photographer due to the liminality of the practice itself. Photographs taken in this sense almost seem to defy the cultural and emotional imperatives of time and place, and exist in a timeless continuum of non-significance until they come to a sudden end. So, is memory implicated or not implicated in the reading of this kind of photography? That is, for memory to be implicated in their reading, do anticipations of memory and recollection in the future via these photographs play any role in the taking of these photographs? In the Introduction, I referred to Orhan Pamuk's contention, 'we were having our photographs taken in anticipation of our own gaze back' (Pamuk 2017). Given that anticipation, embedded into the act of photography itself, 'when we faced the camera, we were "posing" for the future' (ibid.). This is a clear reference to one of photography's major and perennial expectations of memory in many circumstances. To be precise, under most circumstances, particularly with regard to personal photographs, we expect the photos to take us to moments in our past, and that expectation is conventional photography's major implication in memory.

In a sense, this is what Maurice Halbwachs (1992) refers to as 'autobiographical memory', that is, the kind of memory understood as remembering events that individuals have personally experienced in the past. In a photographic sense, such moments of memory would be the photographs of weddings, birthdays, school events, family outings, and so on that an individual has been part of. At any time in the future, an individual can rely on these photographs to take her/him to the moments recorded in the photos. But such recollections should not be assumed to be a reference to a complete event or moment. According to Halbwachs, 'the past does not recur as such, that everything seems to indicate that the past is not preserved but reconstructed on the basis of the present" (ibid.: 39–40). So when we look at a photograph of a significant moment from the past, we would remember aspects of that event as it is seen from the present. However, some of the components that were initially part of what the photograph depicts might no longer be recallable. Image 8.1 depicts a number of former students and teachers (including myself) from the University of Colombo in the vicinity of the southern Sri Lankan village, Koggala, in 1995. This was shared by one of the students in the photo when I was looking for fieldwork photos of that time.

Indeed, this photograph had been taken one morning prior to the students going out for their work. But I had forgotten the exact place and time of the photograph and thought it depicted a colleague (on the left) speaking to a villager. That was primarily because this was the kind of image I was looking for, and also because I had not thought of this moment in a very long time, and had made no investments in time or thought in this photograph. But Jinali Chandrika Hettiarachchi, from whose personal album the photograph comes, had singular clarity on the details of the photograph. She informed me very clearly about the location and temporal details of the photograph, as well as who was in it, including myself.[2] The person I had thought was a villager tuned out to be me. This clarity of detail was possible for her as in her own circumstances, this had not been a casually captured image. Time had been invested in it, as well as thought. And many conversations would have been based on it at different times over the years when old friends met. As a result, it was possible for its guardian to narrate the details of the photograph fairly accurately, even though it had been taken twenty-three years ago. Such a possibility cannot exist with regard to the casual photographs I have focussed on in this chapter.

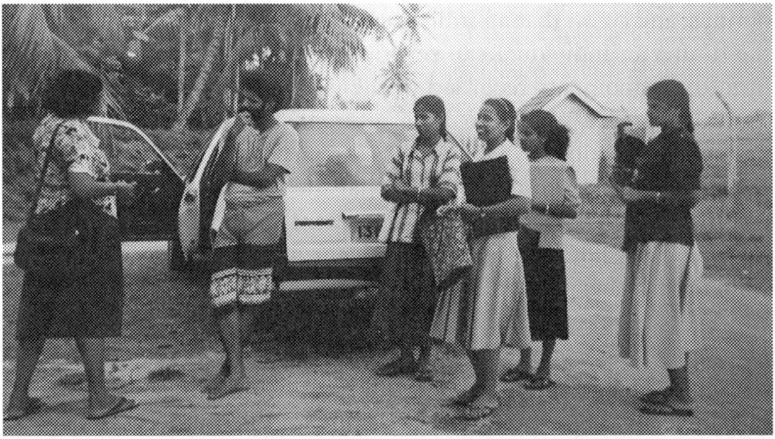

IMAGE 8.1 Fieldwork training by the Department of Sociology, University of Colombo in Koggla, Sri Lanka, 1995.
Photograph courtesy of: Jinali Chandrika Hettiarachchi.

As Halbwachs further notes, 'Most of the time, when I remember, it is others who spur me on; their memory comes to the aid of mine and mine relies on theirs' (Halbwachs 1992: 38). In such situations, photographs of specific events often work in much the same way as 'others spurring one on', in the sense suggested by Halbwachs. It is precisely how Image 8.1 worked once it came into my possession after twenty-three years, where others' memories certainly spurred me on as my own recollections were somewhat cloudy. In such circumstances, where memory plays an important role in offering signposts to the past, photographs as we conventionally understood them, or even photographs of the present time, such as wedding photographs, are triggers that bring back such memories. They are also signposts to a past that is worthy of remembrance and recollection. That is, when photos are triggers that unlock personal memories, such photographs ideally ought to have been the result of considerable effort, or at least of significant moments. But the kind of photos I am discussing in this chapter clearly do not fall into this category. As a result, casually and almost thoughtlessly framed photographs of nondescript objects such as dishes, cultural events, general scenes such as flower beds in parks, or ordinary meetings of friends are unlikely to 'spur' memories due to the lack of specificity in these kinds of photographs.

Bringing the past into the consciousness of the present is not a simple matter of remembering an incident from the past out of context. It is a much fuller and complex experience, even though much can also be left out of that reconstruction. As Kandel notes, it amounts to 'experiencing the atmosphere in which it occurred—the sights, sounds, and smells, the social setting, the time of day, the conversations, the emotional tone' (Kandel 2006: 3). Talking in the very different context of photography and violence, this is also what Tagg tries to explain with regard to the ability of photographs to bring 'feeling' into relatively 'un-feeling' prose (Tagg 2009: xx). As he notes,

> Photographs are there, sure enough. Nothing to remark on here. Except that, as the pain of memory rises, the unaffected prose turns chilled like the stone of a monument, and a thin film passes across the images like the ghost of Vladimir Nabokov, trying to catch something in his net. (ibid.)

Obviously, under most circumstances, including in the extreme conditions that Tagg refers to, photographs are fairly accurate means to specificities, despite possible lapses. That is why, after seeing Image 8.1 and particularly after its contextual parameters were established by others who remembered more clearly, many additional memories of people, situations, incidents, colours, and sounds of the area, and even memories of the sea, came to my mind in subsequent days. The photo was the catalyst for this resurgence of memory. But it cannot work in this manner if such photographs are the result of a fleeting gaze, a passing distraction, or a regularised and almost 'automated' photography of the casual and the thoughtless. Photography under such casual circumstances will not bind people emotionally to the place, the object or the moment referred to in such images. If we were not inherently linked to the 'mental time travel' provided by memory, 'we would have no awareness of our personal history, no way to remembering the joys that serve as the luminous milestones of our lives' (Kandel 2006: 10). It appears that photography of this kind does not readily allow people access to 'mental time travel', as Kandel has argued. If at all, such images have limited memory without its general structures of contextualisation and specificities of anchoring. So if photography of this kind is thought of as an 'unthinking practice', as I have suggested in this chapter, memory is not the route through which they can be made sense of. That is, in such a context, it does not seem reasonable to assume that memory and the anticipation of recalling it in the future is the prerogative that triggers the need to engage in such photography in the first place.

If so, how does one make sense of this specific genre of photography? Every time I think about this question, what comes to mind are the haunting words of George Mallory, uttered sometime before he attempted to scale the heights of Mount Everest in 1924, from which he and his partner never returned. When asked why he wanted to do climb Everest, his answer was, 'because it is there' (Clash 2001). That is, he was attempting to do something because it was thought of as possible, because it was there, and not because it was essential or necessary. It seems to me that more than any sentimental or emotional considerations as would be the case if memory were involved, this genre of photography has to be located squarely in the midst of the sentiment conjured by the words, 'because it is possible', which is quite similar to 'because it is there'. How would 'because it is possible' make sense as an act of photography in our times? In 1995, when Image 8.1 was created, that act could not be that easily encapsulated within the notion, 'because it is possible'. True, it was possible within the technological and attitudinal circumstances of the time. But there was no digital photography, although colour analogue photography was very much in place. There was also no significant internet presence in Sri Lanka at that time.[3] This meant that the kind of sharing that is routinely taken for granted now was not even a thought at the time. This photograph, and others like it in the 1990s and earlier, had to be thought of within scales of necessity as well as economics before the act of photography could begin. That is, is this photograph really needed? Because the act of photography at the time was preceded by a specific cost directly linked to the purchase of film. This was followed by two other costs, for the development of negatives and the printing of photographs. If additional copies were needed for the physical sharing that was possible at the time, then the overall cost increased. My suggestion is not that people thought about cost implications every time they clicked a photo. But it was certainly an important consideration in the overall act of photographing and collecting images in one's private collection, which had to be taken into account. The issue of time, effort, and thought, which I had referred to earlier, come into focus again. If general or personal photography prior to the advent of digital photography is to be considered within the notion 'because it is possible', it will be clear that the realm of possibilities at the time was far more complex than it is today.

However, in the present, when a digital photograph is captured fleetingly, casually, and thoughtlessly, it is certainly 'because it is possible'. And more importantly, within this realm of possibilities in the present, none of the earlier considerations need to be taken into account with any degree of seriousness. Digital photography is free, one does not need a camera as long as a smartphone with an inbuilt camera is available, images captured can easily be deleted if not to one's satisfaction, and they need not be printed to be shared or to be stored in one's private albums. The latter can remain in the phone itself or in electronic storage devices or web-based storage spaces. These general circumstances allow for a very differential interpretation of 'because it is possible'. It is possible because it is easy and has no cost implications, and it is also what many people seem to do on a quotidian basis, which makes it a widely accepted general practice. All of this allows for this genre of photography to readily emerge along with all other genres of photography of the present time, and entrench itself as an acceptable practice. It seems to me that this is also a taste in the sense articulated by Bourdieu (1993). That is, this is a choice made within a field of available practices and properties, 'through, taste in the sense of the principle underlying these choices, manifests itself' (ibid.: 108). Individuals are free to select this kind of photography as something that should define them as individuals and as reflective of their time. And as we know, many in fact make this choice. But if we are to understand this kind of photography as a particular kind of taste, which I think is possible, it is also important to see how tastes as such come into being. As Bourdieu suggests, tastes are created as the result of an encounter between two histories, 'one existing in an objectified state, the other in the incorporated state, which are objectively attuned to each other' (ibid.: 109). Photographs of this kind exist in the objectified state once they are created, while the urge or the anticipation of creating them exists in the incorporated state as an ideal. An individual will adopt this practice as within the structure of her/his tastes when these two conditionalities are met.

However, rather than an acquired taste aimed towards joining the higher echelons of social hierarchy and higher rungs of social mobility, in today's circumstances, this kind of photography is a practice linked to a taste that is widespread, global, generalised, and standardised. In this sense, it is very different from Bourdieu's explanation for the change in tastes. For him, 'all the goods [or practices, as in this case] offered tend to lose some of their relative scarcity and their distinctive value as the number of consumers both inclined and able to appropriate them grows' (Bourdieu 1993: 114). In other words, 'popularisation devalues' (ibid.). Obviously, this reasoning applies to most transformations of tastes. Comparatively, however, this kind of fleeting photography as a practice is not something rare that needs to be carefully acquired and cultivated. Effectively, it is a free, circulating taste in the form of a practice, into which many in the millennial generations are born. But it is a necessary marker of the time, which will indicate that people who have acquired it are in with the times and its sensibilities. Seen in this sense, outsiders to this taste-cum-practice would be people such as myself, who have so far found no need for this specific genre of photography in the personal circumstances of our lives and are therefore not fully in with the times. Given the seemingly natural acquisition of this taste as a matter of routine life, its global standardisation, and its ability to cut across ethnic, gender, class, cultural, and national borders, it has become one of the most recognisable iconic practices of our time.

Given its specific location in the present time, it can also be understood within a discourse of desire, impulsiveness, consumption, and over-consumption. This does not mean that these human attributes did not exist in previous times. But it does mean that these attributes have found wider acceptance and prevalence in contemporary times. More importantly, much of the negative social value attached to them in public discourses in previous times has also diminished in recent times, and has led to their normalisation within many practices, but within limits. The attitudinal and technological possibilities of the present have created a sense of impulsiveness, which is closely related to consumption. But impulsiveness varies between 'benign experimentation' on one end and 'self-destructive acts' at the other extreme.[4] Much of the popular and mental-health discourse on impulsiveness views it as a kind of illness with serious consequences. When I think of the thoughtless, casual, and fleeting photography within an idiom of impulsiveness, I do not think of it as a self-destructive tendency. Instead, it is closer to the 'benign experimentation' suggested above, which can be conducted within the comfort zone of a widespread and taken-for-granted social practice. By and large, most global social formations today prefer some form of capitalist markets and capital-friendly social systems. That is, there exists a pronounced preference for markets not only for goods that are sold for profit, but also for markets for ideas, attitudes, practices, and so on, which are not necessarily sold for profit. The latter manifestations of the market and social systems are instead made available as a field of attitudes, choices, and practices, whose embrace will in the long term enhance the overall circulation of capital and consumerist practices. Such an arena is fundamentally a field of inducement in which the desire to own and possess, and the impulsiveness to put into practice that desire are both privileged and valorised. In the present circumstances, a market-driven society will not work unless a general sense of desire and impulsiveness, as outlined above, are maintained as its core values. Desire for and the impulsiveness to own goods and objects as well as practices and tastes are what make consumption tick.

It is the same desire and its twin, impulsiveness, understood in this sense, which drives this kind of photography as well. This impulsiveness is fired by a desire to possess things, and to do so rapidly. It is this rapidity to possess that creates a sense of impulsiveness. As a person quickly photographs a dish in a restaurant or a flower bed in a park, it is a matter of visually owning that specific object, and therefore also visually consuming it. And once done, you move on to other things, including other objects and sights to desire for, to possess, and to consume visually. But as with most things that are acquired without much reflection, these images also do not have much value, beyond momentary consideration. This is why their lifespan is much more tenuous compared to other kinds of photographs.

However, this kind of photography as an iconic contemporary practice has now moved much beyond desire and compulsion. Through the interrelated operation of these two states, it has now been converted into a fully-fledged need, perceived as necessary to be fulfilled by many people. But in the broader contexts of reality, this is not really a need, in the sense that it is not essential. That is, unlike wedding photography or other event-based photography, which might have both historic and emotional needs embedded in it, this specific practice is too dispersed. Nevertheless, despite this lack of rootedness to issues of memory, history or emotion, this fleeting practice of photography is with us to stay.

Finally, this brings us to the issue of the history of this practice. As I have explained with regard to selfies in Chapter 4 and wedding photographs in Chapter 5, both practices had a considerably long history that could be traced to different moments in the past. In these two practices, what happened in the present was a change in the nature of their practice as a response to and a result of contemporary circumstances, marked by both newer attitudes and the availability of specific technologies. But they clearly did not originate in the present. Comparatively, however, the fleeting, casual, and unthinking photography, as I have attempted to explain the practice here, does not seem to have such a history or sense of provenance that extends into the past. It can only be understood in the present and the recent past of the twenty-first century.

Notes

1. https://fernandogros.com/ode-thoughtless-photographer/ (accessed 13 July 2018).
2. Email commmunication from Jinali Chandrika Hettiarachchi, 14 July 2018.
3. The internet was officially introduced to Sri Lanka in 1995, although conversations on it had been ongoing for at least a decade before that.
4. https://www.nytimes.com/2006/04/04/health/psychology/living-on-impulse.html (accessed 17 July 2018).

nine

Fear of the Visual? Power of 'Writing' in Anthropology and the Eclipse of Photography

... ethnographic enquiries came to depend upon words, words and words, during the period that anthropology was maturing as a science.

Margaret Mead (1995)

Paradoxically, while social researchers encounter images constantly, not merely in their own daily lives but as part of the texture of life of those they work with, they sometimes seem at a loss when it comes to incorporating images into their professional practice.

Marcus Banks (2001)

I*n the previous* eight chapters, I have explored a number of themes with regard to photography which were of interest to me. As I had noted at the very beginning of this book, this was both a personal journey and an academic inquiry that varied from revisiting the combined histories and intersections of photography, anthropology, sociology, and colonialism on the one hand, and dealing with the politics of specific kinds of photography, such as selfies, wedding photography, and what I have very subjectively called fleeting, casual, and thoughtless photography, on the other. In this journey, I have also traversed issues of ethics in visual research and the dynamics that led to the emergence of visual sociology and anthropology. I have undertaken this admittedly incomplete and fragmented history of seeing in the specific intellectual contexts of South Asia, where these issues have not received much attention. And this is clearly the case with regard to the region's sociology and social anthropology, within which I am located. Moreover, my focus has been that of a sociologist with a keen interest in photography in particular and the visual more generally, and not as a photographer or as a visual sociologist. And in this effort, I have situated my undisguised subjective self as well as my anxiety-ridden academic self in the midst of this journey as two related characters walking down the same path, but quite unsure of where they might end up. That itself is perhaps too unorthodox an approach when seen from the perspective of the clinical, and what I consider the boring and often-colourless domains of formal sociology and social anthropology in South Asia. I am sure that for many of my colleagues, what I have said will not be adequately 'sociological'.

But as far as I am concerned, my movement in the direction of photography's implication in sociology is well within my interests in sociology. At the end of this ruptured and non-linear journey, I remain unconvinced of the reasons that led sociology and social anthropology to expel the visual into the sub-disciplinary domains where it now resides. In fact, I think it should be self-evident that one major foundation of my journey was this intellectual rupture and my inability to understand the logic underlying it in both theoretical and methodological terms, despite my readings on the matter and subsequent conversations and reflections with many colleagues, friends, and students who shared some of these interests. My attempt in these concluding pages is to briefly revisit this intellectual rupture in the context of the overall conditions that I have so far discussed, and place in context my own thoughts on why photography in sociology makes sense.

In 1974, in the conclusion of his influential essay, 'Sociology and Photography', Becker had expressed much hope that while the kind of work involving photography and sociology that he was trying to 'encourage barely exists' at the time, 'common and converging interests of social scientists and photographers, often in the same person, suggest that we don't have long to wait' (Becker 1974: 24). Re-reading Becker's essay and reflecting on his hopes, I cannot help but feel how right and how wrong he has been at the same time. He was right to the extent that the visual and photography have generated pronounced interest within visual sociology and anthropology, as well as cultural studies and a number of other domains of study in the social sciences and humanities. But it is quite evident today that his hope has not manifested within the mainstream of either sociology or social anthropology. It almost seems that later twentieth-century criticisms of photography's usefulness in sociology and social anthropology, which I had outlined in Chapters 3 and 6, had assumed to a great extent that photography somehow had to narrate a story that was authentic and autonomous, as well as the ultimate truth, and that it had to be done through images alone. Alternatively, the criticism was that whatever was narrated through images, including photographs, was too soft and smacked of unreliability in discursive and analytical terms. Today, in the era after the 'writing culture' and 'partial truths' debates initiated by the writings of James Clifford, George Marcus, Michel Fischer, Stephen Tyler, and others in the 1980s, such a sense of absolute privilege is not even offered to the written text in the practice of ethnography. Hence the understanding of ethnographic accounts as 'partial truths'—the residue of theorisation, interpretation, and representation of what had been collected from the 'field'. It is self-evident today that the 'perfume' of specific places and moments that Levi-Strauss referred to in the context of his field notes also manifests not as simple 'facts' beyond which there can be no interpretation; instead, they too are snippets of partial truths open to interpretation, just as much as his own photographs, which he had later discarded due to their alleged lapses in sociological value.

Like field notes, photographs in any anthropological work have to be situated and interpreted in the same way as one is expected to when dealing with any other kind of social and cultural material. This is what Bourdieu and Bourdieu mean when they assert, 'photographs should be the object of a reading that one may call sociological and that they are never considered in themselves and for themselves, in terms of their technical or aesthetic qualities' (Bourdieu and Bourdieu 2004: 605). Much of the suspicions about photography's suitability for sociological research in methodological terms also emanated from its situation within an idiom of art and aesthetics. This is why Bourdieu and Bourdieu very clearly emphasise the need to engage in a sociological reading via photographs without reference to its aesthetic sensibilities (Bourdieu and Bourdieu 2004). It is in this context that Wright has noted that 'the status of the visual in much contemporary visual anthropological practice is often achieved largely through a denial of any aesthetics, constructed through a distancing from any potentially polluting "artistic" concerns' (Wright 1998: 17).

It is also in this context that Becker tried to argue in the 1970s that 'photography from the beginning strove toward art just as it did toward social exploration' (Becker 1974: 5). As a pioneer visual sociologist with a great passion for photography, and writing twenty-four years prior to Wright, Becker was not denying the artistic potential of photography. Instead, he accepted it as a matter of fact. On the one hand, he argued that 'the artistic element of photography was held at a substantial distance from photography carried on for more mundane purposes, including journalism' (ibid.). In a certain sense, sociology was also one of these mundane purposes which, to a significant extent, necessitated a conscious shift from framing in the idiom of art or leisure to that of recording 'facts', insofar as photos generated in predetermined research contexts were concerned. On the other hand, Becker also thought that aesthetically oriented photography and discursive practices like sociology need not be seen as separate when he argued, 'art and social exploration describe two ways of working, not two kinds of photographers' (ibid.).

The arguments about photography as art or as an aesthetic practice that could therefore dent the scientific validity of sociological research were used as a tool to disrupt its methodical entry more seriously into mainstream sociology and social anthropology, rather than providing a clear understanding of its fallacies. It is because of this argument that photographs were expected to provide an independent narrative to make themselves sociologically viable if they were to be considered adequate sources of research in mainstream sociology and social anthropology. It is interesting that seminal ethnographies written on the basis of memory and recollection in contexts where field notes were destroyed, such as M.N. Srinivas' *Remembered Village* (1980) and Edmund Leach's *Political Systems of Highland Burma* (1954), have been so well-received as sound ethnographic accounts, while the same reception has never been accorded to photography in mainstream contemporary social anthropology. It would appear that in the received wisdom of conventional South Asian as well as global mainstream anthropology, memory and recollection are far more reliable in methodological terms, despite their countless fallibilities, than the apparent silence and stasis of photography. However, the reality is that photographs are no less or no more partial or mute than field notes or recollections of memory, if carefully situated in context.

Another source of anxiety over photos in social anthropology stems from the fact that they are not always captured while an event was actually taking place. Often, photographs in anthropological contexts might be taken after an event, similar to crime scene photos, which capture the 'residual' by professionals who arrive 'too late', after an incident has already taken place (Bond 2009: 1). But anthropologists and sociologists are not news photographers for whom 'live coverage' should matter, as it does in news reportage, except in very specific circumstances. Images captured by anthropologists and others who arrive at a ceremony, a ritual, or any other event after it has taken place also fall within this category of 'too late' images. Nevertheless, this residuality itself should not become a source of anxiety when considering the research or narrative potential of photographs. In such moments, too, photographs are taken in a specific situation, which is impacted by spatial, temporal, cultural, and political factors. As such, any photograph will be 'read' and situated in that specific context to make sense. This brings to mind the following three questions that Banks had formulated in his book, *Visual Methods in Social Research*, when attempting to make methodological sense of photographs: '(i) what is the image of, what is its content? (ii) who took it or made it, when and why? and (iii) how do other people come to have it, how do they read it, what do they do with it?' (Banks 2001: 7). It seems to me that these three issues are of simple yet direct relevance to any project in any discipline (and not simply in sociology and social anthropology) that intends to utilise photographs as a central object of research, or as main repositories of information. In a similar context, Wright has suggested that three approaches can be utilised to read photographs. These include looking through photographs, looking at them, and finally looking behind photographs (Wright 1999: 38). Effectively, by using these three approaches, what Wright is arguing for is the need to focus on both the contents and the contexts of photographs to bring out their social and political meanings (Wright 1999).

Seen in the sense outlined above, the photographs of the Vedda ritual performances at the Mahiyangagna Raja Maha Viharaya Buddhist temple in southern Sri Lanka that I had captured in 2009 had been taken while the actual performances were in progress (see Image 9.1). This was part of the annual ritual known as *Vedi Perahera*.

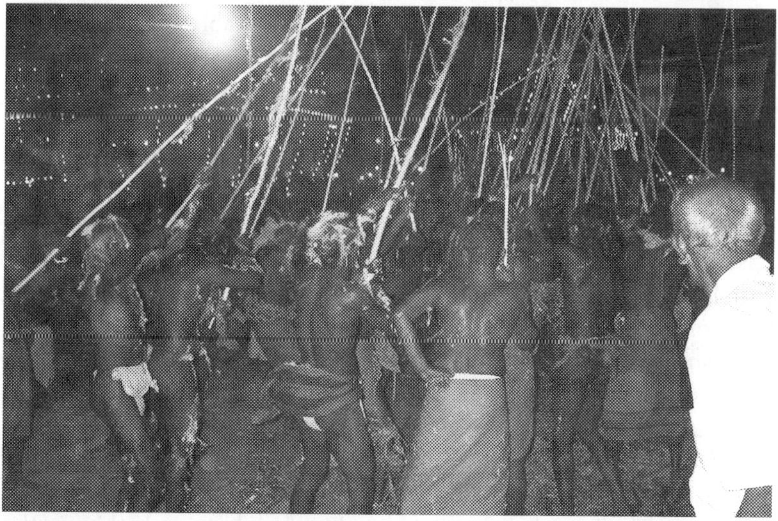

Image 9.1 *Vedi Perahera* in progress, Mahiyangana Raja Maha Viharaya, Sri Lanka, 2005.

Photograph courtesy of: Author's research collection.

There was no time lapse between the event and the act of photography. Effectively, they were captured 'live', and as a result, the issue of residuality that Bond refers to above does not come into play with regard this series of photographs. While I have written nothing so far based on these photos or the work undertaken at the time, these images can 'speak' to me today as well, if I wish to give them voice. Similar images from the collection of the Seligmanns, referred to in

Chapter 3, or in other colonial-period collections will also offer such reading possibilities more than 100 years after they were taken. But while my images were taken as a large-scale ceremony was in progress as part of an annual ritual cycle, some of the Seligmanns' images and many other period photographs of Veddas were posed for. It is this kind of contextual relevance that the three questions suggested by Banks (2001), referred to above, establish. In other words, the answer to these questions with regard to photographs in a research project will establish degrees of reliability. Once the limitations and strengths of a photograph, as well as its contextual circumstances, are taken into account, they will offer considerable information. In this sense, Image 9.1 and others in the series pictorially refer to the changes the ritual has structurally experienced over time, changes in costumes, and what these changes might mean in terms of broader social and cultural transformations, and so on. In other words, they offer signposts for situating these rituals in specific historical milieus within a discourse of social change, and are still open for interpretation based on material from other sources. *Vedi Perahera* is an important ritual that establishes the entry of this indigenous community into the folds of Buddhism, while it also refers to practices of trade that the community was traditionally engaged in. But beyond this symbolism, the costumes that people wear nowadays and the layers of political patronage that precede the ritual outline significant aspects of recent social and political change, while the symbolic references of the ritual are lost to many viewers for whom it has become a mere tourist attraction. The point I wish to make is that this photo and others in the series, when situated in the specific context in which they were taken as well as within the discourse of other material on the Veddas, will allow for considerable information to emerge, along with numerous interpretative possibilities.

Similarly, the photographs I had captured over a sixteen-year period in northern Sri Lanka of war memorials constructed by the guerilla group, the Liberation Tigers of Tamil Elam, and the Sri Lankan armed forces, as well as other sites touched by violence were taken many years after they were constructed, and the incidents of violence associated with some sites had ended. Some of these images were captured in 2005 in the midst of a ceasefire while others were photographed in 2012, three years after Sri Lanka's civil war ended in 2009.[1] But none was taken in the midst of combat in the sense of 'live' photography. As articulated by Bond, what I had captured in these images were the 'residual' of what had happened, after arriving at the scenes 'too late' (Bond 2009: 1)—after the war was over or in the relative safety of a faulty ceasefire. For me, the value of these images has nothing to do with the time in which the monuments or other structures were constructed or when they were photographed, but in what they had to narrate about the kind of politics that ensured the emergence of these objects at one moment and how some of these were removed from the landscape at another moment, as well as what they had to say about the manner in which memory worked. As I have noted on the use of photographs in my book, *Warzone Tourism in Sri Lanka*,

> the extensive availability of images from my own research collection as well as the personal narratives of others allowed for the pictorial contextualization of where travellers went, what they saw, why they recorded specific objects and places and the nature of discourse that emerged with respect to these places. (Perera 2016b: xii)

More broadly, in this context, the

> focus on photography was not a matter of simply attempting to understand what people did in the form of a 'thoughtless' technical practice and getting a sense of what they saw in their travels. More importantly, it was also a methodological prerogative in at least partially creating a parallel narrative that would accompany the written text as a necessary subtext of what it was attempting to outline. (ibid.: xii–xiii)

As far as my use of photographs was concerned, they were not mere illustrations, but were an integral part of what I saw and what I had to say as well as what I hoped others would also see and perceive. While I could have not used photographs in what I wrote, my conviction is that the photographs helped to create an effective secondary narrative, which in some cases necessarily surpassed the narrative potential of the written text in terms of nuance.

In many ways, photographing a place after a specific event has taken place is not very different from interviewing a person about an incident that has already taken place, and making notes of that conversation. In fact, unlike such an interview, a photograph might capture much more information, in the same way that the residue of war and its destructions are clearly embedded in many of my own photographs. The last of these, which were taken in December 2012 in the midst of the former war zone, still narrated stories of war and violence (see Image 9.2), while in many places, the presence of war and its destruction were being actively erased by the State and destroyed homes and burnt Palmyra trees were being replaced with hoardings announcing the rapid influx of private capital into the former warzone (see Image 9.3).

It seems to me that photography's dislocation from mainstream anthropology and sociology emanated partly from not asking seriously enough what to do with photographs and how best to utilise

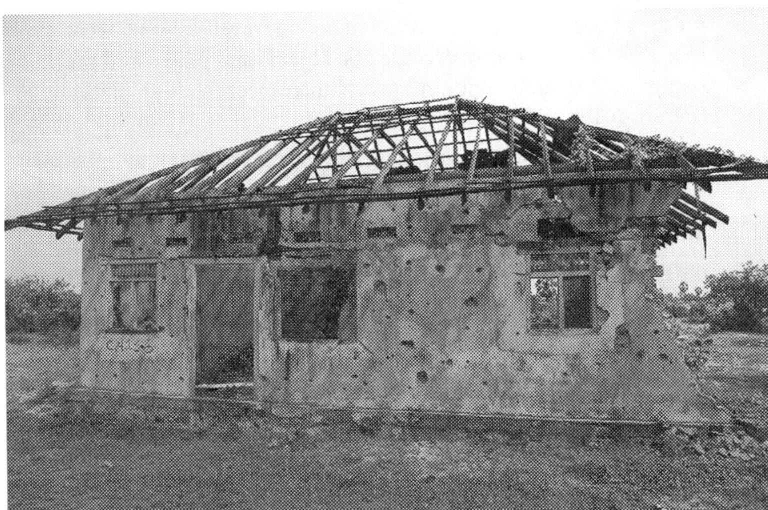

IMAGE 9.2 House destroyed by war, with bullet holes and identification marker placed by the military, Pudumathalan, northern Sri Lanka, 2012. *Photograph courtesy of*: Author's research collection.

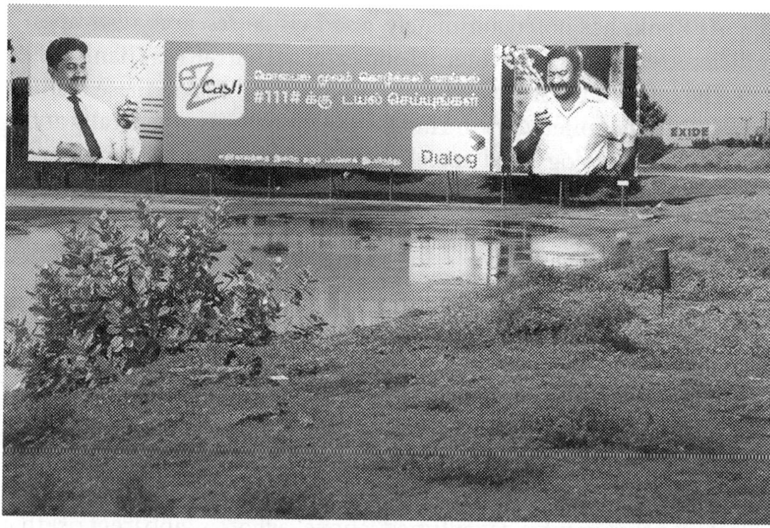

IMAGE 9.3 Post-war commercial advertisement at Elephant Pass, northern Sri Lanka, 2012.

Photograph courtesy of: Author's research collection.

them. This is what Elizabeth Edwards wondered when she asked, 'what "work" is expected from photographs as objects—in albums, on walls, at shrines, in political protests, as gift exchange? Under what material conditions are photographs seen? In which ways are they things that demand embodied responses and emotional affects?' (Edwards 2012: 222). Instead of asking under what conditions and how photography can drive anthropology and sociology in both methodological and theoretical terms, the mainstreams of these two disciplines have felt more comfortable to allow that question to be answered as central issues within visual sociology and anthropology, rather than as part of core interests within the mainstream. And for that to happen, the visual in both sociology and anthropology had to be first expelled to their sub-disciplinary locations. And it is clear that colleagues who have found visual sociology and anthropology a more comfortable intellectual home have welcomed this distancing from the mainstream as well.

As Banks has noted, ultimately, 'good visual research rests upon a judicious reading of both internal and external narratives' (Banks 1999: 12). The question that always comes to my mind is: Are these reading possibilities not offered by the intellectual apparatuses generally at the disposal of sociology and social anthropology even today? Internal narratives are provided by the photograph itself, while the external narratives might have some references within the photograph. But its main sources will be exterior to the photograph and embedded in other domains and contextual materials such as local histories, individual memories, and other temporal resources, which might offer a more nuanced reading to the photograph and its context. This is because, as Banks further notes, 'at root, all visual objects represent nothing but themselves; their very existence in the world as material objects is proof of nothing but their autonomy' (ibid.).

Despite the discursive possibilities embedded in carefully selected photographs as outlined above, what is apparent is that photography's presence in mainstream anthropology was eclipsed more decisively with the forceful establishment of 'literate' sensibilities in social anthropology consequent to the influence of the 'writing culture' debate, particularly in the United States, and later in the rest of the world as well. Although this debate was something that emerged within social anthropology, the power of the written word accompanied by statistics is similarly seen in sociology, and has played a core role in its own distancing of photography and the visual into the sub-disciplinary domain of visual sociology. This eclipsing has been taking place steadily since the 1960s. Rather than a self-conscious expulsion of photographs, this was more the by-product of the emergent theoretical and methodological prerogatives privileging the practice of writing and literary sensibilities in anthropological practice. As Clifford has noted, 'writing' or 'making of texts' is 'no longer a marginal, or occulted dimension' in anthropology, but has 'emerged as central to what anthropologists do both in the field and thereafter' (Clifford 1986: 2). Obviously, this does not mean that anthropologists did not write before. Early armchair anthropologists wrote on what they had not seen, but had heard from others or 'seen' via photographs. Later, with the professionalisation of the discipline and the advent of fieldwork and participant observation, they wrote about what they actually saw on the basis of their comprehension. But in this later incarnation, what was privileged was not the act of writing but participant observation, the act of being in the 'field'. This is what offered anthropology an almost mythologised and romantic identity. Writing was simply the end-product of this over-encompassing and non-transferable personal experience of 'being there'. It was this experience that paved the way for cultural relativism and emic understandings of culture. As we have seen, in both these schemes of anthropology, photography had an important role to play in situating the writing in its overall context, offering 'truth' value or 'scientific' validity to the claims that were made—depending on the circumstances as well as the interests of individual scholars.

However, compared to these earlier modes of anthropological expression, the dominant post-writing culture anthropological practice saw the emergence of writing as its core obsessive object. As Marcus writes, anthropologists became 'more self-conscious than ever before that they are *writers* who, as maturing professionals, routinely outgrow the models of ethnography by which they were inducted into anthropology' (Marcus 1986: 262; emphasis mine). As they become writers in the sense articulated by Marcus, among the things they discarded along the way included the centrality of participant observation as well as long-term research itself as a more embedded and complex process. This was both a theoretical and a methodical re-orientation of the discipline at a time when many perceived that the broader theoretical project of twentieth-century anthropology was in 'disarray', and enmeshed in 'crisis' (Clifford 1986: 3; Marcus 1986: 263). As a result, these circumstances opened up possibilities to discuss more openly the textual expressions of anthropological knowledge and the career-circumstances of individual scholars (Marcus 1986: 263). Under these conditions, the 'literariness' of published anthropological knowledge became far more important than the processes that had made this discursive end-product possible. It is in this overall context that researchers in the social sciences with an interest in the visual—including in sociology or social anthropology—were moved to say that they 'work in a minority field that is neither understood, nor properly appreciated by their colleagues', because given the social sciences' over-emphasis on the written word, 'there is no room for pictures, except as supporting characters' (Banks 1999: 1–2).

As far as social anthropology is concerned, this situation emerged in the general circumstances marked by an interest in literary approaches more generally in human sciences, as well as the intellectual interest in literary theory and practice exhibited by a number of important anthropologists, which included Claude Levi-Strauss, Victor Turner, Clifford Geertz, Mary Douglas, and others (Clifford 1986: 3). Interestingly, in their own differing ways, they have 'blurred the boundary separating art from science' (ibid.). As we have already seen, earlier, in the evolution of anthropology, photography was inducted into the discipline for exactly the opposite reason, that is, to ostensibly take it more squarely into the bosom of science. However, this self-conscious rupture and anthropology's march towards art was mostly predicated upon the emerging importance given to writing. At no point did this process look towards other practices such as photography, which combined both artistic and reasonable discursive possibilities, depending on what kind of photography one was dealing with. But in this context, what might be more plausible is to assume that 'art', in the sense of the literary turn in anthropology, was more a matter of 'skillful fashioning of useful artifacts', as once described by Raymond Williams (ibid.: 6). In this sense, the formulation of anthropological texts, including ethnographies, is 'artisanal, tied to the worldly work of writing' (ibid.).

Seen in this sense, one can generally agree with Marcus that 'textualization is at the heart of the ethnographic enterprise, both in the field and in university settings' (Marcus 1986: 264). But Marcus' assumption is that ethnographic practice begins with orality, and proceeds towards writing 'with difficulty' (ibid.: 264–65). However, orality is only one source of ethnography while visuality is another, which unfortunately does not find much space in the writing culture debate or in the post-writing culture intellectual environments in which we are located today. In the over-emphasis of literary approaches to anthropology and the dominance that writing itself has come to occupy in the hegemonic schools of social anthropology globally, much has been rejected as 'visualism' (Clifford 1986: 11). What has been lost to both mainstream social anthropology and sociology in this context includes 'reflexivity; collaboration; ethics; and the relationship between content, social context and materiality of images' (Pink 2003: 179). But visualism in this context is not merely photography. It refers to ways of seeing or how vision has been hierarchically positioned over other senses in Western literate cultures, and how, in that same scheme of things, photography has ebbed beyond the intellectual horizon of contemporary anthropology. This is because of its inability to compete with the power of the written word in post-writing culture over-literary anthropology. It is at the intersections of these circumstances that one may find the now-established but often unarticulated fear of the visual in contemporary anthropology.

Note

1. For more information, see Perera (2016a, 2016b).

References

Adshade, Marina E., and Brooks A. Kaiser. 2008. *The Origins of the Institutions of Marriage*. Queen's Economics Department Working Paper No. 1180. Ontario: Department of Economics, Queen's University.

Aird, Michael. 1993. *Portraits of Our Elders*. Brisbane: Queensland Museum.

Allana, Rahab. 2013. 'Statuesque Enthrallment: The Body in Early South Asian Photography'. In *Early Portrait Photography from South Asia: Allegory and Illusion*. Hyderabad: Mapin Publishing.

Allana, Rahaab, and Pramod Kumar (eds). 2008. *Painted Photographs: Coloured Portraiture in India*. New Delhi: Alkazi Collection of Photography.

Alessio, Dominic. 1992. 'Capitalist realist art: Industrial images of Hamilton, Ontario, 1884–1910'. *Journal of Urban History* 18 (4): 442–69.

Anderson, Claire. 2004. *Legible Bodies: Race, Criminality and Colonialism in South Asia*. Oxford: Berg.

Appadurai, A. 1997. 'The Colonial Backdrop'. *Afterimage* 24 (5): 4–7.

Azoulay, Ariella. 2008. *The Civil Contract of Photography*. New York: Zone.

Baker, Samuel. 1854. *The Rifle and the Hound in Ceylon*. London: Longman, Brown, Green and Longmans.

Banks, Marcus. 2001. *Visual Methods in Social Research*. London: Sage Publications.

Banks, Marcus, and Howard Morphy. 1999 [1997]. *Rethinking Visual Anthropology*. New Haven: Yale University Press.

Barthes, Roland. 2000. *Camera Lucinda: Reflections of Photography*. London: Vintage.

Baviskar, Amita. 2011. *In the Belly of the River: Tribal Conflicts over Development in the Narmada Valley*. New Delhi: Oxford University Press.

Becker, Howard S. 1974. 'Photography and Sociology'. *Studies in Visual Communication* 1 (1): 3–26.

Berger, John. 2013. *Understanding a Photograph*, edited and introduced by Geoff Dyer. London: Penguin Books.

Berger, L. 2011. 'Snapshots, or Visual Culture's Clichés'. *Photographies* 4 (2): 175–90.

Berlant, Lauren. 2012. *Desire/Love*. Brooklyn: Punctum Books.

Biswas, Jennifer Chowdhry. 2015. 'A Landscape of Desire'. In *Imaging the Isle Across: Vintage Photography from Ceylon*, 52–67. New Delhi: National Museum.

Bond, Henry. 2009. *Lacan at the Scene*. Cambridge, MA: Massachusetts Institute of Technology Press.

Bourdieu, Pierre. 1993. *Sociology in Question*, Richard Nice (trans.). London: Sage Publications.

_____. 1995. 'A Science that Makes Trouble'. In P. Bourdieu, *Sociology in Question*. London: Sage Publications.

Bourdieu, Pierre, and Marie-Claire Bourdieu. 2004. 'The Peasant and Photography'. *Ethnography* 5 (4): 601–16.

British Council. 2000. *Regeneration: A Reappraisal of Photography in Ceylon 1850–1900*. London: British Council.

Brow, James. 1996. *Demons and Development: The Struggle for Community in a Sri Lankan Village*. Tuscon: University of Arizona Press.

Callero, P. L. 2003. 'The Sociology of the Self'. *Annual Review of Sociology* 29 (1): 115–33.

Caulfield, Jon. 1996. 'Visual Sociology and Sociological Vision, Revisited'. *The American Sociologist* 27 (3): 56–68.

Citron, Beth. 2013. 'Rethinking the Figure in Early Photography from South Asia'. In Beth Citron and Christopher Pinney (eds), *Early Portrait Photography from South Asia: Allegory and Illusion*. Hyderabad: Mapin Publishing.

Clark, Andrew. 2012. 'Visual Ethics in a Contemporary Landscape'. In Sarah Pink (ed.), *Advances in Visual Methodology*, 17–35. London: Sage Publications.

Clash, James M. 2001. 'Because it's there'. *Forbes*, 29 October. Available at https://www.forbes.com/global/2001/1029/060.html#716eda532080 (accessed 15 July 2018).

Clifford, James, and George E. Marcus. 1986. *Writing Culture: The Poetics and Politics of Ethnography*. Berkeley: University of California Press.

Clifford, James. 1986. 'Introduction: Partial Truths'. In James Clifford and George E. Marcus (eds), *Writing Culture: The Poetics and Politics of Ethnography*, 1–26. Berkeley: University of California Press.

Coomaraswamy, Ananda. 1956. 'The Traditional Conceptions of Ideal Portraiture'. In *Christian and Oriental Philosophy of Art*, 117–29. New York: Dover Publications.

Cuylenburg, Reg Van. 1962. *Image of an Island: A Portrait of Ceylon*. New York: Orion Press.

———. 2015. *The Green Stick: A Memoir*. Santa Barbara: Blue Palm Press.

Datta, Ankur. 2017. *On Uncertain Ground: Displaced Kashmiri Pandits in Jammu and Kashmir*. New Delhi: Oxford University Press.

Davis, Janet. 1993. 'Spectacles of South Asia at the American circus, 1890–1940'. *Visual Anthropology* 6: 121–38.

Day, Elizabeth. 2013. 'How selfies became a global phenomenon'. *The Guardian*. Available at https://www.theguardian.com/technology/2013/jul/14/how-selfies-became-a-global-phenomenon (accessed 3 July 2017).

Devereaux, Leslie, and Roger Hillman. 1995. *Fields of Vision: Essays on Film Studies, Visual Anthropology and Photography*. Berkeley: University of California Press.

Dewan, Deepali. 2012. *Embellished Reality: Indian Painted Photographs*. Ontario: Royal Ontario Museum Press.

Dreyfuss, Ben. 2014. 'In Defense of Selfies: Rembrandt'. *Mother Jones*, 15 July. Available at http://www.motherjones.com/mixed-media/2014/07/on-this-day-rembrandt-selfie (accessed 29 November 2016).

Edwards, Elizabeth. 1992. 'Introduction'. In *Anthropology & Photography, 1860–1920*. New Haven: Yale University Press.

———. 2012. 'Objects and Affect: Photography Beyond the Image'. *Annual Review of Anthropology* 41: 221–34.

Evans-Pritchard, E. E. 1940. *The Nuer: A Description of the Modes of Livelihood and Political Institutions of a Nilotic People*. Oxford: Oxford University Press.

Fabry, Merrill. 2016. 'Now You Know: Why Do People Always Look So Serious in Old Photos?' *Time*, 28 November. Available at http://time.com/4568032/smile-serious-old-photos/ (accessed 26 November 2017).

Friedman, Thomas L. 2014. 'Four Words Going Bye-Bye'. *The New York Times*. Available at https://www.nytimes.com/2014/05/21/opinion/friedman-four-words-going-bye-bye.html?_r=0 (accessed 28 June 2018).

Garside, Juliette. 2013. 'Huawei banks on the rise of the selfie for world's thinnest smartphone'. *The Guardian*. Available at https://www.theguardian.com/technology/2013/jun/18/huawei-ascend-p6-slimmest-smartphone (accessed 3 July 2017).

Geertz, Clifford. 1988. *Works and Lives: The Anthropologist as Author*. Stanford: Stanford University Press.

Grundberg, Andy, Beaumont Newhall, Helmut Erich Robert Gernsheim, and Naomi Rosenblum. 2017. 'History of photography'. *Encyclopaedia*

Brittanica. Available at https://www.britannica.com/technology/photography (accessed 12 August 2017).

Halbwachs, Maurice. 1992. *On Collective Memory*. Chicago: University of Chicago Press.

Harper, Douglas. 1988. 'Visual Sociology: Expanding Sociological Vision'. *American Sociologist* 19: 54–70.

_____. 2005. 'What's New Visually?' In N. Denzin and Y. Lincoln (eds), *Handbook of Qualitative Research*, 747–62. Thousand Oaks, CA: Sage Publications, 3e.

_____. 2016. 'The Development of Visual Sociology: A view from the inside'. *SOCIETÀMUTAMENTOPOLITICA* 7 (14): 237–50.

Haraway, Donna. 2006. 'A Cyborg Manifesto: Science, Technology, and Socialist-feminism in the Late 20th Century'. In Peter Pericles Trifonas, Joel Weiss, Jason Nolan, and Jeremy Hunsinger (eds), *The International Handbook of Virtual Learning Environments*, 117–58. Springer International Handbooks of Education.

Hastrup, Kirsten. 1993. 'Anthropological Visions: Some Notes on Visual and Textual Authority'. In P. I. Crawford and D. Turton (eds), *Film as Ethnography*, 8–25. Manchester: Manchester University Press.

Hattersley, C. W. 1906. *Uganda by Pen and Camera*. London: Religious Tract Society.

_____. 1908. *The Baganda at Home*. London: Religious Tract Society.

Hawkey, Sean, and Paul Jeffrey. 2016. '"Informed Consent" and Why it Doesn't Work'. *PetaPixel*. Available at ttps://petapixel.com/2016/10/22/informed-consent-doesnt-work/ (accessed 28 June 2018).

Herdt, Glibert H. (ed.). 1998. 'Editor's Preface'. In *Rituals of Manhood: Male Initiation in Papua New Guinea*, xxi–xxxviii. New Brunswick: Transaction Publishers.

Higgins, Charlotte. 2015. 'Julia Margaret Cameron: Soft-focus Photographer with an Iron Will'. *The Guardian*. Available at https://www.theguardian.com/artanddesign/2015/sep/22/julia-margaret-cameron-victorian-portrait-photographer-exhibitions (accessed 12 August 2017).

Hirsch, J. 1981. *Family Photographs: Content, Meaning and Effect*. New York: Oxford University Press.

Italie, L. 2013. 'Is the Rise of the "Selfie" Harmless Fun or a Sign of Society's Growing Narcissism?' Available at http://www.news.com.au/technology/are-selfies-just-narcissim/story-e6frfro0-1226669894830 (accessed 1 July 2017).

Jenness, Diamond, and Andrew Ballantyne. 1920. *The Northern D'Entrecasteaux*. Oxford, UK: Clarendon Press.

Jones, Amelia. 2002. 'The "Eternal Return": Self-Portrait Photography as Technology of Embodiment'. *Signs: The Journal of Women in Culture and Society* 27 (4): 947–78.

Junod, Henri A. 1913. *The Life of a South African Tribe*. Neuchatel: Imprimerie Attinger Freres.

Kandel, Eric R. 2006. *In Search of Memory: The Emergence of a New Science of Mind*. New York: W. W. Norton & Company.

Karlekar, Malavika. 2013. *Visual Histories: Photography in the Popular Imagination*. New Delhi: Oxford University Press.

Kaufmann, P. 2014. 'A Sociological Snapshot of Selfies'. *Everyday Sociology Blog*. Available at http://www.everydaysociologyblog.com/2014/01/a-sociological-snapshot-of-selfies.html.

Kotchemidova, Christina. 2005. 'Why We Say "Cheese": Producing the Smile in Snapshot Photography'. *Critical Studies in Media Communication* 22 (1): 2–25.

Leach, Edmund. 1954. *Political Systems of Highland Burma: A Study of Kachin Social Structure*. London: G. Bell and Son Ltd.

Levin, Adam. 2014. 'The Selfie in the Age of Digital Recursion'. *InVisible Culture: An Electronic Journal for Visual Culture.* Available at http://ivc.lib.rochester.edu/the-selfie-in-the-age-of-digital-recursion/ (accessed 2 July 2017).

Levi-Strauss, Claude. 1961. *Tristes Tropiques*, John Russell (trans.). New York: Criterion Books.

———. 1995. *Saudades do Brasil: A Photographic Memoir.* Seattle: University of Washington Press.

Luhmann, Niklas. 1986. *Love as Passion: The Codification of Intimacy*. Cambridge: Harvard University Press.

MacDougal, David. 1999 [1997]. 'The Visual in Anthropology'. In Marcus Banks and Howard Morphy (eds), *Rethinking Visual Anthropology*, 276–95. New Haven: Yale University Press.

Marche, Stephen. 2013. 'Sorry, Your Selfie Isn't Art'. *Esquire*. Available at http://www.esquire.com/entertainment/a23557/selfies-arent-art/ (accessed 2 July 2017).

Marcus, George E. 1986. 'Afterword: Ethnographic Writing and Anthropological Careers'. In James Clifford and George E. Marcus (eds), *Writing Culture: The Poetics and Politics of Ethnography*, 262–66. Berkeley: University of California Press

Marion, Jonathan S., and Jerome W. Crowder. 2013. *Visual Research: A Concise Introduction to Thinking Visually*. London: Bloomsbury.

Martinka, Paul. 2013. 'My Selfie with Brooklyn Bridge Suicide Dude'. *New York Post*. Available at https://nypost.com/2013/12/04/selfie-ish-woman-snaps-cellphone-shot-with-suicidal-man/.

Matthan, Ayesha. 2015. 'Lens Upon Islanders'. In *Imaging the Isle Across: Vintage Photography from Ceylon*, 70–87. New Delhi: National Museum.

Maxwell, Anne. 1999. *Colonial Photography and Exhibitions: Representations of the 'Native' and the Making of European Identities*. London: Leicester University Press.

Mead, Margaret. 1995. 'Visual Anthropology in a Discipline of Words'. In Paul Hockings (ed.), *Principles of Visual Anthropology*, 3–10. Boston and Berlin: De Gruyter Mouton.

Mellinger, Wayne. 1992. 'Representing blackness in the white imagination: Images of happy darkies in popular culture, 1893–1917'. *Visual Sociology* 7 (2): 3–21.

Metz, Christian. 1985. 'Photography and Fetish'. *October* 34 (Autumn): 81–90.

Montrescu-Mayes, Annamaria. 2015. 'The Ascent of (wo)man: Visual Priming in Early Photographs and Films of Ceylon, 1880s–1930s'. In *Imaging the Isle Across: Vintage Photography from Ceylon*, 90–106. New Delhi: National Museum.

Nafeel, Nushka. 2017. 'Death by Selfie'. *Daily News*. Available at http://dailynews.lk/2017/06/14/features/118801/death-selfie (accessed 4 July 2017).

Norman, Wilbert R. 1991. 'Photography as Research Tool'. *Visual Anthropology* 4: 193–216.

Obeyesekere, Gananath. 1984. *The Cult of the Goddess Pattini*. Chicago: University of Chicago Press.

Pearlman, Jonathan. 2013. 'Australian man "invented the selfie after drunken night out"'. *The Telegraph*. Available at http://www.telegraph.co.uk/news/worldnews/australiaandthepacific/australia/10459115/Australian-man-invented-the-selfie-after-drunken-night-out.html (accessed 2 July 2017).

Pamuk, Orhan. 2017. 'Taking Photographs in Istanbul: On Memory, Authenticity and the Photographer Ara Guler'. *Literary Hub*. Available at http://lithub.com/orhan-pamuk-taking-photographs-in-istanbul/ (accessed 19 November 2017).

Perera, Sasanka. 2016a. *Violence and the Burden of Memory: Remembrance and Erasure in Sinhala Consciousness*. New Delhi: Orient BlackSwan.

______. 2016b. *Warzone Tourism in Sri Lanka: Tales from Darker Places in Paradise*. New Delhi: Sage Publications.

Perera, Sasanka. 2018. 'Photography's Methodological Absence in Social Anthropology in South Asia'. In N. Jayaram (ed.), *Knowing Your Social World*, 299–319. New Delhi: Orient BlackSwan.

Pink, Sarah. 2003. 'Interdisciplinary Agendas in Visual Research: Re-situating Visual Anthropology'. *Visual Studies* 18 (2): 179–92.

_____. 2007. *Doing Visual Ethnography*. London: Sage Publications, 2e.

_____. 2012. 'Advances in Visual Methodology: An Introduction'. In Sarah Pink (ed.), *Advances in Visual Methodology*, 3–16. London: Sage Publications.

Piette, Albert. 1993. 'Epistemology and Practical Applications of Anthropological Photography'. *Visual Anthropology* 6: 157–70.

Pinney, Christopher. 1990. 'The Quick and the Dead: Images, Time and Truth'. *Visual Anthropology Review* 6 (2): 42–54.

_____. 2011. *Photography and Anthropology*. New Delhi: Oxford University Press.

_____. 2013. 'Stirred by Photography'. In *Early Portrait Photography from South Asia: Allegory and Illusion*. Hyderabad: Mapin Publishing.

_____. 2015. 'The Civil Contract of Photography in India'. *Comparative Studies of South Asia, Africa and the Middle East* 35 (1): 21–34.

Prosser, J. 2000. 'The Moral Maze of Image Ethics'. In H. Simons and R. Usher (eds), *Situated Ethics in Educational Research*. London: Routledge Falmer.

Raheem, Izmeth. 2015. 'Imaging the Isle Across: Early Photographers from Ceylon, 1840–1920'. In *Imaging the Isle Across: Vintage Photography from Ceylon*, 30–49. New Delhi: National Museum.

Ramsey, Ellen. 1992. 'Picturing the picturesque: Lucius O Brien's "Sunrise on the Saguenay"'. In Paul Simpson-Housley and Glen Norcliffe (eds), *A Few Acres of Snow: Literary and Artistic Images of Canada*, 189–202. Toronto: Dundurn Press.

Rawlings, Kandice. 2013. 'Selfies and the History of Self-Portrait Photography'. *Oxford University Press Blog*. Available at http://blog.oup.com/2013/11/selfies-history-self-portrait-photography (accessed 1 July 2017).

Rice, Mark. 2011. 'Colonial Photography Across Empires and Islands'. *The Journal of Transnational American Studies* 3 (2): 1–22.

Rose, Nikolas. 1999. *Powers of Freedom: Reframing Political Thought*. Cambridge: Cambridge University Press.

Ruby, Jay. 1996. 'Visual Anthropology'. In David Levinson and Melvin Ember (eds), *Encyclopedia of Cultural Anthropology* 4, 1345–51. New York: Henry Holt and Company.

Samotin, Perrie. 2017. 'The 10 Best Photo Editing Apps to Look Better in Every Selfie'. *StyleCaster*. Available at http://stylecaster.com/beauty/best-photo-editing-app/ (accessed 3 July 2017).

Schlackman, Steve. 2016. 'Is Street Photography Legal?' *Art Law Journal*. Available at https://alj.orangenius.com/is-street-photography-legal/ (accessed 10 February 2018).

Schnettler, Bernt. 2013. 'Notes on the History and Development of Visual Research Methods'. *InterDisciplines* 1: 41–75.

Seligmann, C. G., and Brenda Z. Seligmann. 1911. *The Veddas*. Cambridge: Cambridge University Press.

Shah, Nishant. 2014. 'The Selfie and the Self: Part 1—Hiding and Revealing'. *Connected Learning Alliance*. Available at https://clalliance.org/blog/the-selfie-and-the-self-part-1-hiding-and-revealing/.

Shinde, Srishti, 2016. 'Be Selfie Safe in Mumbai'. *The Times of India*, Mumbai, 20 January.

Sontag, Susan. 1977. *On Photography*. Harmondsworth: Penguin.

Srinivas, M. N. 1980. *The Remembered Village*. Berkeley: Center for South and Southeast Asia Studies.

Srivastava, Vandana. 2017. 'Selfies no longer acceptable in Sri Lanka, Government will arrest people found taking selfies near train tracks'. *India.com*. Available at http://www.india.com/buzz/selfies-no-longer-acceptable-in-sri-lanka-government-will-arrest-people-found-taking-selfies-near-train-tracks-2234999/ (accessed 4 July 2017).

Tagg, John. 1988. *Burden of Representation: Essays on Photographies and Histories*. Minneapolis: University of Minnesota Press.

———. 2009. *The Disciplinary Frame: Photographic Truths and the Capture of Meaning*. Minneapolis: University of Minnesota Press.

Tarr, Jen. 2015. 'Ethics and Visual Research'. In *Thinking Methods: Explorations in Social Research Methodology*. London: The London School of Economics and Political Science. Available at http://blogs.lse.ac.uk/thinkingmethods/2015/07/01/ethics-and-visual-research/ (accessed 24 December 2017).

Taylor, Lucien. 1998. 'Visual Anthropology is Dead, Long Live Visual Anthropology'. *American Anthropologist* 100 (2): 534–37.

Tennent, Emerson. 1859. *Ceylon: An Account of the Island*, Vols 1 and 2. London: Longman, Green, Longman and Roberts, 2e.

Thiranagama, Sharika. 2013. *In My Mother's House: Civil War in Sri Lanka*. New Delhi: Zubaan.

Thomas, Elizabeth. n.d. 'Reading from the Old Family Album'. *New Vision*. Available at http://newvision.photojaanic.com/familyalbum/ (accessed 18 June 2016).

Thompson, Lanny. 2002. 'Representation and Rule in the Imperial Archipelago: Cuba, Puerto Rico, Hawai'i, and Philippines Under U.S. Dominion'. *American Studies Asia* 1 (1).

Thurnherr, Christof. 2012. 'Visual Anthropology as a Discipline of Words: On the Importance of the Verbal in Visual Archives'. *The Newsletter* 61 (Autumn): 32–33.

Tifentale, Alise, and Lev Manovich. 2014. 'Selficity: Exploring Photography and Self-Fashioning in Social Media'. Available at http://manovich.net/content/04-projects/086-selfiecity-exploring/selfiecity_chapter.pdf (accessed 1 July 2017).

Tiidenberg, Katrin. 2018. *Selfies: Why We Love (and Hate) Them*. Bingley: Emerald Publishing.

University of Delhi. 2015. *Syllabus of Courses to be Offered—Core Courses, Elective Courses & Ability Enhancement Courses*. The Department of Sociology, Undergraduate Programme—Courses Effective from Academic Year 2015–16/Choice Based Credit System (CBCS). Delhi: University of Delhi.

Van Gelder, Hilde, and Helen Westgeest. 2011. *Photography Theory in Historical Perspective: Case Studies from Contemporary Art*. Chichester: Wiley Blackwell.

Warfield, Katie. 2014. 'Making Selfies/Making Self: Digital Subjectivities in the Selfie'. Proceedings of the *Image Conference*, Berlin, 30 October. Available at http://www.academia.edu/8991582/Making_Selfies_Making_Self_digital_subjectivities_in_the_selfie (accessed 29 June 2017).

Wendt, Brooke. 2014. *The Allure of the Selfie: Instagram and the New Self-portrait*. Amsterdam: Institute of Network Cultures.

Wiles, Rose, Jon Prosser, Anna Bagnoli, Andrew Clark, Katherine Davies, Sally Holland, and Emma Renold. 2008. *Visual Ethics: Ethical Issues in Visual Research* (ESRC National Centre for Research Methods Review Paper). Swindon: Economic and Social Research Council.

Wilkinson, Sophie. 2014. 'Women Who Eat on Tubes: I was Hurt and Humiliated when My Photo Appeared Online'. *The Independent*. Available at https://www.independent.co.uk/life-style/gadgets-and-tech/features/women-who-eat-on-tubes-i-was-hurt-and-humiliated-when-my-photo-appeared-online-im-never-going-to-9249512.html (accessed 28 June 2018).

Wolbert, Barbara. 2000. 'The Anthropologist as Photographer: The Visual Construction of Ethnographic Authority'. *Visual Anthropology* 13: 231–343.

Wright, Chris. 1998. 'The Third Subject: Perspectives on Visual Anthropology'. *Anthropology Today* 14 (4): 16–22.

Wright, Terence. 1991. 'The Fieldwork Photographs of Jenness and Malinowski and the Beginning of Modern Anthropology'. *Journal of Anthropological Society of Oxford* 22 (1): 41–58.

_____. 1999. *The Photography Handbook*. London: Routledge.

Index

Index

Index